Interactive Television
Production

Interactive Television Production

Mark Gawlinski

OXFORD AMSTERDAM BOSTON LONDON NEW YORK PARIS
SAN DIEGO SAN FRANCISCO SINGAPORE SYDNEY TOKYO

Focal Press
An imprint of Elsevier Science
Linacre House, Jordan Hill, Oxford OX2 8DP
200 Wheeler Road, Burlington, MA 01803

First published 2003

British Library Cataloguing in Publication Data
A catalogue record for this book is available from the British Library

Library of Congress Cataloguing in Publication Data
A catalogue record for this book is available from the Library of Congress

ISBN   0 240 51679 6

For information on all Focal Press publications visit our website at:
www.focalpress.com

Typeset by Keyword Typesetting Services Ltd
Printed and bound in Great Britain

Contents

This book

This book is for anyone interested in getting a general understanding of interactive television and how to produce it. You will find it useful if:

- You already work in new media or television (whether in design, production, marketing, business development, human resources, programming, engineering or any other area). The book will give you a clear idea of how your skills and experience could fit in with the practice of interactive television and how interactive television could support your existing projects.
- If you are a company director, lecturer or student. You'll get enough down to earth information to draw your own conclusions about the commercial and cultural importance of the medium.
- If you are about to become involved in the production of new or existing interactive television (iTV) services or have an interactive television idea. You'll get an introduction to the end-to-end processes required to make things happen – plus numerous examples of existing services to stimulate your creative thinking.

If you are interested purely in the engineering and electronics of interactive television, in detailed country-by-country market projections or in academic analysis, other books will serve you better.

This book covers each of the elements required to understand the production of most interactive television programmes or services:

- Chapter 1 answers the question 'what is interactive television?'
- Chapter 2 covers the technology. The material can be understood by anyone: a PhD in electronic engineering is not required.
- Chapter 3 outlines how companies have made money and delivered benefits with interactive television. The need to provide a return to investors is at the heart of every interactive television development (even publicly funded projects measure success against something – or should do).
- Chapter 4 takes a close-up look at the tools and processes that can be used to produce the best possible services, on time and to budget. This includes an outline of the people required to get a project off the ground and a way to go about doing it.

- Chapter 5 looks at the most important people in the interactive television business – the viewers. The best examples of interactive television are designed with the viewers in mind at all times: the ones that are not invariably fail.

- Finally, in Chapter 6, industry experts look to the future, predicting how interactive television is likely to develop through to 2007.

The book takes a practical, production-based approach, based on my hands-on experience of building interactive television services – and based on the knowledge and experience of a number of the United Kingdom's leading interactive television producers. To maintain the flow, detailed references for research reports and surveys are not listed. However, there is a general summary of sources at the back of the book.

You can pick and choose sections that interest you or throw yourself into the book from beginning to end. Either way, you may find it useful to spend two minutes glancing over all the 'Chapter in 30 seconds . . .' summaries, which are located at the beginning of each chapter. This will give you a quick overview of interactive television production and the structure of the book – and perhaps enough information to bluff meetings or discussions on interactive television at work or college!

On the web site, *www.InteractiveTelevisionProduction.com*, there are pages of links designed to help with common iTV questions and issues. There are also entertaining quizzes for each chapter, so you can test your knowledge of some of the concepts introduced in the book.

Acknowledgements

Many thanks to everyone who gave their time to work on this book. In particular, I would like the thank the book's editor, Sue Wingrove, for her tireless effort and skill commissioning case studies, commenting on drafts and sub-editing. Also, thank you to Bill Goodland, director of internet, NTL Home, and Andrew Curry, director, The Henley Centre, for helping to structure and focus the book throughout production.

Furthermore, I'd like to thank the following people who have provided invaluable help and feedback:

- Innes Ballantyne, senior producer, interactive television, BBC New Media.
- Madani Boughnounou, product manager, Canal+ Technologies.
- Patrick Brown, director, CentricView.
- Keith Cass, director of technology, ITN.
- Duncan Cranna, journalist and writer.
- Richard Kydd, director of technology, Two Way TV.
- Paul Lancefield, director, Infinite Reason.
- Matthew Stratfold, manager, enhanced television, NTL.
- Christophe Declerck, chief technology officer, Canal+ Technologies.
- Hugh Griffiths, Video Networks Ltd.

And thank you to the following people for writing case studies and in-depth pieces:

- Billy Ingram, producer of Tvparty.com.
- Rod Clarke, technical consultant, NDS.
- Sandra Gorel, producer, BBC New Media.
- Andrew Howells, managing director, AH Associates.
- Mervyn Metcalf, vice president, media investment banking, Merrill Lynch International.
- Mike Constantine, head of electronic services, HSBC Bank.
- Ismail Vali, head of interactive development, Ladbrokes e-Gaming.
- Ronnette Lucraft, general manager, Living Health, Flextech.
- Richard Steel, head of information and communication, Newham Council.

Acknowledgements

- Martin Hart, the Independent Television Commission.
- Andy Wyper, producer, Victoria Real.
- Humphrey Lau, senior technical manager, BBC New Media.
- Vlad Cohen, head of design, BBC New Media.
- Damian Rafferty, executive producer, BBC New Media.
- Michael Atherton, manager new media, Oktobor.
- Owen Daly-Jones, manager, Serco Usability Services.
- Dr Guy Winter, senior behavioural scientist, BBC Research and Development.
- Andy Mayer, business analyst, NOP Research Group.
- Ian Pearson, futurologist, BTexact Technologies.
- Scott Gronmark, head of interactive television, BBC New Media.
- Andrew Curry, director, The Henley Centre.

I would also like to thank my colleagues and managers at ITN and the BBC for their understanding and flexibility during the time I've spent writing. In particular, thank you to Paul Grice, director of technology, BBC Resources; Richard Tait, former editor-in-chief, ITN; and Garron Baines, former managing director of ITN New Media and now managing principal, media and entertainment, IBM.

Finally, thank you to my wife Aldona for her even greater levels of understanding and flexibility during my time of egomaniacal absorption.

Chapter **1**

What is interactive television?

Chapter 1 in 30 seconds . . .

▷ Interactive television can be defined as anything that lets the television viewer or viewers and the people making the television channel, programme or service engage in a dialogue. More specifically, it can be defined as a dialogue that takes the viewers beyond the passive experience of watching and lets them make choices and take actions.

▷ Interactive television services can be classified in different ways. This book classifies interactive television services according to the terminology that producers use and the experience that viewers have of those services. Examples of different types of interactive television include 'walled garden', teletext-style and enhanced television.

▷ Recent developments in technology have opened up new possibilities for interactive television. However, interactivity doesn't necessarily need the latest technology. Simple types of interactivity, like telephone call-in shows, have been around for years.

▷ One early example of interactive television that didn't require advanced technology was *Winky Dink and You*, a children's show first broadcast in America in 1953. Kids were asked to further the on-screen action by drawing pictures on transparent sheets attached to the screen.

" A mighty maze of mystic magic rays is all about us in the blue . . . **"**

Singer Adele Dixon at the opening of the BBC television service, November 1936

Introduction

I n 1936, the BBC powered up the first ever television broadcast. Sir John Reith, the director general of the publicly funded radio broadcaster, was decidedly under-whelmed by the new technology. His sober diary entry for the day read: 'To Alexandra Palace for the television opening. I had declined to be televised or take part.'

Sir John had no way of knowing that television would become such a huge medium, so we can forgive his initial scepticism. But what would he say about interactive television today? It could be heralding a fundamental change to the medium. But it's difficult to tell. Drastic change may not happen for a long time – or may not happen at all.

One thing is certain, interactive television is having an impact already and millions of people are affected. Declining to take part, as Reith initially did with television, is becoming more and more difficult every day.

This book concentrates on the here and now – the technology and techniques of today – focusing on the job of producing real interactive television programmes and services. It will equip you with enough down-to-earth information to rise above the hype and to draw your own conclusions about the future.

The United Kingdom interactive television industry

Most of the material in this book refers to work done in the United Kingdom. The United Kingdom is particularly worthy of detailed study because it is the most well-developed interactive television market in the world. This is due to its extensive rollout of digital television (the main transmission platform for interactive television). At the beginning of 2003, there were more than nine million households with digital interactive television – that's over 40 per cent of the viewing public (of around 24.5 million homes). Although there have been several hiccups (including the closure of ITV Digital, the pay-television part of the digital terrestrial network), hundreds of interactive television services are available on the mass-market digital interactive platforms (digital satellite, digital cable and digital terrestrial), as well as on smaller-scale television platforms that use the telephone network (by means of DSL technology); and many interactive service producers have built up several years of experience.

This level of development means it is possible to draw some firm conclusions about what's working with interactive television and what isn't, simply because the services are being used by so many people and have been around for so long – and the producers in charge have had a chance to learn lots of hard lessons. The United Kingdom has got to a stage where the focus is very much on producing down-to-earth services that add real value to people's lives as well as making money, rather than experimental and pilot works (although there is always a place for these). Moreover, the production tools and techniques for interactive television have achieved a level of consistency across the industry.

It is likely that the lessons learnt and the technologies that have become stable and successful in the United Kingdom will be applied in other countries as they develop interactive television services. It is certainly the case that the big players in the United Kingdom interactive television industry have an almost constant barrage of requests from executives in the United States, Asia and continental Europe, asking for demonstrations and explanations of what they have achieved.

What is interactive television?

Interactive television isn't new. Since the very earliest days of television, producers have been trying to make their programmes and channels more dynamic and participatory. In the case of children's television, for example, the interactive element often involved desperately trying to get the viewers to sing along, jump up and down or dance around the room. One early children's programme pushed the boundaries of the often passive relationship between the broadcaster and the viewer. It was called *Winky Dink and You* and featured the adventures of a cartoon character with a star-shaped hairdo. American children in the 1950s were asked to help Winky Dink out of difficult situations by drawing on the television screen using special transparent sheets, which were sold in shops and by post. Viewers would draw a bridge to help Winky Dink move around and draw a parachute to stop Winky Dink crashing to the ground. From the child's point of view at least, the fate of a television programme's star had passed into the hands of the viewer. (*Winky Dink* is sometimes criticised as being gimmicky and irrelevant to modern interactive

1.1 *Winky Dink and You.* © *CBS.*

television. However, one only has to read some of the memories of *Winky Dink and You* viewers, 50 years on, to see that its effect was way beyond that of a gimmick. See 'In-depth: *Winky Dink and You*' at the end of this chapter.)

Adult viewers have been won over to the idea of interacting with television in a number of clever ways too. Anything and everything has been tried: asking for feed-back, running prize competitions, giving out leaflets with extra information. The telephone, in particular, has proved itself to be a powerful interactive television tool. Nearly every daytime television chat show asks viewers to ring in with their views or problems. And fund-raising shows focus all their energy on trying to per-suade viewers to pick up the phone and give money. One memorable example was Bob Geldof looking directly into the camera during *Live Aid* and imploring: 'Just give us your fucking money'. More recently, music channels like The Box have installed technologies that allow viewers to ring in, on a premium rate line, to choose a video. The video is then put in a queue and eventually shown to everyone watching the channel.

Interactive television can be defined as anything that lets the television viewer or viewers and the people making the television channel, programme or service engage in a dialogue. More specifically, it can be defined as a dialogue that takes the viewers beyond the passive experience of watching and lets them make choices and take actions – even if the action is as simple as filling in a postcard and popping it into the mail, or drawing a picture on the television screen.

Recent developments in technology have really opened up the possibilities for inter-active television. In particular, digital transmission technologies have made it pos-sible to cram a lot more information into a given piece of broadcasting space (bandwidth). This allows broadcasters and television platform operators (cable com-panies, for example) to more easily parcel extra information alongside the television signal, and for viewers to send information back to the television companies. By using digital and other technologies, viewers and television producers now have a myriad of new and exciting ways to interact.

Interactive television: the players

The companies involved in interactive television fit into five camps:

Broadcasters. Broadcasters own television channels and commission pro-grammes for these channels, either from their own in-house production teams or from production companies. They also buy in shows from other broadcasters. United Kingdom examples include the BBC, MTV UK and ITV.

Production companies. Production companies make programmes and/or interactive television services for broadcasters and other customers. They spend most of their time pitching ideas for new programmes and services to broadcasters. They also develop programme brands, like *Who Wants to be a Millionaire*, which they sell around the world. United Kingdom examples include Rag Doll, Wall to Wall, and Endemol UK.

Platform operators. Platform operators own the networks that carry video and interactive services into people's homes. In the main, they deal with the delivery of data via either satellite, cable, terrestrial or telephone (using DSL technology) networks. Platform operators sometimes pay broadcasters for their channels; sometimes broadcasters have to pay platform operators for carriage. Platform operators occasionally commission content directly from production companies. United Kingdom examples include BSkyB, Freeview, NTL and Telewest.

Technology companies. These guys provide the hardware and software required to make television programmes, channels and interactive services. Examples include NDS, OpenTV and Liberate.

Retailers and consumer goods companies. Retailers and other companies and organisations want to get messages to and sell products to the viewers of television channels, using whatever means works best – mainly advertising. Examples include Domino's Pizza, Unilever and government departments.

There are numerous large-scale and hybrid companies that fit across two or more of these camps.

The different types of interactive television

One of the difficulties with interactive television is that there's no generally agreed framework for describing different types of interactivity. Everyone involved in the industry uses different jargon.

For example, Microsoft (producer of interactive television software Microsoft TV) has a taxonomy that includes:

- Enhanced television – services that allow viewers to interact with a television show.
- Internet on television – services that allow viewers to view and use information currently available on the internet.
- Personal television – services that allow viewers to record and pause television programmes.
- Connected television – services that allow the television to share information with different devices in the home, like personal organisers and personal computers.

On the other hand, consumer research organisation The Henley Centre breaks down interactive television into three principal modes:

- Distribution interactivity – where the viewer interacts to control the delivery of a piece of content, but not the content itself. This covers functionality similar to that provided by a video recorder, where the viewer can decide when to view a particular programme.

- Information interactivity – where the viewer can get to different types of information. This includes anything from playing an arcade game on the television, to ordering a pizza, to checking the weather.

- Participation interactivity – where viewers are able to choose between options during a programme or advertisement. This includes the ability to play along with a game show or choose a particular player for the camera to follow during a sporting event.

To muddy the waters even more, I'm going to introduce yet another list of the different types of interactive television. This is a practical book, concerned with the realities of producing interactive television. Therefore, this list is based on the terminology that many of the producers who work in the industry use. The list is not definitive, but is designed to be a framework that will simplify explanations later in the book. (And provide a few buzzwords to use at parties.) Be warned, some interactive television experts and other publications will use different names or different classification systems. There are also hybrid services that combine two or more of the different types.

Each of these types of interactive television is described in terms of the viewer experience of interactivity rather than the technology behind that experience. This is because it is often the case that any given piece of technology or software that makes interactive television happen can be used to produce more than one, even all, of the different types of service listed here. The main types of interactive television, for the purposes of this book, are also all displayed on a television screen (rather than a personal computer monitor).

The different types of interactive television covered by this book are:

- Electronic programme guides (EPGs).
- Teletext-style services.
- Walled gardens.
- Internet on television.
- Enhanced television.
- Video-on-demand and near-video-on-demand.
- Personal video recorders.

Electronic programme guides

One of the most useful and important types of interactive television is the electronic programme guide (EPG). Its core job is to tell viewers what's on the television, effectively replacing newspaper- or magazine-based television guides. EPGs display information about schedules directly onto the television screen and viewers can select programmes to watch from the on-screen list – which is a must-have on services that have tens and sometimes hundreds of channels to choose from. To access an EPG, viewers usually press a button on the remote control (marked *TV Guide* or something similar) that is supplied with the television service.

Electronic programme guide

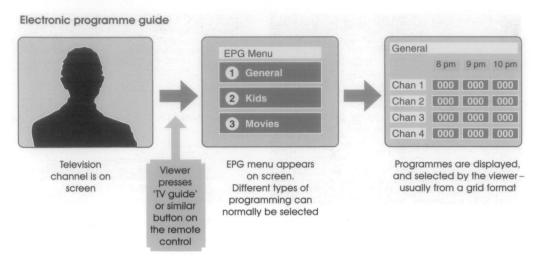

1.2 A typical EPG works by putting television listings information on the screen.

Some EPGs simply have a list of television programmes and start times. Others have more detailed information (such as programme reviews and cast lists for movies) and can display information in a variety of ways, depending on what the viewer prefers. Some have useful interactive functions, like the ability to set reminders that pop up on screen when a programme is starting on another channel.

A typical modern EPG will include a mode that displays television listings across the whole television screen. Lots of channels can be displayed – usually in a grid format. Viewers can quickly compare programmes, select a listing by genre and, if the functionality is available, set reminders for programmes that look interesting. The programme information is usually shown to viewers in text format, but some trail-blazing EPGs incorporate photographs and video windows showing the live picture from each channel on offer.

1.3 The Sky Digital electronic programme guide. © *BSkyB*.

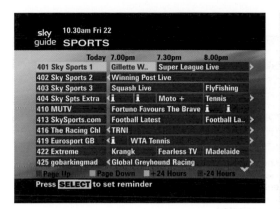

1.4 Searching for sports content using the Sky Digital electronic programme guide. © *BSkyB*.

1.5 An EPG reminder – the viewer can set this to come up when a programme is about to start on another channel. © *BSkyB*.

Now/next boxes

Some EPGs can display information about what's on televison now and what's on next in boxes that are overlaid on top of the television picture. Viewers can then keep watching television while reading the EPG information. The boxes may even be semi-transparent (so the video picture can be seen underneath), so they are less likely to distract people's attention from the programme. These are sometimes called now/next or present/following boxes.

Viewers can use these boxes to quickly check whether anything else interesting is on (without needing to switch channel) and read information and reviews. Usually, different options are selected using the arrow and other keys on the remote control. If viewers see a programme they are interested in on another channel they press a button to switch channel. Usually these now/next boxes appear for a few seconds every time a viewer changes channel.

1.6 A now/next EPG box appearing over a video channel. © *BSkyB*.

Teletext-style services

Analogue teletext

Teletext-style interactive television services take their name and style of presentation from a technology first developed over 30 years ago. Millions of viewers – particularly in Europe, where the technology became much more widespread than in the United States – are familiar with the useful services that analogue teletext technology provides. It works by transmitting text and simple graphics to suitably equipped sets.

Analogue teletext technology has a particular style of on-screen presentation for the content. Viewers usually press the *Text* button on the remote control, while watching a particular television channel. This directs them to information carried with that channel. The information tends to be relevant to the channel. So, for general entertainment channels, viewers can usually find information like television listings, news and weather. For more specialist channels, like MTV, there is often more specialist information (in MTV's case, music news, reviews and so on). The audio from the channel usually continues in the background – giving the viewer the impression of keeping in touch with the channel. Viewers access different pages of information by pressing numbers on the remote control. They type the number identifying a page (for example, page 100), then wait for that page to be displayed on-screen.

1.7 An analogue teletext service. Fast-text options are on the bottom line. © *Teletext Ltd.*

In the 1980s, an extra piece of functionality was added to analogue teletext. Known as fast-text, this makes it possible for viewers to very quickly access up to four other pages that are likely to be requested (in the broadcaster's view) after the one currently on-screen. So, for example, on a news page, the fast-access pages might be a news headline page, a sports news page, the top news story page and the main index page. Viewers can jump to any one of the four other pages by pressing one of the four coloured buttons that were added to the remote controls of televisions with the fast-text function.

Digital teletext

The technologies of interactive television have moved beyond the bulky graphics of analogue teletext. Today, photographs and thousands of colours are possible – and even groovy functionality like email and text messaging. However, analogue teletext

Digital teletext

| Television channel | Viewer presses 'Text' or similar button on the remote control | Teletext menu appears (specific to each channel) (The TV channel sometimes continues in small window) | Viewer can select different types of information |

Teletext

1 News 4 Sport
2 Fun 5 TV
3 Lottery 6 Weather

Weather

1 World
2 UK Regions
3 UK Outlook
4 UK Long range forecast
5 Back to main Menu

1.8 Digital teletext is usually associated with a particular channel or series of channels. It is usually available by pressing a button on the remote while watching the channel.

technology has set expectations within the minds of some viewers – expectations that continue when people upgrade their television service. Because of this, some broadcasters, like the BBC and Sky in the United Kingdom, have decided to keep analogue teletext-style presentation up to a point, even on their latest and most high-tech digital services. Specifically, these broadcasters have kept the idea that the viewer can access information by pressing one button (usually a button marked *Text* on the remote) while watching a television channel. They have also kept the idea that some kind of connection remains with the television channel that the viewer is watching, after he or she has pressed the *Text* button. This is done by continuing to have the audio from the television channel in the background of the interactive information or by having the television picture from the channel inserted into the interactive page.

Some digital teletext services have kept the concept of page numbers, and viewers are able to press the number keys to jump directly to specific pages. Others have

1.9 The front page of a digital text service. *Courtesy of the BBC. Images supplied by kind permission BBC/BBC Worldwide.*

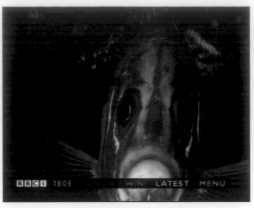

1.10 The weather section of a digital text service. *Courtesy of the BBC and the BBC Weather Centre.*

1.11 Viewers pressing *Text* on many BBC digital channels will actually see an overlay bar appear first. Using this, they can select digital text and other services. *Courtesy of the BBC.*

redesigned the navigation completely, with viewers only able to find information by selecting items on menus. In a number of services, the coloured fast-text keys have new-found importance as key elements of the navigation system.

Some digital teletext content can be accessed in ways other than using the *Text* button. For example, on the United Kingdom's digital terrestrial platform, digital teletext services from the BBC and Teletext Ltd are available via their own television channel numbers (which viewers access using the EPG). And, just to add to the confusion, some digital platforms provide both analogue teletext services and modern digital text services, although these are usually accessed in different ways.

Walled gardens

Some interactive television platform operators offer a whole collection of different interactive content and services from a variety of different companies under one umbrella. They aim to provide a secure, controlled and easy-to-understand environment for different types of interactive television – a so-called 'walled garden'.

Each one of the services in a walled garden is usually specially prepared for use on television and has a commercial arrangement with the operator of the platform. The services are accessible via a set of on-screen menus. To access the menus, viewers press a button on the remote control that is normally labelled something like *Interactive* or *Services*. The term walled garden is used because a defined boundary stops viewers accessing unregulated content like that found on the internet.

Telewest in the United Kingdom has a typical walled garden on its digital cable service. This is made up of a series of menus that offer different types of content and service – games, news, email, banking, shopping and so on. Usually, the operator of the interactive television platform will either own or control the walled garden. However, some broadcasters put their content within platform operators' walled gardens as an alternative or addition to their digital teletext services.

Walled garden

Television channel
(any and all channels
on the platform)

Viewer
presses
'Interactive'
or similar
button on
the remote
control

Main menu
1 Shops
2 Games
3 News

Walled garden main
menu appears – usually
with sections for shops,
games and so on.
The walled garden is
not specific to a
particular channel

Shops
1 WH Smith   2 Domino's
3 Last   4 Holiday
  Minute   Shop

The viewer can select
services from a range
of different companies

1.12 A typical walled garden is a collection of content and services from various companies.

There is nothing stopping platform operators from offering an assortment of walled garden services from different sources. In fact, in the United Kingdom, the regulator has decreed that Sky Digital, a satellite platform, must allow other companies to build their own walled garden services on its platform. Therefore, if the viewer presses the *Interactive* button on their remote control while they are watching any television channel, they are taken to a menu that includes a number of companies supplying a range of different walled gardens. Each walled garden has its own set of retailers and/or other services.

1.13 The main menu of the Telewest walled garden. *Courtesy of Telewest Broadband.*

1.14 The travel section of the Sky Digital walled garden service. © *BSkyB.*

Usually, the most popular part of a walled garden is the games section. Indeed, some walled garden services only contain games. Games on interactive television include anything from fast-action arcade-style zapping to strategy or word games. There were a number of walled garden games services launched in the UK in 2002 and 2003, including GoPlayTV and Sky Gamestar.

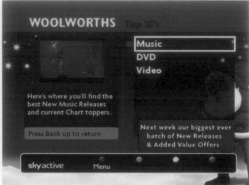

1.15 Shopping services in the Sky walled garden. © *BSkyB*.

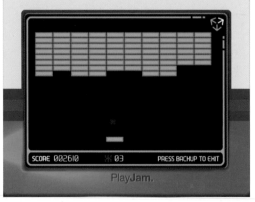

1.16 A selection of interactive television games and games menus. *E-Victor and Big Brother news and voting was produced by Two Way TV Ltd under licence from Channel Four Television Corporation and Endemol Entertainment UK Ltd. © Two Way TV Ltd 2001. Two Way TV is a registered trade mark of Two Way TV Ltd. E-Victor and the Two Way TV stylised logo are pending trade mark applications of Two Way TV Ltd.*

1.17 © *Static2358*.

1.18 © *Static2358.*

1.19 © *BSkyB.*

Internet on television

Internet on television allows viewers to access the millions of pages and communication services already available on the internet. Internet on television services break down the garden wall to give viewers the opportunity to roam beyond the confines of what the platform operator thinks is suitable. The theory goes that viewers can then get all the advantages of the PC-internet but at a much reduced cost, compared to a computer – and all in the comfort of their own living rooms.

The practice, unfortunately, is that many web sites, which are designed for viewing on a personal computer, look awful when viewed on television, and some don't work at all. Compounding the problem, television remote controls do not lend themselves to being used for navigating PC-internet sites that are designed for a mouse, while graphics designed for a personal computer monitor can look terribly small when viewed from two metres away on the living room sofa.

Perhaps because of these problems, many internet on television services attract only small numbers of customers. NTL's analogue TV-internet service (which used a box attached to a normal phone line to access the internet) closed down in 2001, due to lack of interest. Production of the Dreamcast, a games machine that had internet on television functionality, stopped the same year. And the biggest web on television service, MSN TV (formerly Web TV), has been relaunched several times in the United States in unsuccessful efforts to achieve mass market appeal.

The solution to layout and readability problems with the internet on television is to ask the owners of PC-based web sites to spend some time designing alternative versions of their sites that will work on television. Unfortunately, to date there are very few sites on the open internet that have alternative versions that work really well on television. Companies are not prepared to spend the time and money involved in redesigning their sites and services for television, until the number of users and the level of usage make it worthwhile. Users won't sign up to an internet on television service until there are lots of good-quality services. Catch-22.

Internet on TV

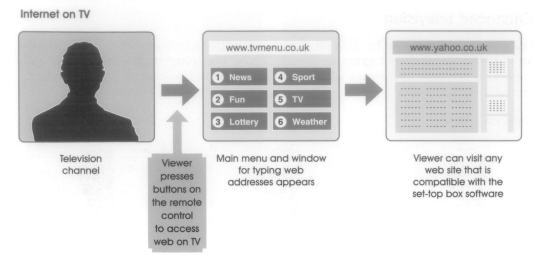

Television channel	Viewer presses buttons on the remote control to access web on TV	Main menu and window for typing web addresses appears	Viewer can visit any web site that is compatible with the set-top box software

1.20 A typical internet on television experience.

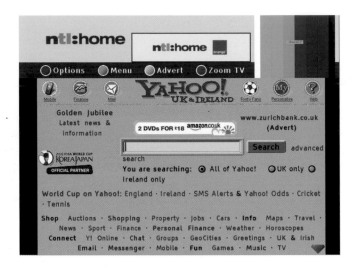

1.21 A web site designed for a personal computer monitor displayed on television. © *Yahoo!/NTL.*

Most surviving internet on television operators have focused on trying to get a small number of specially redesigned sites and pieces of content to work well on their services. In effect, they have become walled garden services with internet on television access as an added attraction.

An innovative variant on the internet on television model involves producers offering video content via the television and complementary web content designed to be accessed on a personal computer positioned in the same room. In the United States, this is called two-screen interactive television and is reasonably popular. Scarborough Research in 2002 reported that more than one-quarter of American adults aged 18–34, who took part in a survey, said they surfed the internet and 'always' or 'often' watched television at the same time.

Enhanced television

Enhanced television can be defined as any interactive television service that makes an existing television programme better, while that programme is running and shortly afterwards. Enhanced television service providers typically add overlays, text and graphics to programmes, so viewers can interact while they watch.

Enhanced television

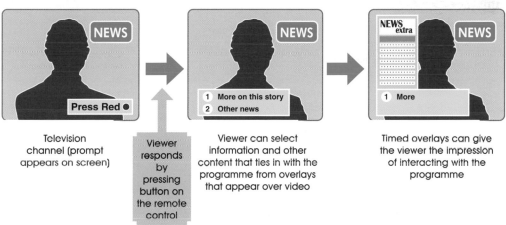

1.22 A typical enhanced television experience.

A great example of enhanced television comes from games company Two Way TV. As well as providing walled garden games (which don't involve television programmes), they put graphical and text overlays on top of television quiz programmes and sports events. Enhanced television services like this give viewers at home the opportunity to try to answer questions before the contestants on the television or to predict what will happen during football matches and so on. Just as the host has finished asking a question or just before a player takes a shot, for example, a range of different answers or options pop up on-screen. The graphic overlays are timed perfectly so they appear and disappear at exactly the right moment – and the key strokes required for choosing the correct answer will only be accepted from the remote control for a very specific period of time that corresponds to the on-screen graphics. The quick-fingered viewer

1.23 An enhanced television sports event.
Screenshot reproduced courtesy of Sky Sports.

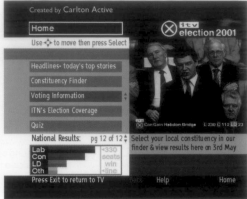

1.24 ITV *Election 2001* using enhanced television. *Courtesy of Carlton Active/ITN.*

can then try to guess the right answer before the contestants in the studio or predict what will happen next in the sports event.

In the case of quiz shows, the Two Way TV service records the viewer's score so they can see how they are doing compared to the studio contestants. Even better though, different family members at home can compete against each other, each person with a different remote control. At the end of the programme, everyone can see how he or she has performed against other interactive viewers around the country. This kind of enhanced television completely transforms the experience of watching a quiz show or sports event, from a relatively passive affair to a dynamic event, played out with the rest of the family and the rest of the country.

Another example of enhanced television, this time without such close synchronisation, was the *Election 2001* programme from ITV, one of the United Kingdom's major television stations. At the beginning of the programme, viewers were prompted (by a graphical overlay) to press the red button on the remote control. Once they chose to do this they were taken to pages with detailed election results for different parts of the United Kingdom. The programme's presenters would never have time to read out the results in full for more than 650 constituencies in the United Kingdom, but on the enhanced television service the detailed results for every area were available on demand. This information was accessible during the programme, so the viewer could continue to watch television while they checked the results. Unlike the channel's teletext-style service, at the end of the programme the enhanced television content was removed.

The big advantage of enhanced television is that the interactivity takes place in close conjunction with something that is proven to be immensely popular and compelling – a television programme. Because viewers can continue to watch a programme, they are more likely to interact. What's more, the interactivity can add value to the programme itself, perhaps even changing the viewer's experience of it.

Video switching

In addition to enhancing programmes with text and graphics, it is also possible to enhance programmes and channels by allowing viewers to switch between a selec-

Video switching enhanced television

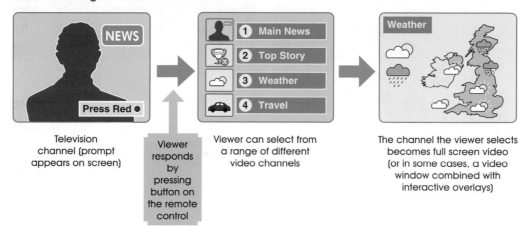

Television channel (prompt appears on screen)

Viewer responds by pressing button on the remote control

Viewer can select from a range of different video channels

The channel the viewer selects becomes full screen video (or in some cases, a video window combined with interactive overlays)

1.25 The viewer experience of video switching enhanced television.

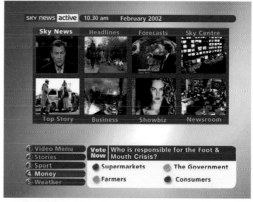

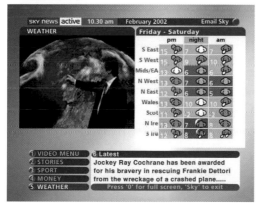

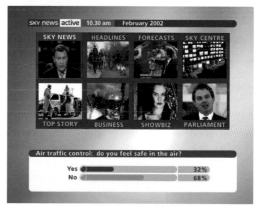

1.26 Sky News Active, an example of a service where viewers can switch between video channels using the interactive functionality. © *BSkyB*.

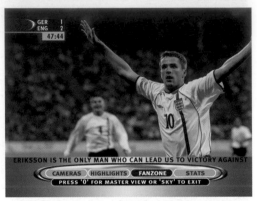

1.27 With Sky Sports Active, the viewer can choose multiple camera angles from the same game, watch highlights, listen to commentary from fans and check the latest statistics. © BSkyB.

tion of different video and audio streams, based around a single event or programme. With this type of service, viewers are normally taken to some kind of menu, where they can select the video and audio streams they wish to use.

Sky Digital pioneered video switching to mass markets in the UK. It has produced Sky News Active, which gives viewers the opportunity to choose entertainment, weather and other video feeds instead of the main news channel. For major stories, it's also possible for viewers to choose to stay with a press conference or event, while the main news channel moves on to other items. Voting, weather graphics and text headlines are also part of the package.

Similarly, Sky Sports Active allows viewers to choose different video and audio sources during big sporting events. Viewers can follow a particular player around the field or choose to hear commentary from fans rather than the professional commentators.

There are endless creative possibilities with video switching services. Other examples include Channel 4's *Big Brother*, the BBC's *Walking with Beasts*, and the BBC's Wimbledon and World Cup coverage. A case study on how *Walking with Beasts* works appears at the end of Chapter 2. A case study on the production of *Big Brother* appears at the end of Chapter 4.

1.28 *Walking with Beasts* viewers could choose the original or an in-depth narration and they could jump to other video segments during the programme. *Courtesy of the BBC and Walking with Beasts*™; © *BBC 2001.*

1.29 *Big Brother* allowed viewers to use video switching to see the action in different parts of the house. © *Channel 4 (© Endemol).*

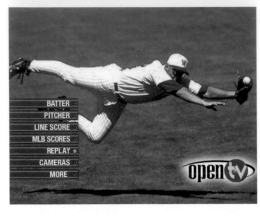

1.30 Video switching can work for lots of different sports and is particularly good for covering tournaments, as viewers are able to choose between simultaneous matches on different courts or pitches. © *Open TV*.

Individualised programming

A variant of video switching interactive television, which was pioneered by ACTV in the United States (although not adopted fully on digital television in the UK), gives viewers the chance to work their way through a television programme by choosing the course of action at certain key points. This is like a television version of those children's books where readers can choose, from a pre-set selection, what page to jump to – depending on what they want the protagonist to do. In the books, for example, the hero might reach a crossroads at the end of the first section; the reader is then told to turn to page 50 if they want the hero to go left, page 60 for right and so on. In the television version, the viewer is able to choose which channel to switch to totally seamlessly, by pressing keys on the remote control. The key feature is that, after making a choice, the video changes without any perceptible jump in the picture, so viewers get the impression that the main programme is continuing (the BBC's *Walking with Beasts*, *Pyramid Challenge* and *Life of Mammals* went much of the way towards this, although the channel changing wasn't always seamless). As more choices are made, the viewer jumps back and forth between video streams or segments, all of which have been prepared to begin the appropriate action at the right point. The original ACTV system could also remember a long list of previous choices and on that basis switch the viewer seamlessly to a programming stream that reflected those choices.

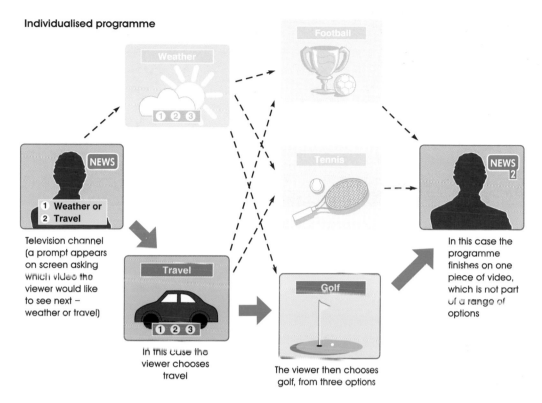

Individualised programme

Television channel (a prompt appears on screen asking which video the viewer would like to see next – weather or travel)

In this case the viewer chooses travel

The viewer then chooses golf, from three options

In this case the programme finishes on one piece of video, which is not part of a range of options

1.31 Viewers make choices at different points during the video. The picture then jumps to the appropriate stream and continues the narrative. The other possible options are also shown here (but, in this case, the viewer has chosen not to view these).

It's possible to produce all sorts of compelling interactive programmes like this: dramas where the viewer decides what should happen to the actors; betting programmes where the viewer decides whether to bet and how much; and advertisements where the viewer decides which products they would like to learn more about. It can be quite expensive to produce (as video has to be shot for as many video channels as are needed and it all needs to be synchronised perfectly so the viewer can't see the jumps), but it does mean that viewers get to experience television in a completely new way. The same sort of effect can also be reproduced with some video on demand services.

Video-on-demand and near-video-on-demand

From the point of view of the viewer, video-on-demand (VOD) services do pretty much the same thing as video rental shops. Video-on-demand allows the viewer to watch television programmes, sports events and films at any time of day or night. Unlike video shops, however, the viewer chooses from a list of shows displayed onscreen, rather than nipping down the high street. Some services also allow the viewer to pause, rewind and forward wind during the programme. There are innumerable ways of providing video-on-demand technology to the home. Pioneers in the field include Video Networks Ltd in the United Kingdom and SeaChange and nCube in the United States – there are many others.

[23]

Video on demand

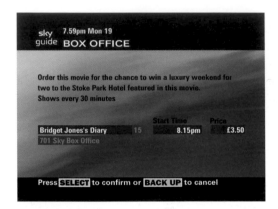

Viewer presses 'Video on demand' or similar button on the remote control

Video on demand category menu

List of films

Films start to order

1.32 The viewer experience of video-on-demand.

1.33 Near-video-on-demand. © *BSkyB.*

A similar service, from the viewer's point of view, is near-video-on-demand (NVOD). Rather than giving viewers the opportunity to select the exact start time of the programme, near-video-on-demand suppliers play the same programme out repeatedly on different channels. The start times of the show are then staggered across these channels. This way, whenever the viewer wants to start watching, let's say the latest James Bond movie, they will only have to wait for the next start time. On these kind of services, the most popular movies usually start every 15 minutes, although it is not uncommon for viewers to have to wait a couple of hours for films or programmes that are broadcast on only two or three channels rather than several.

Personal video recorders

As with video-on-demand services, personal video recorders (PVRs) were developed because of the popularity of video cassette recorders. But, rather than recording programmes onto video cassette, personal video recorders record programmes into a set-top box. This is achieved by using a storage device inside the set-top box, usually a personal computer-style hard drive. Once recorded, the programme can be watched at any time and the viewer can rewind or forward wind any bits they miss or get bored with.

Personal video recorder

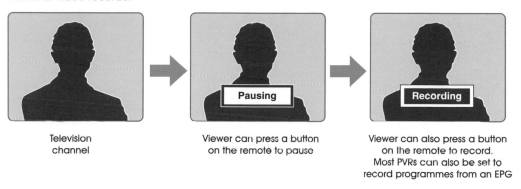

| Television channel | Viewer can press a button on the remote to pause | Viewer can also press a button on the remote to record. Most PVRs can also be set to record programmes from an EPG |

1.34 With personal video recorders, viewers can pause and record television. The EPG can sometimes be used to control the PVR functions.

Unlike VCRs, personal video recorders can play back and record at the same time, so they can also be used to stop live television. If a viewer fancies a cup of tea during the big game, he or she just presses stop and the personal video recorder starts recording in the background. After the kettle has boiled and the tea bag soaked, the viewer can pick up the action at the point they left off, and the actual live coverage continues to be recorded in the background ready for later. Clever stuff.

1.35 Recording television programmes onto a PVR. © *BSkyB*.

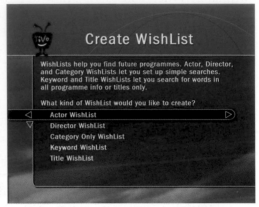

1.36 PVRs often have advanced functionality that can work out what kind of programmes viewers like, then record those programmes automatically for them. Viewers can also set preferences for the programmes they like. © *TiVo; reproduced courtesy of TiVo.*

On top of this, with electronic analysis of the viewer's favourite television programmes and access to the television schedule, personal video recorders can predict what programmes the owner is likely to want to watch. They can then record these programmes without being asked. *Star Trek* fans, for example, will find a whole galaxy of episodes waiting for them when they get back home each day.

Most of the material in this book is relevant to all of the different types of interactive television service listed in this chapter. However, the book is particularly relevant to digital teletext, walled gardens and enhanced television. There's an emphasis on these, because it's these services that the wider production community (broadcasters, production companies, retailers and so on) tend to be closely involved with.

Why bother with interactive television?

Do viewers really want their televisions to be interactive? Even considering telephone polls, mail-in competitions and Bob Geldof-style calls to action, television is generally a rather passive experience. And that's what people seem to like. Does it really need to be changed?

There are two good reasons why interactive television is likely to become more popular and more common: it can make television more appealing and it makes television companies richer. Evidence for this is outlined in Chapter 3. Unfortunately, when considering how to build a popular and profitable service, it's not just a matter of 'you build it and they will come'. The interactive television producer has to bring together a number of different strands: the technology has to work, the commercial model has to deliver, the production has to be on schedule and to budget, and the content and user-experience has to be right. These are all covered in turn in the following chapters.

A concise history of interactive television

1930s to 1960s

The first widely available television broadcast takes place in November 1936, from Alexandra Palace in the United Kingdom. During the war years, most television development gets put on hold. After the war, the number of televisions and the number of broadcasts in the United States, Europe and around the world grows quickly. The 1950s is very much a golden age of television, when the medium moves beyond rehashing radio formats. In the 1950s, television numbers get an enormous boost from people buying sets to watch big sporting and other events (the lure of exclusive sporting events has more recently been used to sell European digital television platforms too). In 1953, the first television programme that can claim to be truly interactive begins in the United States. *Winky Dink and You* is about the adventures of a cartoon character. Children help Winky Dink out of fixes by drawing objects on a transparent sheet that is fixed over the television screen.

In 1959, the first telephone call-ins are used on the *Today* show from NBC. In the 1960s, colour television is perfected and builds in popularity over the course of the decade. In 1964, the first video telephone is demonstrated in the United States.

1970s

A decade of community television, participation and feedback. By the end of the 1970s, the idea that viewer participation can be an important part of television programmes is widespread.

In 1973, the first public demonstration of a teletext system called Ceefax (after the words see and facts) is held in the United Kingdom. This system, developed by the BBC, allows text and simple graphics to be transmitted to specially adapted televisions. It takes advantage of some unused parts of the broadcast signal to carry the data. The viewer is able to call up different pages of information by typing page numbers into the remote control. Although the service is carried in the broadcast stream and there is no way for a signal from the viewer to get back to the broadcaster, the effect is of interaction with the television – information arrives to order.

In 1974, the United Kingdom Post Office demonstrates Viewdata, the world's first videotext system. It is officially launched in 1979 and later marketed in the United Kingdom as Prestel. Videotext systems allow simple text and graphics to be transmitted to televisions via a telephone line and special terminal. Unlike early teletext technology, the system uses two-way communication. The viewer is able to send a signal (usually a page request or a short message) back to the operator who holds the content. Prestel builds up a user base of several hundred thousand people over the coming years, particularly in business, and is extended to personal computer users too. Ultimately, the subscription and usage prices are too high and the service is closed in 1994.

In 1977 in the United States, Warner Amex launches Qube in Ohio. This is the first major interactive television service that allows viewers to send messages back to the broadcaster and participate in surveys and votes during television programmes. It rolls out to some other cable franchises around the United States but, dogged by technical problems and high costs, it is closed within a few years.

In 1978, the first trials of a French videotext system begin. Called Minitel, the system allows viewers to look up phone numbers and post information, using specially produced mini-television terminals. It is a roaring success, mainly because France Telecom subsidises the cost of the terminals (in an attempt to cut the costs of having to produce paper-based telephone directories) and because a micro-payments system makes it easy for content providers to charge directly to customers' phone bills.

1980s

United States cable companies experiment with simple teletext and videotext services. There's the two-way Index service from Cox Cable and Time Teletext from Time Inc. Both services are pulled, after backers conclude that they are not commercially viable. Knight Ridder and Times Mirror develop videotext services, similar to Prestel, using the phone line to transmit information to television and personal computer screens. Because of over-ambitious content plans and prices that are too high for customers, they are also shut down.

In 1988 the BBC launches a children's show, *What's Your Story*, where viewers can ring in to help decide what happens next.

Online services (like Dow Jones, CompuServe and the Prodigy) for personal computers, using the videotext model, start to build up large numbers of users. These are the forefathers of today's online giant AOL, which has at its heart a proprietary videotext-style system.

1990s

There are trials of various different types of interactive television service around the world. Many end disastrously after the investment of huge amounts of cash to test services on very small numbers of customers. There's Bell Atlantic's trial of a video-on-demand system, called Stargazer. Meanwhile, TCI, AT&T and United States West hold trials of a movie-on-demand service in Denver.

Videotron launches a service in Canada, and later in the United Kingdom, with text and graphics, video switching and individualised enhanced television technology from United States-based ACTV. Viewers can switch cameras and decide what happens at key points in programmes. The technology proves popular but is expensive to run due to the bandwidth required by the analogue video channels.

Time Warner cable launches the Full Service Network, offering a range of interactive television services. It is later closed down due to the heavy cost of the technology – the set-top box is based on an SGI system, one of the most powerful and expensive available at the time.

Between 1990 and 1992, physicist Tim Berners-Lee initiates the World Wide Web – a way of presenting information on the internet using hypertext markup language (HTML). Throughout the 1990s, the PC-internet and World Wide Web become more popular.

In 1992, Jim Clark, the founder of Silicon Graphics, announces his idea for the Telecomputer. He wants to turn ordinary televisions into computers, allowing shopping, messaging and movies on demand. Two years and millions of dollars in investment later, the technology isn't working. Jim Clark quits to set up Mosaic Communications (later changed to Netscape), after realising that the Telecomputer was ahead of its time. It disappears into obscurity.

During the mid to late 1990s, a number of channels, like MTV in the United States and Channel 4 in the United Kingdom, put live computer chat rooms on-screen during television programmes. These are the first examples of so-called two-screen interactive television, where viewers use a computer at the same time as watching television.

From 1996, British Telecom, the United Kingdom's biggest phone operator, runs interactive television trials, although it closes the services down at the end of the trials.

By the end of the 1990s, after years of trials and many failures, a variety of advances in technology converge to make digital and interactive television cheaper and easier to produce. In the United Kingdom and parts of Europe, the low proportion of households with multi-channel pay-television (compared to the United States) makes the initial investment in digital technology look attractive (there is the potential to take subscription revenues from viewers signing up to pay-television for the first time and extra advertising revenue from new channels). Also governments encourage digital transmission technologies because they hope to be able to sell off the radio spectrum that is subsequently freed up.

Television Par Satellite in France is the first broadcaster to launch digital interactive services commercially, followed by its rival Canal+. Sky Digital launches on digital satellite in the United Kingdom in 1998. This is followed by different services, using different technology, from the UK digital cable and digital terrestrial platform operators. The United Kingdom pursues one of the most ambitious rollouts of interactive digital television services in the world.

Early 2000s

By mid-2002, the pioneer digital platforms in the United Kingdom (and some in Europe) are suffering cash-flow problems and ITV Digital, the operator of a commercial service on the United Kingdom's digital terrestrial network, goes bust. It's a similar story for the interactive television services that are carried on the digital platforms – a number of services that started in 1999 or 2000 have been closed by 2002. Fortunately, the interactive television producers that are left can reap the benefits of several years of practical experience. And by 2003 there's a second wave of interactive television services, which are much more closely targeted at real customer needs and have much more appropriate commercial models.

In the United States, there is less incentive for platform operators to invest large amounts of money in the rollout of new television technologies, as the penetration of multi-channel pay-television is already very high. The situation is also complicated by the existence of legacy technologies that need to be replaced or integrated as part of any new systems. However, the United States government has backed the launch of digital television and many United States platform operators are making serious investments in interactive digital television systems. A number of pilot interactive television services, by 2003, are transforming into large-scale commercial operations.

In-depth: *Winky Dink and You*

Billy Ingram, producer of TVparty.com. TVparty is a web site covering television history and nostalgia.

Winky Dink and You was a favourite of kids everywhere, a show that was first broadcast in the 1950s, but I've met other people who remember it being on in the early 1960s.

It originally ran at 10 a.m. on Saturday mornings from 1953 until 1957 on the CBS network in the United States. Joining host Jack Barry was Dayton Allen (from *Howdy-Doody*) as Mr Bungle, the assistant that never gets anything right. The voice of Winky Dink was Mae Questel, who also voiced Betty Boop. Broadcast in glorious black and white, the programme featured the adventures of a star-headed cartoon lad named Winky Dink and his dog Woofer – interspersed with the in-studio antics of a host and an audience of kids. The gimmick was that the boys and girls at home were asked to help Winky Dink out of a jam by drawing

1.37 *Winky Dinky and You. © CBS.*

whatever Winky needed (rope, ladder, bridge and so on) on the television screen. This was done with the aid of a Winky Dink kit, which was sold by mail for 50 cents. 'We sold millions of those kits,' the show's host Jack Barry commented, 'It was well thought out.' You would place the clear piece of plastic that came in the kit over the television screen and connect the dots to create, for example, a bridge for Winky Dink to cross to safety, then trace letters at the bottom of the screen to read the secret messages broadcast at the end of the show.

A viewer explains her connection to the show: 'Every Saturday morning as a six-year-old in 1953 I would wander up the back porch steps from my parents' flat in Chicago to my grandparents' flat. They had a television! My grandmother would tune in and my favourite show as a child would appear: Winky Dink. My grand mother would spoil me by taking me to local dime stores on every shopping trip and buy me a toy. I knew I would not have a problem asking for and getting my Winky Dink screen. I will always cherish the time I was able to spend with my grandparents (now deceased) and in saving Winky Dink from his perils.' Of course, it goes without saying that scores of kids without the kits drew on the television screen itself, ruining many a family's first television set. 'I remember that my Mother didn't want to buy me a Winky Dink screen,' viewer Charlie Jamison says, 'That was not going to stop me from helping my old pal Winky Dink, I just used a permanent marker! The next week, I had a Winky Dink screen.'

'There were actually two Winky Dink kits,' says viewer Alan Rosen. 'The one for 50 cents that you could order from television or a deluxe Winky Dink kit with a screen and extra crayons and erasing cloth that was sold in toy stores for the then hefty price of $2.95.' Another viewer says: 'I used to watch Winky Dink when I was a kid in the 1950s. I had the kit, but I would intentionally draw the wrong things. When Winky needed a ladder to get out of a hole, I would draw a cover on the hole. When he needed a parachute, I would draw an anvil to pull him down. I would tease my younger sister and tell her that I was making Winky die! Whenever she left the room crying, I would laugh and laugh. Winky was cool.'

Actions

✓ Watch some video examples of different interactive television services at www.broadbandbananas.com.

✓ Pay a visit to http://directory.google.com/Top/Arts/Television/Interactive/ (case sensitive), part of the Google search engine directory, for an updated list of useful iTV sites.

✓ Try some of the links available at www.InteractiveTelevisionProduction.com.

✓ Take a quiz on Chapter 1 interactive television concepts at www.InteractiveTelevisionProduction.com.

Chapter **2**

The technology

Chapter 2 in 30 seconds . . .

▷ Interactive television productions involve and are dependent on a range of technologies – including television sets, transmission platforms and set-top boxes.

▷ The introduction of digital transmission technologies made it easier to distribute interactive television services.

▷ The main transmission platforms for interactive television are digital cable, digital satellite, digital terrestrial and, using digital subscriber line (DSL) technology, the telephone network.

▷ The hardware and software in television set-top boxes usually control the on-screen presentation of interactive television services.

▷ Interactive television services on different transmission platforms often have to be created in completely different ways, using different technologies; they are rarely interoperable. This makes multi-platform production time-consuming and expensive, although the backers of standards like Multimedia Home Platform are trying to address this issue.

" Well informed people know it is impossible to transmit the voice over wires and that were it possible to do so, the thing would be of no practical value. "

Boston Globe *editorial, 1865*

Successful film directors – Spielberg, Scorsese, Lucas and so on – almost always have a deep understanding of the tools of their trade. They know how to get the most from lighting, the effect of different types of film stock and how to use editing for emotional effect. With this thorough understanding of the technical potential and limitations of the medium, film directors can push the creative and commercial boundaries. The same can be said to be true for interactive television. The technology can look formidable, but focused research into this fast-changing area can bring great creative rewards.

The main challenge with interactive television is that different transmission platform operators use very different technologies and standards are not widely adopted. This can make production complicated, particularly since most of the technology is still at a relatively early stage of development: problems are still being solved and products are constantly being upgraded. And to add to the challenge, interactive television technologies have not simply replaced traditional television technologies: the two are deeply intertwined.

This may change. As interactive television technologies are standardised and production tools perfected, production will become much more straightforward, like regular television. But this is likely to take several years. For the time being, like the best film directors, interactive television producers with a good understanding of interactive television technologies are the ones who are best equipped to create the best possible final results.

Interactive television technologies

There are a number of technologies involved in interactive television, all of which can have a dramatic effect on how the end-product looks and works:

- The viewer.
- The television set.
- The transmission network or platform.
- The set-top box.
- The production tools.

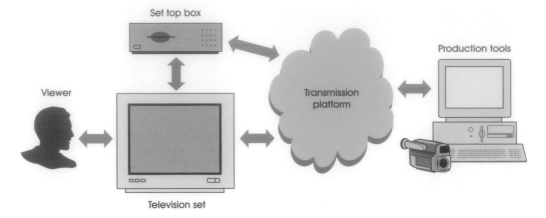

2.1 The technologies involved in interactive television.

This chapter looks at each of these in turn, except production tools, which are covered in detail in Chapter 4. It also goes on to outline some of the issues associated with synchronising video with interactive information and to summarise the main technical standards that are relevant to interactive television production.

The section on television sets and the section on transmission platforms may initially seem rather removed from interactive television. They've been included because the technologies of both are instrumental in making interactive television possible and because both have implications for how interactive television services are produced. Interactive television graphics, for example, have to be designed in the right way to work on television screens, while transmission network technologies define the parameters of what an interactive television service can achieve.

If, however, you already understand the basics of how television sets work and the make-up of television transmission platforms, feel free to skip to the section on interactive television set-top boxes.

The viewer

Okay, so viewers aren't really pieces of technology. But the 'biotechnology' of people's brains is important for television and interactive television, which both work by playing tricks on people's visual perception. There are two characteristics of the brain that make these tricks possible. First, human beings naturally look for meaning in anything they see. If an image is broken into a series of dots, the brain will try to put those dots back together into something meaningful. Take a close look at Figure 2.2. If you stare at the image from a few inches away, it's not always possible to see what it is – the dots (or pixels in this case) are too big for the brain to see as a whole. However, if you move the book further away from you, you can see an image. The brain is able to tie all the dots together into a meaningful whole.

The second feature of the brain that makes television possible is that it retains an image for a fraction of a second after it views it – a property called visual persistence.

2.2 Difficult to see close up, easier from further away.

If a series of identical images are displayed quickly enough, the brain won't see the gaps between them. It will register one persistent image. If you make minor changes to the images, the brain is likely to see these as movement – just like the children's books that show cartoon figures jumping up and down as you flick through the pages.

There's more detail on how viewers relate to television and interactive television in Chapter 5.

The television set

Scan lines

A cathode ray tube is at the heart of most television sets. In a standard colour set it fires three beams of electrons at the glass screen at the front of the set. The beams move quickly from the top to the bottom of the screen, hitting photo-reactive chemicals (phosphors) behind the glass and making them glow. Each beam targets a different phosphor red, green or blue. In response to electrical pulses that represent the brightness and colour of different parts of the picture, the intensity of each beam changes as it moves, making different parts of the screen glow different colours.

The beams move from the top to the bottom of the television screen, painting across it, left to right, in straight lines (called scanning lines) until the whole screen is covered. At the end of each line, the beams turn off and jump to the next line. At the bottom of the screen, the beams turn off and jump back up to the top. The whole process then starts again. This all happens so quickly that the human brain reassembles the collection of thousands of individual glowing dots into an understandable whole – the television picture.

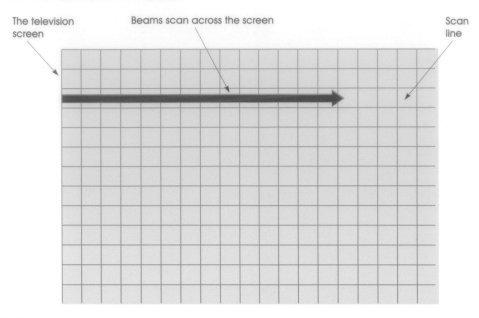

2.3 Electron beams scan across the television screen.

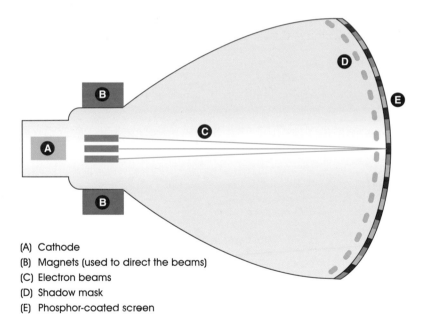

(A) Cathode
(B) Magnets (used to direct the beams)
(C) Electron beams
(D) Shadow mask
(E) Phosphor-coated screen

2.4 Inside the television.

Go and switch your television on now and stick your nose a few centimetres away from the screen. On a colour television, you'll see the thousands of tiny red, green and blue phosphors arranged in dots or stripes. Behind the dots is a perforated sheet, known as the shadow mask. This helps the electron beams strike individual dots cleanly and minimise unwanted illumination of neighbouring dots – a problem that can be caused by very rich colours, and one that interactive television graphics have to be designed to minimise.

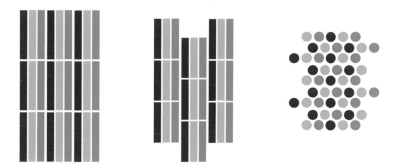

2.5 Various types of shadow mask phosphor patterns.

Interlacing

The next task for a television set is to tie these pictures together to create the illusion of movement. Years ago, movie makers worked out that you need to produce more than 40 pictures every second to fool the brain into thinking the picture is moving continuously. However, these movie pioneers could only work with enough film to get 16–24 frames per second. This is why cinema became known as the flicks: everyone could see the flicker as the frames changed. In cinema, the problem was solved by using special projectors that effectively showed each picture twice – doubling the frame rate to 48 and making the action look much smoother.

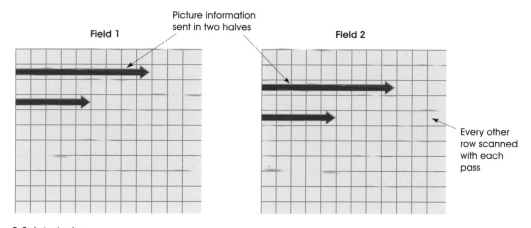

2.6 Interlacing.

The same problem occurs in television. Ideally, you need more than 40 frames per second, but that was too expensive and technically difficult in the early days. To deal with this problem, television pioneers found a clever solution. Televisions paint the screen (and cameras record the image) using alternate lines, completing the picture in two runs. After each run, top to bottom, the electron beams switch off and quickly jump back to the top of the screen to do the other lines. This tricks the brain into thinking that the image is being viewed at a faster rate, and makes any motion look much smoother – even though only half the screen (known as a field) has been drawn each time. The technique, known as interlacing, has a number of implications for interactive television design – particularly when graphics are designed on PC monitors, which update the whole screen with every pass (a technique known as progressive scanning).

Both the unwanted effects of rich colours and the problems for interactive television production associated with interlacing are covered in more detail in Chapter 5.

Country-by-country differences in television sets

The number of scans per second and the number of lines painted varies between different television systems around the world. Twenty-five whole pictures (50 fields) are built up each second in the European PAL and Secam systems, using 625 lines. In the United States and Japan, which use the NTSC-M system, it's 30 whole pictures (60 fields) per second, across 525 lines. The difference is partly due to the mains electricity used in the different areas. Television pioneers needed to use the electrical current to synchronise the timing of equipment, so settled for 50 and 60 frames per second respectively, which tied in with the frequency of the mains electricity, 50 Hz in Europe and 60 Hz in the US.

The transmission network or platform

The signal that most televisions require to continuously operate the electron beams contains three main types of information:

- Information that can be used to reproduce the colour and brightness correctly for each part of the image.
- A synchronisation pulse to tell the television when to move the beams to the start of a line.
- A synchronisation pulse to tell the television to move from the bottom to the top of the screen.

Televisions expect to get this information in a particular way, so they can use it to control the cathode ray tube at high speed.

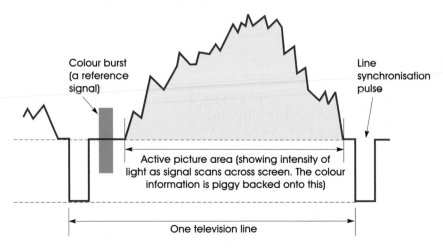

2.7 Close-up view – a signal used by the television to paint one line of the screen.

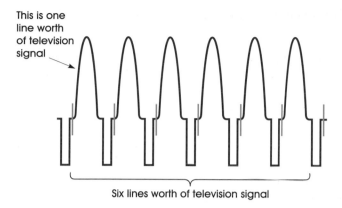

This is one
line worth
of television
signal

Six lines worth of television signal

2.8 Several lines worth of television signal.

These television signals can make their way from the location where they are produced to television sets in two forms: analogue or digital. Nearly all televisions eventually work only with an analogue signal to control the intensity of the electron beams. However, before this final stage, the signal can, and often is, converted back and forth between the two forms, on its journey from the supplier to the viewer. Whether a television transmission platform is marketed as digital or not, really depends on the exact points when a digital signal is used – and what actually constitutes a 'digital' system is very much a matter of opinion.

Analogue transmission

With analogue television transmission, the television signals are imprinted directly onto a carrier radio wave, in a process known as modulation. The carrier wave is altered in proportion to the changes in the level of the television signal. An antenna can then pick up the carrier wave and feed it into a television set, which can then extract the original signal and use it to control the electron beam.

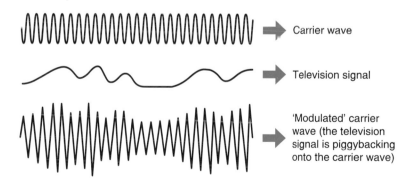

Carrier wave

Television signal

'Modulated' carrier
wave (the television
signal is piggybacking
onto the carrier wave)

2.9 A signal being added to a carrier wave – amplitude modulation.

The vertical blanking interval

In the 1970s, engineers at the BBC realised that some spare parts of the analogue television signal could be put to good use. The extra space, called the vertical blank-

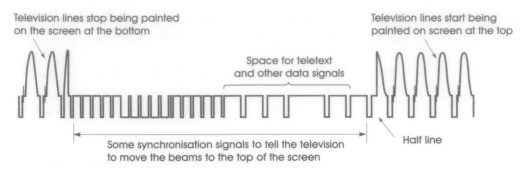

Television lines stop being painted on the screen at the bottom

Television lines start being painted on screen at the top

Space for teletext and other data signals

Some synchronisation signals to tell the television to move the beams to the top of the screen

Half line

2.10 The vertical blanking interval (VBI).

ing interval (VBI), was designed to allow the electron beams to jump back up to the top of the screen after painting each field. It is called VBI because the beams are blanked out during the interval it takes for them to jump vertically from the bottom of the screen to the top.

The VBI contains pulses that help synchronise the timing of the beams inside the television after they have made the jump from bottom to top. The BBC engineers put some extra signals carrying other information into this. If the television set at the other end was equipped with a suitable adapter, it could read this extra information and, for example, display words on-screen. The BBC started using this space to transmit television listings, news, weather and other useful information. Within a few years, millions of people across the United Kingdom and Europe were using services developed using this teletext technology.

The VBI can also be used for other types of data: subtitles, computer software or even web pages. All that is required is a box inside or connected to the television that can monitor the television signal, interpret any data sent in the VBI and process it in the right way. The VBI is the main delivery platform for interactive television in analogue broadcast environments. Many of the services provided in the United States – for example, versions of Wink TV enhanced television advertising and some versions of the Microsoft TV internet on television system – use the VBI.

The VBI is a particularly good method of transmission for interactive television because it is very easy to synchronise data with the underlying television picture. The data is inherently connected to the frame of video that it is sent along with, as it is carried in the spare capacity for that frame. To put up an interactive icon on-screen, for example, all the broadcaster has to do is make sure the instruction to put up the icon is contained in the VBI lines for the video frame that it needs to appear over. The disadvantage of using the VBI is that there is usually a relatively small amount of space available for data (especially if analogue teletext and subtitles are already being carried). Also, the VBI solution has rather been overtaken by big changes happening to television.

Changing television

The principles of television haven't changed a great deal since the first song in the first broadcast from Alexandra Palace in 1936. For anyone that wants to make fundamental changes to the technology of television (like changing the picture size or adding interactive television services), there are basically three choices:

- Replace every single television, transmitter and camera in the world with ones that incorporate the new technology.
- Try to find a way of piggybacking new technologies on the existing systems.
- A bit of both of the above.

The introduction of colour television was achieved by piggybacking the new technology onto the existing system (by squeezing the colour information into the existing black and white signal), combined with a slow upgrade of people's television sets over the course of the 1960s. Similarly, teletext was created using a space in the television signal that was originally designed for something else, combined with upgrades to television sets. The same sort of combined approach, the 'bit of both' option, is happening with interactive television.

On one hand, set-top boxes have been devised that can be used as an add-on to existing television sets. These allow viewers to use new services (like video-on-demand or enhanced television) without having to go to the expense or effort of buying a new television. The television itself doesn't need to be changed. On the other hand, the owners of television transmission platforms (cable, terrestrial and satellite operators) have replaced their old technologies with newer systems that make interactive television and other improvements (like more television channels) possible. By far the most important of these new technologies is digital transmission.

Digital transmission

People usually think that digital technology must be a good thing – but often can't explain why. Marketing executives have capitalised on this confusion and wasted no time branding all sorts of different products as digital: everything from music formats to electric toothbrushes.

Digital crash course

The principle behind digital is that information is coded into lists of ones and zeros known as binary. This system has the advantage of being able to be represented by an electric current as either an 'on' or an 'off'.

If you and I are trekking in the mountains and we agree that six blows on a whistle in quick succession (that is, the code 111111) means 'help, I'm in distress', then we have devised a digital communication system. Computers, and now television transmitters and set-top boxes, use digital systems. Once a system of meaning has been agreed between the sender and the receiver, almost any type of information can be communicated using ones and zeros – television pictures, computer programs, photographs, anything.

With an analogue television signal, the wave varies according to the intensity of the different parts of the picture. The conversion of analogue television signals to digital ones is done using sampling. Sampling involves breaking the original analogue signal into sections and measuring the signal in each section. Each point in the

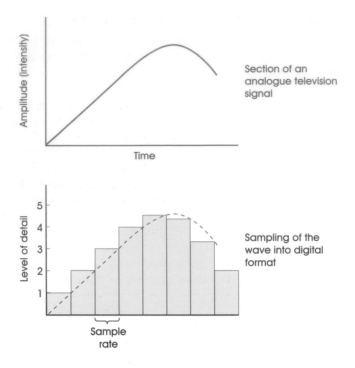

2.11 Sampling.

video signal is then given a binary value (for example 0100 or 0011), representing the size of the sample at that point.

In the case of the computer programs that are interactive services, the digital data represents the individual instructions that the computer processor running the interactivity should follow, such as what graphics to put on screen. There is no analogue equivalent of this.

With digital transmission, video signals, audio signals and interactive programs all combine to become part of one long stream of ones and zeros. The different types of data are identified by marker codes, which are themselves made up of binary code.

Video and audio sample quality

Digital samples are expressed in terms of the sample rate and the number of bits. The sample rate is how frequently the signal is measured (along the horizontal axis); the bit rate is the number of ones and zeros that can be used to define the size of the signal at each point (giving the level of detail available on the vertical access).

A two-bit sample rate (00, 11, 01 or 10) has four different values, giving any level between 0 and 3. An eight-bit sample (0000 0000, 1111 1111, 0101 0101 and so on) gives up to 256 different levels of signal that can be expressed with the ones and zeros – anything between 0 and 255.

The benefits of digital transmission for interactive television

The use of digital technologies for transmission has a couple of big advantages for interactive television services, far surpassing the value of the humble vertical blanking interval in the analogue transmission environment.

The first is that digital data transmission is very robust. Digital data, whether information about a television picture or an interactive service, is attached to a radio carrier wave by modulation (the binary code is transmitted by changing the characteristics of the carrier wave). Although both digital and analogue signals weaken (decrease) as they get further from the transmitter, digital ones will suffer much less from interference. If you've ever stood in front of a television with a coat hanger stuck in the back in lieu of an aerial, you'll know that weak analogue signals cause problems such as double images and ghost images from other channels. However, if the television receiver is close enough to get a signal at all, it should be able to detect whether a one or a zero is being transmitted. So digital signals are more likely than analogue ones to work better across a given distance. It's like being in the mountains and having to listen for the sound of a whistle rather than hearing the exact words someone is shouting. You either hear the whistle or you don't. This means digital transmitters need less power than analogue ones in order to cover the same area, making it easier to cover particular regions with a digital signal carrying television channels and interactive television services - and if the viewer normally gets a poor analogue signal, digital could offer a major improvement.

Another major benefit of digital transmission is that more information can be sent to viewers in a given piece of bandwidth (the space in the radio frequency range available for sending information on carrier waves – see the 'Bandwidth' definition). This is mostly thanks to the fact that digital television data can be compressed. Basically, to transmit an image using analogue transmission, every pixel has to be represented in the carrier wave in some way. With digital television, on the other hand, systems have been developed that take advantage of the way the brain perceives pictures and motion to remove data that isn't required. For example, if the background behind a presenter isn't changing, the information about that background only needs to be sent once – at least until the background changes. The most popular video compres-

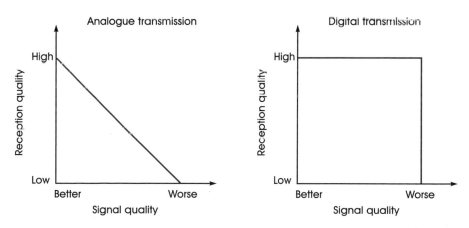

2.12 Analogue versus digital television transmission. Digital reception quality is mostly better, but will fail more dramatically.

sion standard with broadcasters and platform operators is MPEG-2 (see 'In-depth: MPEG-2'). MPEG-2 and other compression formats make it possible to send more channels and to fit interactive services, or anything else, in the space freed up by reducing the size of the video streams. In fact, in the space occupied by one analogue video channel it's possible to send five or more digital video channels (depending on the quality of picture required).

This bandwidth efficiency, more than anything, has led to the massive growth of interactive services on digital television transmission platforms. Interactive television, consequently, tends to be associated with digital platforms – and as digital platforms are built and developed, so interactive television services are built and developed.

It is possible to get interactive television to work on analogue transmission platforms, using the VBI for example, but there tends to be less bandwidth available. Conversely, it is also sometimes the case that digital platforms do not have interactive services. This is usually because the platform is newly launched and the operator is concentrating on getting the television working first, because the platform has very little bandwidth available for some reason, or because the platform is using one of the very early digital formats that doesn't have the capability to deal with interactive data. This is the case with some of the digital services launched in the 1990s in the United States.

The rest of this chapter refers to interactive television services on digital transmission platforms (although much of the information will be relevant to interactive television services running on analogue transmission platforms as well).

Bandwidth

Bandwidth is the amount of information that can be transferred in a given amount of time. Imagine it as a pipe with water flowing down it – the bigger the pipe, the more water that can flow down it. Interactive television producers often get into arguments with the television platform operators about the amount of bandwidth that will be made available for their interactive service: generally, the more bandwidth that is available, the more features can be added to the service.

In the analogue world, bandwidth is expressed in terms of the section (band) of the radio spectrum that is available or required for transmitting a signal. This is expressed in hertz (Hz), a unit of measurement of the number of changes in state or cycles of a radio wave in a second. An analogue television signal needs around 6 MHz range, or bandwidth, to carry enough information to build a picture (6 MHz bandwidth means there must be enough space to fit in six million cycles per second). To put it another way, if you own carrier waves between 600 and 624 MHz in the radio spectrum, you have enough space to transmit four television channels.

In the digital world, the term bandwidth has been hijacked and changed a little in meaning. Here it refers to the number of bits of information that can be transferred in a given time. A bit is a one or a zero. Broadcast-quality video generally requires around 3 Mbps (that's three mega, or million, bits per second) once it has been compressed, although this is partly a matter of opinion and depends on the compression system. Some broadcasters use 6 Mbps or more, while others will go as low as 1 Mbps. Using a half- or quarter-screen size or not worrying too much about quality also means the video data can take up much less bandwidth. In the internet world, technologies like Real Video and Windows Media have managed to squeeze watchable video down to 56 kbps (that's 56 kilo, or thousand, bits per second) and even less, but this is still nowhere near good enough for relaxed living room viewing on a big television screen.

Interactive services usually take up a lot less bandwidth than broadcast-quality video channels. This is because the number of ones and zeros needed to describe a computer program and simple graphics is much less than required to describe a high-quality moving video picture. It's been known for enterprising broadcasters to run passable digital teletext services in less than 50 kbps (50 000 bits per second) bandwidth. Generally, the more complicated the service and the more content it contains (be that photos, products for sale, text or – worst of all – video), the more bandwidth it will require. Text on its own without photos and graphics generally takes up the least bandwidth (information about how to draw letters on-screen is generally stored at the receiving end, so doesn't need to be sent in transmission).

Be careful not to confuse bits with bytes. A byte is the information carried by eight bits. Bytes are generally used as a measurement of computer storage.

Digital platforms

Some jargon that platform operators use

There are usually two routes for signals and, therefore, the data that makes up particular interactive television services, to get to viewers via digital transmission platforms:

- Broadcast via a one-way route, which is used to send information from the broadcaster to the viewer. This is known variously as the one-way channel, the broadcast channel, forward path or in-band channel.
- Transmitted via a two-way route, which can be used to send information back and forth between the broadcaster and viewer. This interactive communication channel is variously known as the two-way channel, interaction channel, return path, back channel or out-of-band channel.

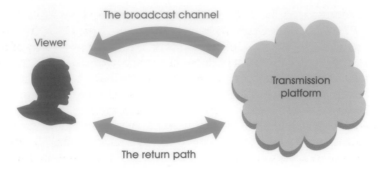

2.13 Broadcast channel, return path and the viewer.

The broadcast (one-way) channel

A typical television platform operator will take a range of video and interactive data feeds from different broadcasters (for example, MTV, Sky, CNN) and interactive service suppliers. They will then combine the different bits of data into one signal, in a process called multiplexing, add this onto a carrier wave (using modulation) and send it out to viewers. Basically, there only needs to be one version of each bit of data, as it will be broadcast to everyone.

You may be wondering how interactive services sent by a one-way channel can really be interactive. After all, there is no way for the viewer to send a response or instruction back to the broadcaster. Some commentators don't believe that it is possible to have 'true' interactive television using the broadcast channel. Nevertheless, from the viewers' point of view, the experience can certainly feel interactive. The way this works is that every single thing that the viewer could do is planned for in advance. All the instructions for these various possibilities are bundled together and sent down the one-way stream. Although the communication is not two-way, it appears so to viewers. Everything the viewer does is followed by what looks like an interactive response. Analogue teletext usually works on this kind of one-way broadcast system, but the pages still appear as if they are arriving to order.

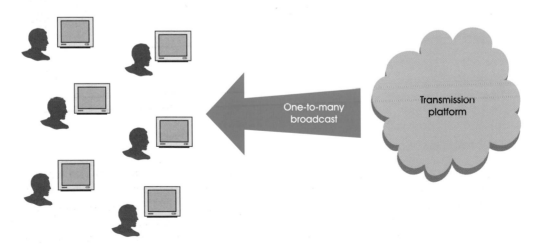

2.14 A one-to-many broadcast system.

There is a limit to the size of interactive information that can be sent in the broadcast stream. That limit depends on the bandwidth allocated. Bandwidth, in this case, is a measure of the amount of data that can be sent in a given time. If a lot of bandwidth is set aside by the operator, then lots of data can be sent quickly – and the viewer will have to wait less time for the interactive service to load and the content to be displayed. If there is very little bandwidth, then less data can be transmitted in a given time. It will then take longer for the interactive service and its content to load. If the wait time becomes too long, the viewer may give up and go and do something less boring instead. The earlier the bandwidth requirements can be planned, the better. A number of UK digital television channels found that in the early days they didn't allocate enough bandwidth for interactive services and therefore had to limit development – or offer services that ran very slowly.

Most broadcast-channel data that relates to interactive services is sent on a carousel system. This means that once all the data has been broadcast once, it is sent again and again, just like a fairground ride turning around. The data needs to be sent many times on a loop, because it's often impossible to know when a viewer will need to download a particular item.

The data is often split into two parts:

- The application (that is, the master control program for the service).
- The data that goes with the application (such as photos, graphics, pages of text and so on).

Whenever a viewer requests a particular interactive service or piece of content, they have to wait for the right blocks of data to come around in the carousel, before they can start downloading it. Any changes to the data made by the broadcaster are reflected the next time that particular piece of information goes out on the carousel.

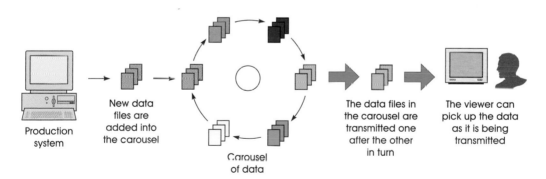

Production system · New data files are added into the carousel · Carousel of data · The data files in the carousel are transmitted one after the other in turn · The viewer can pick up the data as it is being transmitted

2.15 Carousel update of interactive data.

Data that is likely to be popular (like the front page of a news service) can be sent more often on the carousel, so it arrives more quickly to viewers. Analogue teletext also usually works on a carousel system: whenever you type in a page number, you have to wait for that page to come around on the carousel and download into the television before it can be displayed on-screen. The front pages of teletext services tend to be included in the carousel more often than other pages.

Popular data can also be pre-stored near the receiver's end (in a process known as caching). The fast-text function in analogue teletext, which allows viewers to jump quickly (by pressing coloured buttons) to up to four pages linked to the one being viewed, works by pre-storing these four pages in a cache in the television set. This helps increase access speeds.

Multiple interactive services often share the same data carousel.

The return path (two-way channel)

With a return path (two-way channel) there is a two-way relationship between the viewer and content supplier. Each time a viewer makes a request for something (for example, a page of weather information), the interactive service supplier is able to act on that request and send the information out. In other words, there is a direct interaction or point-to-point transfer of data.

Return paths can operate at anything from a very slow 2.4 kbps modem (only good for sending the simplest information), to a super-fast DSL line, which is able to carry enough data to construct a high-quality video picture (at the same quality level as might be found in the broadcast channel). Most – although not all – digital transmission platforms include some kind of return path. The ones that don't have one are limited to providing interactivity via the broadcast channel.

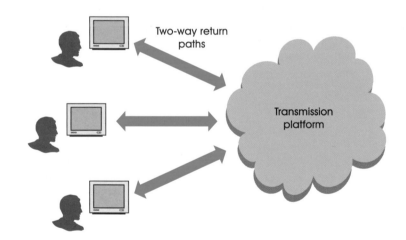

2.16 A return path means the the viewer can talk back to the platform owner.

The disadvantage of a two-way point-to-point model using the return path is that if lots of people request information at the same time, the system can get clogged up. This is the reason that the internet, which is also a two-way point-to-point system, slows down sometimes and on certain web sites, because too many people are trying to access information at the same time.

Interactive television is particularly susceptible to this problem. If a piece of inter-activity is promoted on a television programme (using a graphical overlay, for example), lots of people are likely to request that information at the same time. If the data needs to be sent to all of them individually (that is, lots of versions of the same bit of data), it's likely to cause congestion in the return path. If the information requested takes up lots of bandwidth – video, for example – the problem is likely to be even more severe.

Platform operators sometimes use caching on their return paths to get round this. By pre-storing popular content, there's likely to be less waiting for data to be transported across the network and less likelihood of congestion.

The other way around the problem is to make sure that any service or content that is likely to be in heavy demand is put in the broadcast channel, rather than sent via the return path. In the broadcast channel, everyone can receive the data without fear of congestion.

Broadband

Broadband is one of those terms that everyone bandies about, but there are often contradictory views on what it means. One definition is that broadband means a two-way connection between a user and an operator, where the bandwidth available is significantly higher than what was available in earlier systems. There isn't much agreement about exactly what this extra bandwidth needs to be in order to justify the name broadband. Generally, though, if the connection is two-way and over about 250 kbps you won't embarrass yourself at parties by calling it broadband.

Standards

In the area of interactive television – as in many other forms of telecommunications and technology – certain standards have been agreed to allow manufacturers and broadcasters around the world to build technologies and types of content that work together. This keeps the cost of development down for everyone and makes the industry as a whole more likely to succeed. These useful, but often very dry, standards often have odd names like DSM-CC and MPEG-2.

Because technology is always moving forwards, there are also organisations and groups of engineers who constantly review new ideas to see if they should be included in the latest versions of existing standards. These groups are sometimes formal, sometimes informal, sometimes commercial, sometimes not.

The evolution of standardisation of interactive television is, however, relatively young, compared to the broadcast television and internet worlds – and many standards used by interactive television are borrowed from these areas anyway. Some of the attempts at standardisation are outlined at the end of this chapter.

Data transport protocols

Whether data for an interactive application is sent via the broadcast channel or the two-way return path, there are a number of standard ways for describing and transporting it. These protocols are effectively the traffic police and taxi drivers of the interactive television world – directing data in the right direction and then transporting it from place to place.

For example, for the broadcast channel, parts of video compression standard MPEG-2 can be used to specify how to carry different types of data in addition to television pictures, while a set of protocols under the rather military sounding name Digital Storage Media – Command and Control (DSM-CC) can be used to control data streams. Certain types of data can also be carried using protocols designed for television listings information. Two different systems for this are DVB-SI and ATSC-PSIP (see 'In-depth: DVB and ATSC' later in this chapter).

For the two-way return path, internet standards are often used. For example, internet protocol (IP) is a format for addressing information that is often used by interactive television platform operators. IP addresses are a string of numbers that act as unique identifiers for a particular computer – or, in this case, the interactive television set.

The distinction between one-way broadcast and two-way return path protocols is increasingly blurred. For instance, IP contains a standard called Multicast IP, which allows a single set of data to be sent to many different receivers (effectively a broadcast model using an interactive channel), while, on the other hand, parts of the DSM-CC protocol can also be used for one-to-one communication via either channel. It is also possible for data to be dynamically moved between the broadcast and return path channels (for example, in response to changes in demand) and for requests sent via the return path channel to be fulfilled via the broadcast channel rather than back through the interactive channel.

Types of platform

The main digital transmission platforms that carry interactive television in the United Kingdom are:

- Cable. The main operators in the UK are NTL and Telewest.
- Terrestrial. The main operator in the UK is a consortium consisting of the BBC, Crown Castle International and BSkyB. The service is called Freeview.
- Satellite. The main operator in the UK is BSkyB. The service is called Sky Digital.
- The phone network (using DSL technology). UK operators include Video Networks Ltd and Kingston Communications.

Cable

Cable companies use a physical cable connection between themselves and their customers; that's why they spend a lot of time digging up the streets. Cables can

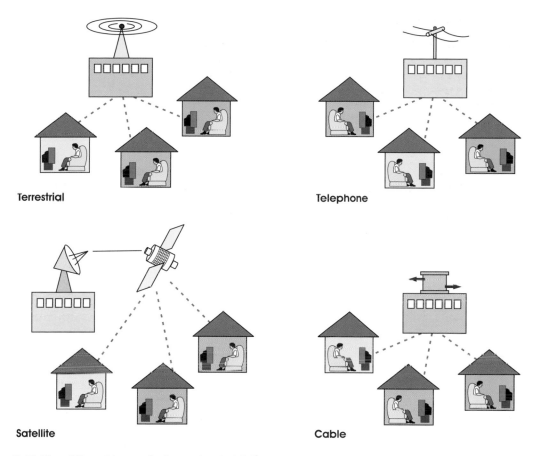

Terrestrial

Telephone

Satellite

Cable

2.17 The different transmission networks/platforms.

carry lots of data (there is usually a large amount of bandwidth), partly because they are closed systems, protected from interference (from the weather, for example).

Fibre-optic cable, which utilises light for data transfer, is often used to move information around the central parts of the cable company's network. At a physical location called a headend, bits of data from different sources (broadcasters and so on) are combined and pumped down to customers in a particular area. Big cable companies will have several headends, one for each region. Once the signal reaches street level it is sent down a co-axial cable (it's generally too expensive to have optical fibre in the home, although this has been tried in some areas). Co-axial cable is so called because it is made of one wire that carries the signal, surrounded by a layer of insulation, plus another wire, which serves as a ground. A network made up of optical fibres and co-axial cables is known as hybrid fibre co-axial (HFC), and is a common mix in the UK.

The advantage of cable platforms for interactive television is that there is usually enough capacity for a high-bandwidth two-way return path as well as a high-bandwidth broadcast channel. Using the return path, cable customers and the cable

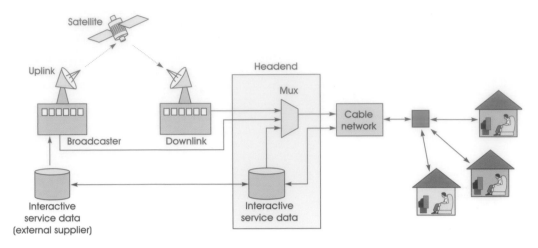

2.18 A typical cable platform.

company can communicate with each other at high speeds. To do this, cable platforms use cable modems. These facilitate two-way communication between ten and 100 times faster than the normal telephone modems that you see attached to personal computers.

Cable companies will also often provide a separate twisted-pair cable (so called because it is made of two copper wires twisted around each other) into the home, along with the co-axial cable. This is used to provide plain old telephone services (POTS).

The disadvantage of cable platforms for interactive television producers is that the transmission platform only reaches the customers that have cable in their street. This is not a big problem in the United States, where cable penetration is high, but more of an issue in some European countries, where the amount of homes passed by cable is relatively small. The UK arguably has a reasonable cable penetration – around 50 per cent of homes can get it if they want it.

Satellite

Satellite platform operators broadcast their signals from transmitters sitting about 38 000 km (23 000 miles) up in the sky. From this geostationary position, one satellite can transmit its signal to large parts of the Earth's surface – the whole of Europe along with parts of the Middle East and Russia, for example. As with cable and terrestrial platforms, satellites convey information on carrier signals. Viewers pick up the signal by using directional antennas, commonly known as satellite dishes. These improve the strength of the signal at the reception point. They work by reflecting the radio waves (using a curved surface called a reflector) into the centre of the dish. The radio waves are then converted into signals that are sent down to the set-top box. The bigger the reflector is, the greater the strength of the signal. Digital dishes can be quite small.

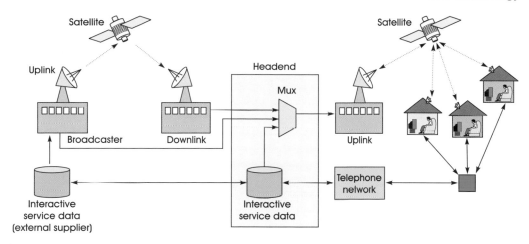

2.19 A typical satellite platform.

As with cable, television channels and interactive services are first combined together at a headend. Satellite operators then send the data up to the satellite using powerful transmitter antennas sitting on the ground, known as uplinks. Up at the satellite, the signal is amplified and transmitted back to earth from a transponder. Most satellites have hundreds of transponders, carrying different sets of television channels and other types of communication signal.

The big advantage of satellite is that the only big cost is for the radio bandwidth on the satellite (which is generally hired from the company that owns the satellite) and for the uplinks. There's no need to worry about digging up the street to every house, or building a network of transmitters around the country.

A disadvantage of satellite is that digital and analogue signals can suffer interference or be weakened by bad weather (particularly rain) and from solar activity. Another disadvantage, particularly for interactive television, is that it is difficult for viewers to send a signal to the broadcaster or platform operator back up via the satellite (unless the viewer fancies having a 100-tonne uplink dish in the back garden – along with a few technicians drinking tea in the shed). To get round this, satellite set-top boxes can usually be plugged into the phone network to allow two-way communication, albeit at a relatively low bandwidth.

Terrestrial

Digital terrestrial television (DTT) uses ground-based transmitters to get radio signals into homes. The big advantage here is that digital signals can be transmitted from transmitters attached to existing installations built for analogue television. Furthermore, viewers are usually able to pick up the signal with their existing aerial. This means that, in theory, the entry costs for digital terrestrial television are low and it should be easy to move people across from analogue to digital using the terrestrial system. In the UK and other countries, the reality has been somewhat different: digital terrestrial systems have been dogged by problems with interference and signal loss. In the UK, the pay-TV digital terrestrial system ITV Digital was forced to close in 2002. Viewers were leaving in droves, which was due, among other things,

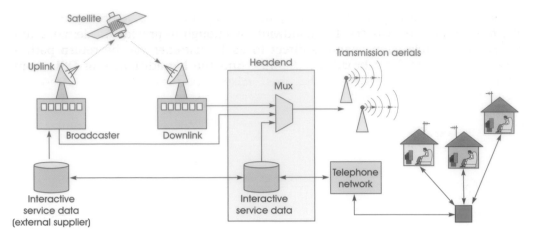

2.20 A typical digital terrestrial television platform.

to people having problems getting a good picture. At the end of 2002 it was reborn as Freeview, which carries less channels and suffers less from picture problems.

As with satellite, the disadvantage of digital terrestrial is that there is no inherent two-way communication channel. To circumvent this, set-top boxes can be attached to the phone network. Another problem is that there tends to be less bandwidth available in the terrestrial spectrum for data – meaning that digital terrestrial platforms tend to have fewer television channels and interactive services than satellite or cable platforms.

The telephone and other networks

Although cable, satellite and terrestrial are the main ways to get television and interactive services, there are others. Several up-and-coming platforms, such as VideoNetwork's HomeChoice service in the UK, use the twisted-pair copper wires of the existing phone network. Standard PC-modems already use these wires to communicate with the PC-internet at relatively low speeds up to 56 kbps. However, platforms like VideoNetworks use a new technology, called DSL (digital subscriber lines), which allows data to be transferred over the same copper cables at much higher speeds. One common form, called ADSL (asymmetric digital subscriber line), provides speeds of between 144 kbps and 1.54 Mbps, back and forth between the viewer and the platform provider.

ADSL works by using frequencies to transmit data down the wires that are not required for voice phone calls (in this way, it's possible to use an ADSL modem at the same time as making a voice telephone call on the same line). The frequencies used for data are then further split up into multiple streams and data is transferred on each one. At the telephone company's office or exchange sits a box, called a DSL access multiplexer (DSLAM), which combines multiple data streams into a single signal with the outside world.

Satellite and terrestrial operators often work in partnership with telephone operators to offer DSL technologies to their customers. DSL gives these platforms the opportunity to erase the competitive advantage cable has from its fast two-way return path connection. DSL also gives phone companies and platform operators the opportunity to become broadcasters. The bandwidth is enough to provide on-demand and live streaming television channels direct to each customer via the return path – negating the need for a broadcast channel. And the big advantage of DSL, from the customer's point of view, is that their existing telephone line can provide all this – there's no need to put up a dish or connect a cable.

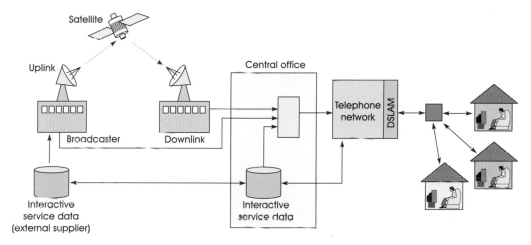

2.21 A typical broadband telephone network.

The disadvantage of DSL is that the distance from the main exchange limits DSL connections. ADSL, for example, is only really possible up to around 5 km from the DSLAM. It is therefore generally only available to people in built-up areas. DSL is also still relatively expensive for the platform provider to install (more expensive even than cable modem equipment).

There are several other less popular (so far) methods for getting television and interactive television into customers' front rooms. For example, it's possible to receive data via microwave radio signals to small antennas on the roof (known as wireless cable), via networks usually used by computers (like Ethernet or ATM), and via the electricity system.

Simultaneous analogue and digital

Platform operators often transmit analogue television pictures along with digital data. They do this because they can't change all their customers to digital equipment at the same time. The digital and analogue services are allocated different frequencies – the digital ones tend to be able to occupy space that wasn't suitable for analogue signals because of problems with interference. As more analogue channels are switched off, additional bandwidth is freed up for digital channels and interactive services.

In-depth: MPEG-2

The most common digital video compression standard used in broadcast television is MPEG-2. Interactive television services often include video streams in MPEG-2 format, so it is worth knowing a little about how it works.

The Moving Pictures Experts Group (MPEG) is made up of a number of industry luminaries and academics who want to standardise digital video and multimedia compression and transmission technologies. It started with only 25 experts but has grown to include hundreds of people and companies from around the world. Many of the participants are involved for academic reasons, others because digital video standards have massive commercial implications for the companies they work for.

MPEG covers a whole family of standards, which are used for different types of data in different ways, each one with a different identifying number (the numbers do not, however, imply that one format is better than the next – just different):

- MPEG-1 is used for putting sound and video on CDs.
- MPEG-2 is the most widely adopted standard for professional high-quality digital television transmission and is likely to stay that way for some time.
- MPEG-4 is used for the transmission of multimedia content across television platforms and the internet (see the 'MPEG-4' section later in the chapter).
- MPEG-7 and MPEG-21. These are standards for classifying and managing video and other types of data (see the 'MPEG-4' section for a little more on these).

MPEG-2 compression works by cutting unnecessary information out of the digital video signal. First, it looks at individual frames and records only enough details to make the picture work on a television screen. (This works in the same way with JPEG images on internet sites, which remove unimportant parts of the image, like the very fine details, to make the file size smaller.) Next it compares adjacent frames and records only the parts of the picture that have moved or changed in some way. If a television presenter is shown against a static background, only the movement of their head and mouth is recorded. Information about the background needs be sent just once – until it moves or changes.

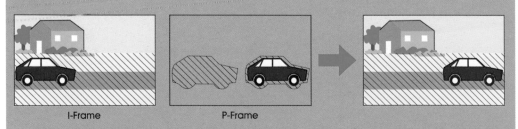

I-Frame   P-Frame

2.22 The I- and P-frames – predicting the picture.

To work the compression across time, MPEG-2 works on groups of frames. The first frame is used as a reference frame and is recorded relatively uncompressed. This is known as the I (or intra)-frame. The I-frame is then used to construct another frame a bit further along in the video sequence. Each part of this frame, known as the P (predictive)-frame, is constructed by looking at the I-frame to see if it is the same. If it's the same, there is no need for that information to be sent again.

Another smart feature of MPEG-2 is that it can also detect whether something has moved to another part of the screen (a ball flying across the scene in a football match, for example). Then, rather than sending the information again, it simply sends details of where that screen element has moved. The final stage of the process is that the I- and P-frames are compared with the other frames, known as B (bidirectionally predictive)-frames. These B-frames are then compressed at very high rates. To enable all this comparison work to happen, the MPEG-2 coding often reorganises the order of frames, and B-frames are often transmitted after I- and P-frames.

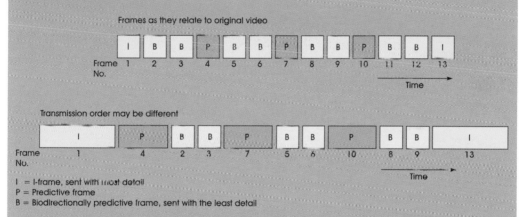

I = I-frame, sent with most detail
P = Predictive frame
B = Biodirectionally predictive frame, sent with the least detail

2.23 A group of MPEG-2 frames. The transmission order can be different from the original video and some frames need to contain more data than others.

Interactive services sometimes grab single I-frames for use as part of the user interface (perhaps as a background). It's possible to send just an MPEG-2 stream with I-frames and nothing else, which can then be picked up and used by a range of interactive services. However, the way MPEG-2 works can also make building some types of interactive television services more difficult. Specifically, MPEG-2 makes it tricky to synchronise interactive content with video content (compared to the VBI, which can carry interactive service information in exactly the right part of the television signal). The problem is that there is no specific part of the MPEG-2 system that defines a frame of video and what interactivity should be associated or overlaid with it. This problem is compounded by the fact that frame order is mixed up and that only I-frames are sent with all the picture information intact.

The new MPEG-4 standard avoids some of these problems, although it is not widely adopted on major digital television platforms. There's more on MPEG-4 later.

In-depth: DVB and ATSC

Two of the most powerful television bodies in the world are the Digital Video Broadcasting group (DVB) and the Advanced Television Systems Committee (ATSC).

The DVB group provides a forum for setting standards used for the delivery of digital television content between the different devices in the broadcast chain: multiplexers, transmitters, set-top boxes and television sets. The DVB group aims for interoperability between all the devices in this chain. The standards it has produced for ratification by various bodies (like the European Telecommunications Standards Institute) have widespread acceptance in Europe, as well as South America and Asia.

As well as adopting MPEG-2 as the digital video compression system, the DVB group has developed standards for all the other bits of information that need to be sent between pieces of equipment to make them interoperable. This includes: modulation standards (which have different forms for cable, satellite and terrestrial); a conditional access standard (DVB-CA) that controls access to channels and services; a subtitle standard (DVB-SUB); and a standard for transmitting service information about the programmes and channels contained in the MPEG-2 stream (called DVB-SI).

The DVB-SI (service information) standard defines tables of information that, once transmitted, allow set-top boxes to, among other things, group channels and programmes into categories (like news, comedy and film) and monitor the start time of programmes (so on-screen reminders can come up at the right time). Needless to say, EPG applications tend to make very heavy use of DVB-SI data, although other interactive services can draw on it too. Additionally, some platform operators are starting to use the optional tables in DVB-SI to send extra information about interactivity (for example, whether a television programme has enhanced content and what that content is). DVB-SI tables can only be taken so far, however. The SI structure is not designed for complex instructions. To address this problem, the DVB has defined what could be the most significant standard in interactive television production ever: DVB-MHP. The Multimedia Home Platform (MHP) standard promises broadcasters and content suppliers the ability to create an interactive service once, in the secure knowledge that it will work in the same way whatever digital platform it is transmitted on and whatever kind of set-top boxes it is displayed on. There's more on this important standard later in this chapter.

The Advanced Television Systems Committee (ATSC) is effectively a rival to the DVB group and is dominant in the United States. ATSC has also been adopted in parts of Asia and in Canada. It initially focused on high-definition television (high-quality widescreen television with more lines and smaller pixels than normal television), but has expanded its remit. As with DVB, ATSC has chosen MPEG-2 as its video compression system. It has also defined modulation and other systems that are required for interoperability between equipment. It has its own equivalent of SI data tables, called the Program and System Information Protocol (PSIP). It also has an equivalent of MHP, called DASE. Unfortunately, although the chosen video system (MPEG-2) is the same with DVB and ATSC, the other standards are a little different. This means that even if Europe and the rest of the world manage to agree a consistent system for creating and displaying interactive services (and even this won't happen until MHP is widely implemented), these will not necessarily work in the United States and vice versa.

A further complication is that the Japanese have another approach in the form of the Integrated Services Digital Broadcasting (ISDB) standards. This is different again from both DVB and ATSC.

Interactive television set-top boxes

Digital set-top boxes are one of the keys to the modern communications world. A typical digital set-top box takes digital data and converts it into analogue signals the television can use, runs interactive services and operates stereo sound. Simultaneously, the box manages purchases, protects children from unsuitable material and maintains multiple lines of communication with the outside world. The good ones almost never crash or break down. And sometimes, they are given away completely free – as pawns in great political and commercial gambles.

2.24 Parental control systems in the set-top box being accessed using the EPG. © *BSkyB*.

Most set-top boxes work with an analogue signal or a digital signal, not both; they usually work only on one television delivery platform – cable, terrestrial, satellite or DSL. This is because each platform uses a different frequency range to transmit its television signals and uses different modulation techniques for adding channels and interactivity into a given piece of bandwidth. Hardware in the box needs to be constructed to deal with the modulated signal for a particular platform. It is possible for a box to work with more than one transmission platform, but it requires expensive extra hardware. (It is also theoretically possible with some set-top boxes to add an attachment called a sidecar. This adds the electronics needed to receive an extra platform onto an existing set-top box designed for another platform.) The UK competition regulators have always been keen to enforce this kind of interoperability between set-top boxes and transmission platforms – but have always failed.

Set-top boxes are sometimes integrated into televisions rather than stuck on top of them. These integrated digital televisions (idTVs) have all or most of the functionality of a set-top box incorporated within the normal television electronics.

The set-top box is central to the work of interactive television producers: it makes interactive services happen. The hardware specification of the set-top box defines the capabilities of the interactive services, while the software processes provide the tools for producers to turn their interactive ideas into reality.

Opening the box: hardware

Set-top boxes are computers. They use the same electronics and the same basic architecture. However, the hardware inside set-top boxes is often less powerful than on the latest computers, because set-top box manufacturers usually need to keep prices down. This is either because box prices need to be competitive or because a platform operator is going to be subsidising the cost (perhaps even giving the boxes away for free) and will want to minimise the outlay. (Imagine having to justify the purchase of one million set-top boxes in your business plan. It makes a big difference whether each box costs you £250 rather than £350 to manufacture.) The memory and processing power of new set-top boxes usually equates to the home personal computers that people were buying three or four years previously.

Core components

After the television signal has gone into the set-top box, the first stop is the tuner. The tuner isolates the radio frequencies that carry particular channels of information from the range of frequencies being sent into the box. After the tuner, the radio wave carrying any digital information is sent to the demodulator. This converts the pulses carried on the radio wave into a digital data stream.

Demultiplexer

After the demodulator, a digital box is left with a string of ones and zeros that have been unpacked from the carrier wave. It sends the data to the demultiplexer to be interpreted. The demultiplexer identifies the different elements within the digital stream and separates them. Different parts of the data will be marked up as either information about the video picture, information about the audio, data about programme schedules or data that can be used to build an interactive service.

Conditional access

After demultiplexing, the box checks whether the television channel or interactive service in the data stream have been paid for by the set-top box owner or – more crucially for parents – whether it needs to be protected with a password screen. All this is handled by the conditional access (CA) system. This compares the type of programme, channel or interactive services against a list of services that the set-top box owner is allowed to access. The conditional access system also deals with any video signals or interactive services that are sent in a specially encrypted form to protect against unauthorised use. It decrypts these, before passing them on.

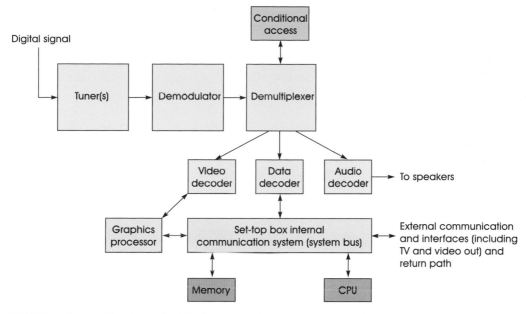

2.25 The physical hardware inside the set-top box.

Video and audio cards

The different bits of digital information are sent to appropriate parts of the box for specialist processing. The video data is sent to a video card. This converts the video data back into a signal that the television can understand. The signal is then sent out to the television via a Scart (or similar) or turned back into a radio signal and sent via the RF lead. The video card works in close conjunction with an audio card, which deals with the audio sections of the data stream and converts it into an output that is suitable for home hi-fi.

CPU and memory

Any interactive data segments, which could be television listings information or interactive services, are sent to a data decoder, which marks them up for appropriate action by the central processing unit (CPU). The CPU, with its processor chip, is the brain of the set-top box. It manages all the hardware components, runs software programs and monitors for problems. The CPU also has access to a graphics processor and to memory. The graphics processor renders interactive text, colours and pictures to the television screen – it is the core display tool for interactive services.

There are several different types of memory in a typical set-top box, each of which performs different functions. Random access memory (RAM) is used as a temporary storage area. When the set-top box is switched off, information held in RAM disappears. Read-only memory (ROM), on the other hand, keeps its information when the set-top box is switched off, but capacity is usually very limited. There are two particular types of ROM memory that set-top boxes use. The first is called EEPROM, which holds information permanently on chips and is typically used to hold the programs that are required to start the set-top up. The other is Flash memory, which can be erased and reprogrammed more easily than EEPROM. Flash memory is used for computer programs that need to be constantly available in the box but might need to be changed – upgrades to the core software, for example.

Some set-top boxes (such as the TiVo and Sky+) have extra storage capacity. These use personal computer-style high-capacity hard drives (and sometimes other storage devices) to record television programmes and interactive applications for later use. This hard drive makes it possible to record, stop, rewind and forward wind television programmes at any time. And it makes it possible to store very large interactive applications, like 3D games. Some games consoles (like the Microsoft Xbox) have similar functionality. See the TV Anytime section towards the end of this chapter for more on these personal video recorder (PVR) technologies.

External communication and interfaces

Most set-top boxes receive most information via the broadcast tuner. However, there are other ways for the boxes to receive and send information.

Smart cards

Most set-top boxes contain a smart card reader (usually in the front panel). Smart cards store information about the channels and interactive services to which the user has subscribed, and keep a running total of pay-per-view programmes or pay-per-use interactive services. The conditional access system then draws on this information in deciding whether a viewer is allowed to use a service.

Pay-per-view services typically work by keeping count of the number of orders on the smart card using a token system. Each time the user views a video programme (such as a boxing match or some porn) or uses an interactive service that needs to be paid for, one unit is removed from the balance on the smart card. Once all the tokens are gone, nothing more can be ordered. Periodically, the platform operator checks the content of the smart card via the two-way return path, adds the price of the tokens used to the customer's bill and resets the token balance. If the box isn't connected to a two-way channel (a phone line or other means of sending information back to the operator), the pay-per-view operator will require the viewer to contact customer services using a telephone. In this case, the central office, not the smart card, records the number of movies viewed and sends permissions to the conditional access system in the broadcast stream.

Smart cards can be taken in and out of the box, although the latest versions will code themselves electronically to a particular box the first time they are used and will not work with other boxes. (With these new boxes it's no longer possible to take a smart card over to your friend's house or down the pub so you can all watch the big game there).

Advanced smart cards can also be used as electronic purses. Although still quite rare, viewers can deposit money onto these cards (using, for example, a specially adapted bank cash point), then slot them into the box to spend the money on various services. Alternatively, some set-top boxes have credit card readers. These can be used to read the identity information off credit cards. Viewers can then make purchases at home simply by slotting the credit card into the set-top box.

Development of the smart card was the basis for much of the modern UK pay-per-view environment: it enabled Sky Digital to charge for football and movies, and to make the content exclusive. However, smart cards have to be continually evolved to keep ahead of a flourishing counterfeit operation.

Modems

The modem in a set-top box allows communication back and forth with the outside world via the return path, by modulating and demodulating data onto a carrier wave. There are many species of modem, which use various standards for communicating back to base and with the outside world, based on the type of modulation they employ. These include the V.22/V.22bis standard used in modems in older set-top boxes, with transfer rates no more than 2400 bps, all the way through to V.90 and K56Flex standard that can send and receive information via the phone line at speeds up to 56 kbps.

Cable modems use one of two main standards. The United States-based Multimedia Cable Network System (MCNS) has developed a standard called Data Over Cable System Interface Specification (DOCSIS). The European based Digital Audio Visual Council (DAVIC) has its own alternative. Theoretically, cable modems can squeeze around 30 Mbps out of a cable line, but in reality viewers usually get up to 1.5 Mbps or so, which is sometimes shared between several people on the same street. Cable companies will also sometimes put limiters on cable modem connections, keeping them down to 512 kbps or less, useful to stop your customers running their own internet service providers from their living rooms.

ADSL modems, which squeeze large data-transfer speeds out of copper telephone wires, use either the discrete multi-tone (DMT) standard or the carrierless amplitude phase (CAP) system. Both these provide up to around 1.5 Mbps into the home.

With most types of modem, the bandwidth allocated or available to send data from the platform operator to the customer (known as downstream) is usually higher than that between customer and platform operator (known as upstream). This reflects the fact that it is the operators that normally send the bulk of data, in response to relatively small (in data terms) requests from viewers.

Interfaces

Interfaces are added to set-top boxes to extend their functionality to other devices. Interfaces also help to make a set-top box future proof. As functionality and new devices are developed, these can be added to the original box using the different interfaces.

Boxes often include one, two or more of the following:

- Parallel (known as IEEE 1284) and serial (known as RS-232) ports, so they can be connected to printers and devices that don't need terribly fast data-transfer rates.
- Universal serial bus (USB) interfaces, which can be used for a wide range of equipment, from scanners to hard drives to networking.
- The relatively new IEEE 1394 (sometimes known as Firewire) interface, for attaching kit that requires high rates of data transfer (like video cameras).

- Common interfaces, which take hardware modules like the Personal Computer Memory Card International Association (PCMIA).
- Base-T (Ethernet) connections, which have been used for years in offices to network computers.
- Bluetooth and other systems that enable wireless communication between devices.

Unfortunately, just because a set-top box has some of these great interfaces doesn't mean they actually work. The manufacturer of the set-top box, and the people who make equipment to plug into them, often have to do quite a lot of software development to get them working. Consequently, set-top boxes often come with interfaces that do not have drivers (the software in the set-top box that tells the box how to access the interface). They are therefore useless. Manufacturers and platform operators put the interfaces on the boxes with the expectation that they may make them work at some point in the future.

Remote controls

Viewers can send instructions to set-top boxes to perform functions using infrared (IR) remote controls or IR keyboards. Set-top boxes themselves can also tell video recorders and other devices what to do by using IR blasters. This is a remote control that is fitted to the set-top box, so it can send out its own instructions.

Infrared waves are just past visible light on the electromagnetic spectrum (and just before micro and radio waves), and so a line of sight between the sender and receiver is required, although bouncing the signal off walls is possible.

Wireless keyboards are designed to sit on people's laps and are usually much smaller than personal computer keyboards – they are a must-have for anyone who wants to write a lot of emails using their television. There are also a variety of other devices that can work using IR, from joysticks to speakers, removing the need for ugly cabling to be strung across the front-room floor.

One interesting piece of technology allows set-top boxes to work with and identify more than one remote control. Each remote is given its own unique identification code in the IR signals it sends. This facilitates games being played on television by different members of the family at the same time – and the set-top box can tell whether Mum or little Johnny answered the on-screen question correctly.

Opening the box: the software

Software programs are the building blocks of interactive television. Interactive television producers tend to have a much closer working relationship with set-top box software than anything else.

Software, processed in the CPU, manages the hardware on the set-top box, communicates back with the platform operator, and controls the presentation of information and interactivity. Although interactive television software can work in many different ways, the structure is broadly the same across almost every set-top box. This structure is composed of three key elements, which work in layers:

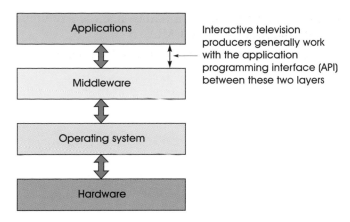

2.26 A typical set-top box software architecture.

- Operating system.
- Middleware.
- Applications.

The operating system

The foundation layer of set-top software architecture is the operating system. This performs broadly the same function as Windows XP and Mac OS X on personal computers. The operating system controls the use of the CPU, tells the various bits of hardware what to do, manages communication around the box, monitors use of memory and generally makes things happen. However, in the case of set-top boxes, unlike personal computers, the operating system does not usually provide an on-screen interface for users to be able to control various parts of the underlying system – television viewers don't need this level of access.

Operating systems are usually held in ROM memory and kept running at all times – although the platform operator can make upgrades to the operating system by downloading new software into Flash memory. (Depending on the amount of Flash memory available, this can involve stopping the box working for a while as the upgrade is made, or switching between two sets of Flash memory to allow the box to keep working while the upgrade is made.) Set-top box operating systems are usually designed to be able to take up very little space in terms of processing power and memory (they have a small 'footprint' in technical terminology), because they need to work on cheap and basic boxes that aren't very powerful.

There are a number of elements that make up an operating system. There's the kernel, which is the core of the system. It includes the most basic functions, such as the ability to manage memory and transfer data. There's a program to allow the operating system to run more than one task at a time (known as multi-tasking), a loader (used for searching for and integrating upgrades and other programs) and different drivers (control programs) for the different pieces of hardware in the box. In addition, there are sometimes programs, known as resident applications, that are stored permanently in the set-top box and that work in close conjunction with the operating system.

There are a wide variety of set-top box operating systems. They tend to be written to support particular processors. Examples include Windows CE, Linux, pSOS and VxWorks. It is unlikely that an interactive television producer will ever need to access the operating system functions directly. This is because there is software that talks directly to the operating system that is specially designed for producers of interactive television services: middleware.

Middleware

Middleware takes all the worry out of developing interactive services by doing two things. First, it communicates with the operating system in a controlled way, which reduces the possibility of interactive services crashing the box or damaging the hardware. Second, it provides a standardised system of commands and programming tools. Interactive service producers have no need to worry about the way the operating system works or details of the hardware in the set-top box – the middleware works all that out. The middleware programming language will also be consistent, whatever platform or hardware the particular middleware is used on (be it cable, satellite; advanced or basic set-top box).

There are a number of different types of middleware on the market, including OpenTV, Canal+ Technology's MediaHighway and Liberate's TV Navigator. Each brand of middleware on the market is significantly different – both in the way they are built and in the way that interactive television producers communicate with them to make things happen. This means that although middleware means that producers don't have to worry about different set-top box specifications, it can be time-consuming and expensive to produce services for more than one type of middleware. Writing the code is often the most time-consuming part of any interactive television project. And rather than an application working automatically across the different types of middleware, it often has to be rewritten from the ground up for every single one.

Table 2.1: A selection of middleware systems	
Middleware	**Produced by**
OpenTV	OpenTV (www.openTV.com) (Used in Sky Digital set-top boxes in the UK)
TV Navigator	Liberate (www.liberate.com) (Used in NTL and Telewest digital set-top boxes in the UK)
MediaHighway	Canal+ Technologies (http://www.canalplus-technologies.com) (Used in some digital terrestrial set-top boxes in the UK)
MicrosoftTV	Microsoft (www.microsoft.com/tv)
PowerTV	PowerTV (www.powerTV.com)
CableWare	Worldgate (http://www.wgate.com/)
Netgem	Netgem (http://www.netgem.com)

The method of communication with the middleware is known as the application programming interface (API). APIs allow producers to create the computer applications that viewers actually use (like EPGs, email, games and enhanced television). They do so by calling on functions of the middleware and, through the middleware, the functions of the hardware in the set-top box.

Some types of middleware use APIs that are based on computer programming languages (like Java or C). A programmer with some knowledge of the language should be able to learn the API specific to interactive television after some extra training. Other types of middleware provide special application development toolkits. These offer PC-based interfaces and short cuts that make creating the programs and content templates easier than using raw computer programming code. There's more on this in Chapter 4.

Virtual machines/engines

Some middleware producers, in an attempt to make their systems very easy to use, have built software modules that allow the middleware to be controlled using existing and well-known programming or content markup standards.

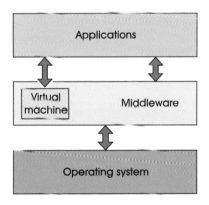

2.27 A virtual machine sits inside the middleware.

A programmer with knowledge of the language will be able to use the module without any extra training. These environments are known as virtual machines or engines. Some of these work very much like mini-middleware systems, with wide-ranging functionality; others (known as presentation engines) are only designed to display information on-screen. A virtual machine created by two different middleware suppliers can be programmed in exactly the same way, as long as they are designed to work with the same programming standard.

There are a number of different types of virtual machine/engines. For example:

- Java virtual machines can be used for developing advanced programs based on the computer language Java. A Java virtual machine is at the heart of the Multimedia Home Platform middleware standard.
- WML presentation engines that layout pages of WML, a low-bandwidth markup language similar to HTML but originally designed for mobile phones. (This works particularly well in the television space because the data required for

WML takes up so little broadcast bandwidth.) Sky Digital in the UK has a WML engine running in the OpenTV middleware.

- HTML and JavaScript presentation engines. The middleware supplier Liberate, a company that was spun out of the PC-internet browser company Netscape, has HTML and JavaScript presentation engines running right in the heart of its system, called TV Navigator. Developers can build applications using the tools Liberate provides or just write code using the same text editor that they use for creating web sites (or even using extensions to off-the-shelf layout programs like Dreamweaver – although this only works for simple interactive television services). The digital cable platforms in the UK use the TV Navigator middleware.

- MHEG-5 presentation engines. MHEG-5 is a standardised way to represent multimedia content on television, sanctioned and developed by the Multimedia Hypermedia Experts Group – an organisation set up by the International Standards Association (ISO) for storing, exchanging and displaying multimedia content. MHEG-5 was adopted by the Digital Television Group as the standard for interactivity to be used in the digital terrestrial environment in the UK. Digital terrestrial television set-top boxes and televisions in the UK generally have presentation engines that can understand MHEG-5.

Set-top boxes can sometimes switch between different virtual machines if required. And powerful set-top boxes can run two or more at once. Interactive television producers can then choose which virtual machines or engine to work with, or whether to work on the middleware directly.

Server-side technologies and thin clients

It is not necessarily the case that all the important software (like the middleware) has to run on the set-top box. Certain platforms have so much bandwidth available between the platform operator and the viewer that it is possible to produce a very cheap set-top box with almost no memory and processing power. Known as a thin-client, these type of boxes do nothing other than run the most basic functions. Powerful computers at the platform provider's office (the server side) run most of the middleware and interactive functions, and instruct the set-top box (the client side) directly what to put on-screen. This obviously only makes sense if there's lots of bandwidth available and the price of set-top boxes has to be kept to an absolute minimum.

Applications

Applications are the software programs that run the interactive television services that viewers actually use. These are what interactive television producers build: electronic programme guides, video-on-demand services, digital teletext services, walled gardens, shopping services, information sites, internet access interfaces, different types of enhanced television and so on. There's more on producing interactive television applications and how to develop for different types of middleware in Chapter 4.

Synchronisation of video and interactive content

One of the most difficult problems that interactive television technologists have had to solve is how to synchronise interactive content with the digital video streams. This is important for a number of applications, including interactive television advertising (where the viewer has to be prompted to do something at exactly the right time during a 30-second slot), enhanced quiz shows and enhanced sporting events involving predictions during the game. There are two key issues that need to be addressed:

- The problem of how to bring up the first interactive graphic on-screen at exactly the right time (for example, an overlay graphic that says, 'Press *Red* now for interactivity').
- How to keep any subsequent interactive overlays in synchronisation with the video stream.

2.28 The 'red button' prompt has to appear on-screen at the right time. *Courtesy of Carlton Active.*

2.29 During this enhanced version of *Antiques Roadshow*, the viewers had to guess the value of each item. The interactive options need to be synchronised very closely with the underlying video. *Courtesy of the BBC and BBC TV Antiques Roadshow.*

Taking the example of an enhanced television quiz show, the first interactive prompt has to be put on-screen at the start of the show. The viewer then has to choose answers from on-screen overlays to questions from the presenter in the video. The different answers need to appear at exactly the right moment and disappear before the next question is asked. The challenge is that they need to come up at the right time across the whole broadcast network, even if viewers in one part of the country are liable to get the video signal a fraction of a second after others (as happens sometimes on cable and digital terrestrial television platforms). They also need to appear at the right time, even if the advertising break runs for an extra two seconds or if the programme starts late because the sports event beforehand overruns.

Unfortunately, MPEG-2, the most common form of video compression used by broadcasters and platforms, doesn't have a standard method for including synchronised interactivity with the broadcast data stream (unlike MPEG-4, which is designed to tie in very closely with interactivity, but isn't widely used by television operators). Therefore, digital platform operators have had to define their own solutions, while working with standards bodies (like MPEG, DVB, the ATV Forum and ATSC) on systems to deal with the problem.

The result is that there are a very wide variety of ways that digital transmission platforms are addressing the synchronisation issue. However, taking a very high

2.30 In this enhanced sports programme, after a suspected foul an overlay comes on the screen at the right time. Viewers can submit their prediction for what will happen right up until the referee makes a decision. © BSkyB.

2.31 After the ref makes a decision, if the viewer made the right prediction he or she wins points. © BSkyB.

level approach, it is possible to describe a broad synchronisation architecture that will apply to at least some of the systems currently in use. Although the terminology varies, what many of these systems do is graft an interactive play-out architecture onto the existing video play-out data stream. This is achieved by adding up to three new streams of data to the existing broadcasts. These can be called:

- The announcement stream.
- The trigger stream.
- The content stream.

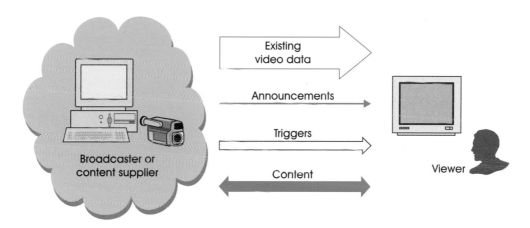

2.32 A broadcast architecture for synchronised enhanced television.

An announcement stream is a relatively low-bandwidth flow of data that tells the set-top box that an interactive application needs to start and where the instructions for how to run that application are held. A process in the set-top box middleware needs to be running at all times to monitor this announcement stream. If the process sees that an enhancement needs to start, it instructs the middleware to direct more of its attention to the place where the television programme's interactive triggers and content are held. The announcement stream is usually in a proprietary format, although some work has been done with integrating announcements into the programme information tables defined by the DVB-SI and ATSC-PSIP.

The trigger stream is where the middleware looks, after it has been told to pay attention by data in the announcement stream. The trigger stream is a flow of data that contains information about the exact time interactive icons need to be shown on-screen throughout the programme. It will contain instructions like 'put this icon on-screen at this point in the programme for this amount of time'. Trigger streams can also contain information that will move overlays or events back or forward in time if the programme is delayed or if the triggers go out of synchronisation.

The content stream (which can be in the broadcast channel or return path) carries content that the application can pick up when necessary during the programme.

For pre-recorded programmes that are unlikely to change in start time or length or unlikely to have their advertisement breaks changed, the process of timing triggers to put up overlays is relatively straightforward. The first overlay and subsequent overlays can be set off at particular times, synchronised to clocks in the programme information streams or in the set-top box. However, for live programmes (like a sporting event), where overlay triggers have to be moved frequently, the process can be a lot more complicated. The synchronisation of interactivity to live programmes usually requires either several people managing the overlays or complex content management systems – or both.

Attempts at standardisation

There's a gaggle of technology standards that are particularly relevant to interactive television production. Most are still in their infancy and none of the main ones are adopted globally. But with powerful organisations like DVB and ATSC behind some of them, it may only be a matter of time. Here are some of the standards that are worth watching.

Multimedia Home Platform

Members of the DVB group realised some time ago that it would be difficult and expensive for content providers to produce commercially successful services if they had to rebuild them for all the different middleware programs (be it OpenTV, Liberate or MediaHighway) used on the big platforms. This has certainly been the case in the United Kingdom, which has three different digital platforms that all use different types of middleware. Only the richest providers have been able to afford to produce services for all three.

In an attempt to get round this problem, the DVB-Multimedia Home Platform (MHP) specification defines standard ways for interactivity to work across different platforms and across different set-top boxes. MHP defines not only a structure for the middleware software and its application programme interfaces (APIs), but also defines all the other areas needed to create interoperable interactive services (including data transport protocols, hardware requirements and content types).

The middleware definition part of MHP is so detailed that MHP is often referred to as a middleware itself. However, because it is standardised and completely open (the specification is published on the internet for anyone to see and use virtually royalty-free), each existing middleware supplier is free to adapt its own product so it fits the MHP specification. This is exactly what OpenTV, Liberate, Canal+ and others have done and there are a number of MHP-compliant middleware products on the market.

When, eventually, all the major middleware suppliers and digital platforms adhere to the MHP specification, interactive television producers will only need to author a service once. It will then work on all the different broadcast systems around the world that adhere to MHP. Great stuff. The only problem is that MHP requires a reasonably powerful set-top box to work (it can take lots of memory) and can use lots of bandwidth. And, unfortunately, many viewers already have set-top boxes that aren't powerful enough to run MHP. And these can't be upgraded overnight. Consequently, the MHP standard is likely to be rolled out gradually over a period of many years, as new platforms are built and set-top boxes in people's homes are upgraded.

DVB-MHP Profiles 1, 2 & 3

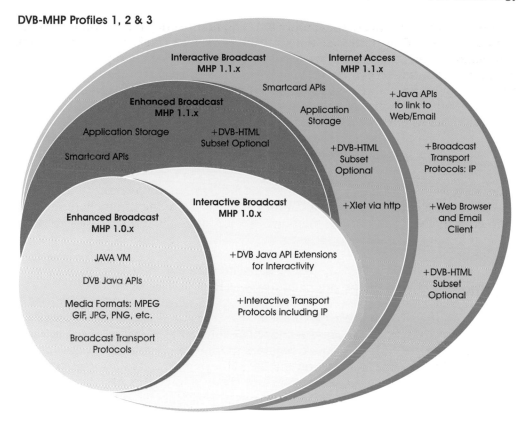

Interactive Broadcast
MHP 1.1.x

Internet Access
MHP 1.1.x

Smartcard APIs

+Java APIs
to link to
Web/Email

Enhanced Broadcast
MHP 1.1.x

Application
Storage

Application Storage

+DVB-HTML
Subset Optional

+DVB-HTML
Subset
Optional

+Broadcast
Transport
Protocols: IP

Smartcard APIs

Interactive Broadcast
MHP 1.0.x

+Xlet via http

+Web Browser
and Email
Client

Enhanced Broadcast
MHP 1.0.x

JAVA VM

DVB Java APIs

+DVB Java API Extensions
for Interactivity

+DVB-HTML
Subset
Optional

Media Formats: MPEG
GIF, JPG, PNG, etc.

+Interactive Transport
Protocols including IP

Broadcast Transport
Protocols

2.33 The DVB-MHP – the technical spec.

MHP can be seen in action on a number of the newer and more advanced European interactive television platforms. It has also been adopted by CableLabs, the research and development consortium representing American cable companies. CableLabs has made it the middleware choice for its OpenCable digital set-top box standard.

The MHP specification has three areas, or profiles, that define different types of interactivity. The profiles are:

- Enhanced broadcast.
- Interactive broadcast.
- Internet access.

In DVB terms, the enhanced broadcast profile is the simplest. It focuses on providing standards for interactivity predominantly via the broadcast stream, in a way that ties the interactivity in with television channels. The DVB-MHP group has specified that a Java virtual machine (called MHP-J) is the primary tool for creating enhanced broadcasting content. Java is a powerful language created by Sun Microsystems, but it can be used without paying royalties. The disadvantage of Java is that its virtual machines can take a lot of memory to run.

The interactive broadcast profile adds more standards to fully utilise a two-way return path, such as internet protocols (IP). Both profiles 1 and 2 also have an optional method for allowing set-top boxes to display HTML.

The final, most complex, profile focuses very much on internet on television. It specifies methods for broadcasting internet content and the particular internet programming standards that MHP set-top boxes will need to understand. These include HTML, ECMAScript (which is the basis of the JavaScript language that is used to add animation and interactivity to web sites) and cascading style sheets (CSS), which is a method for making changes to multiple internet pages by changing the code in only one place, making it much easier to make bulk changes. There's more on the tools needed to produce an MHP-compliant interactive service in Chapter 4.

DASE

While the DVB has been developing the MHP standard, its United States equivalent, the Advanced Television Systems Committee (ATSC), has been developing its own version: the Digital Television Applications Software Environment (DASE). The DASE standard is very much like MHP in that it defines a way to produce both layouts and more advanced code. It also includes specifications for the other aspects of interactive television production that are required to make services interoperable across different platforms and middleware.

Like MHP, DASE has chosen HTML and JavaScript as the layout formats. Also like MHP, DASE uses a Java virtual machine as the mechanism for producing more complex interactivity. Unfortunately, there are some differences between the two standards, and DVB-MHP and ATSC-DASE are not specifically designed to be interoperable. This means that a service built to work on MHP middleware will need to be changed to some extent to work with DASE.

ATVEF and the ATV Forum

The Advanced Television Enhancement Forum (ATVEF) was born in the United States in 1997. It consists of a variety of television and technology companies interested in standardising the way interactivity is authored for television and other receivers (like personal computers with video cards).

ATVEF's most important piece of work defines a set of content formats and delivery mechanisms required to get internet pages from broadcasters to viewers. In contrast to MHP, ATVEF is totally focused on languages that define how the screen is laid out (that is, HTML and JavaScript), not ones that can run complex processes and algorithms. ATVEF does not cover languages like Java, which can be used for this kind of complex programming.

Pretty much everything in the ATVEF standard is based on internet technologies. The idea is that broadcasters can create interactivity in languages that are well understood (that is, HTML and JavaScript) using familiar content formats (like jpeg, gif and so on). ATVEF also has specifications that standardise the way interactive content is synchronised and delivered via video streams.

ATVEF delivery mechanisms are called Transport A and Transport B. By defining how these streams work, ATVEF aims to provide a level of consistency across platforms, allowing synchronised content to be created without producers having to be too concerned about the detail of the broadcast systems:

- Transport A defines a standard for a delivery platform where the triggers for interactivity are included in the broadcast stream but the content is sent via a separate return path (for example, a modem in a set-top box).
- Transport B defines a delivery platform where announcements, triggers and content can all be sent in the broadcast stream.

ATVEF is no longer active. But the work of promoting the standards that ATVEF devised and of promoting interactive television using internet and open standards has been taken over by an offshoot body, the ATV Forum.

MPEG-4

The Multimedia Hyper Media Experts Group (MPEG) has defined a range of different video compression standards for different purposes. MPEG-4 is a standard designed especially for multimedia applications. It is particularly useful for interactive television programmes that require synchronisation between video content and multimedia content (such as timed overlays, on-screen prompts and interactive advertising).

The advantage of MPEG-4 is that a platform operator does not have to work out its own play-out system architecture to make synchronised interactivity work (for example, by adding trigger and announcement streams). All the systems required to tie in interactivity with the video are defined within MPEG-4.

Another advantage of MPEG-4 is that it is designed to work well across a range of bandwidths. So, if the video material can only be sent over a narrowband pipe, with very little room for data (for example, an internet connection using a 56 kbps modem), it will adjust the video to work within these parameters. Equally, if the MPEG-4 signal has plenty of bandwidth (a satellite broadcast channel, for example) then the video picture will become high quality. In fact, high-bandwidth MPEG-4 is comparable to MPEG-2 video, even though MPEG-2 was designed specifically for professional broadcast-quality bandwidths. (MPEG-2 produces an excellent picture when there is plenty of bandwidth available, but doesn't really work at all once the bandwidth starts to become limited.)

MPEG-4 also defines standard ways to represent virtually any unit of sound, video or multimedia content that could be needed. Called media objects, these can be recorded with a camera (for example, a presenter reading the weather) or created by a computer (for example, a three-dimensional computer character of a presenter reading the weather). The objects can then be manipulated in a huge variety of ways by the broadcaster or the viewer. Taking just one example, within MPEG-4 data there can be instructions to treat a weather presenter as an object. The viewer could then decide to change the background that the presenter is on – perhaps he or she wants a forecast from a paradise island rather than a rainy studio rooftop. Or the broadcaster may decide to change the accent of the presenter depending on where the show is being broadcast.

Although the standard is well defined, it is not widely adopted on television transmission platforms. The platform operators are having enough trouble getting their transmission networks, broadcast partners and set-top boxes to work with MPEG-2, without worrying about new functionality. The standard also covers many different things and, to run it all, the set-top box would have to be super-powerful.

It's also worth quickly noting two other MPEG standards:

- MPEG-21 addresses the issue of how multimedia content in different formats (like MPEG-2 and MPEG-4) is used across several different platforms – not just television. It's a high-level standard for people who own platforms.
- MPEG-7 offers ways of describing and cataloguing multimedia content, so it can be easily searched and retrieved.

MPEG-7 is particularly relevant to personal video recorders and has been drawn on heavily by one of the standards bodies dealing with these – the TV Anytime Forum.

TV Anytime

The TV Anytime Forum is dedicated to producing standards for set-top boxes with personal video recorder (PVR) functionality. These boxes can store programs and other data on hard disk or other storage media for later viewing. TV Anytime aims to make all the personal video recorders that come onto the market interoperable. They hope that, ultimately, viewers will be able to plug their new boxes into cable, satellite or terrestrial without any problem, and platform providers will be able to relay one set of standardised signals to help customers make use of advanced personal video recorder functions.

TV Anytime addresses a range of useful personal video recorder functions. Foremost among these are the standards for metadata – or data that describes other data. Metadata, among other things, allows television programmes to be broken up into segments, each identified by particular data packets (the metadata). The metadata for each segment describe exactly what the segment is about and how it can tie in with other programmes and segments. Viewers can then set their personal video recorders to, for example, capture just the sports stories from a number of news programmes across several channels; use metadata to help manage *Star Trek* collections; or add a personal bookmark in a film, so it is possible to jump back quickly to the same shot again and again.

Another element of the standard applies to rights management. This can be used to stop viewers illegally copying films and sending them to their friends, perhaps by using a recordable DVD attached to the personal video recorder. One part of the standard also defines how programmes can be tagged so that they only play a set number of times or so they only play on a particular piece of equipment.

All this wonderful technology counts for nothing, of course, if the people footing the bill don't see some kind of return on their investment. Next: making that return.

Case study: MTV Europe Music Awards

Rod Clark, technical consultant, NDS. NDS is a supplier of end-to-end digital pay-TV solutions for the secure delivery of entertainment and information to television set-top boxes and personal computers.

MTV Networks Europe wanted to create new revenue streams, attract more viewers and add a new dimension to the viewer experience through a range of innovative and exciting interactive services. They therefore decided to broadcast the 2001 MTV Europe Music Awards with a difference. The partnership between MTV and NDS enabled viewers to actively participate in determining the results of the awards by allowing them to vote with their remote control. To further enhance the awards event, viewers could also enter daily quizzes, read about the artists and take a look at all the latest news during the run-up to the MTV Europe Music Awards.

Reinforcing MTV's position as the leader of music television, the success of the European Music Awards interactive applications has substantiated the value of this service and the relevance to the MTV audience. The success of the interactive television service has been recognised at the Revolution Awards in 2002 with MTV receiving the award for best interactive television service.

2.34 The MTV Europe Music Awards with technology by NDS. © *MTV*.

The MTV audience is used to interactivity and expects high standards, and this high-profile event was certainly no different. Within demanding timescales, NDS delivered the technology that successfully processed 710 000 votes between the 5th and 8th of November.

The service was developed by NDS in partnership with MTV, using the Value@TV solution. This system provides standard interfaces for interactive data broadcasting and return-path applications on a multi-platform basis. The NDS infrastructure is flexible and can be configured to support whichever return-path provider is chosen. This meant that MTV were offered the choice to shop around for a return-path partner that best suited their requirements.

The application as a whole was broken down into three different stages:

- Pre-Europe Music Awards (EMA).
- Live EMA.
- Post-EMA.

The pre-EMA stage launched at the start of the week of the event and gave the viewer even more control over the results. Viewers were allowed to vote in 12 different categories, browse through several pages of latest news, read about information relating specifically to the event and were given the opportunity to win a prize in a daily quiz. The data for this stage was all prepared in advance where possible and delivered to the headend as an XML file for compilation. Nominees for the awards were sent from the set-top box, via the point of presence computer (a connection point to the network), to BSkyB's authentication server and via the interactive router at the headend to be collected by one of MTV's application servers. These results were then analysed offline and stored for future broadcast.

The live EMA stage of the interactive service enabled viewers to vote for a new award for the best live performance. This gave the interactive television user the opportunity to influence the choice of artist selected for an evening special on the United Kingdom channel.

The post-EMA stage provided similar functionality to the pre-EMA stage. Again, a quiz was available, with details of the EMA results along with voting for the alternative EMAs such as worst speech, worst haircut and so on. MTV's first interactive television audio application was also developed, giving viewers the chance to choose from an exclusive commentary from celebrities such as Jordan, Ricky Gervais and Ralf Little during the repeats of the awards.

Since NDS are in the business of conditional access, we are used to broadcasting data to millions of set-top boxes. The MTV application brought further challenges that tested NDS technology to the full, because this was the first time that an interactive application was enhancing a live show.

Broadcasting a live event with a two-way enhanced television application required painstaking attention to all the operational details and called for careful consideration of technical issues. For the return path, NDS had to think about finding a method of managing the peak response patterns surrounding the event and then relay that data back to the broadcast carousel to provide voting feedback to the viewers.

For the majority of interactive events, the issue of scheduling interactive data with video content needs to be considered carefully. The NDS system supports interfaces to the content provider's scheduling and automation systems. In the first instance, a series of interactive data events are associated with a particular item in the broadcast schedule. An interactive data event may be the launch of a trigger, the display of a particular piece of data or an instruction to kill the application. In an ideal world, everything runs according to plan, but we know otherwise. A programme often overruns, the unexpected happens and, consequently, schedules slip.

This is where the interface to the automation system can solve the problem. The NDS headend can broadcast data by manual operation, according to the system clock or in total synchronisation with the video broadcast. What the latter actually means is that an interactive data carousel will not be broadcast until the automation system has sent notification that a particular broadcast event really is imminent.

Such synchronisation between interactive data and video managed by the automation system is by no means an easy nut to crack. However, our technology does mean that applications don't suffer from the problems that out of synchronisation interactive data can bring. If the programme schedule slips, then interactive data slip with it, keeping tightly synchronised – and all without human intervention.

During the awards show, viewers were able to vote for each artist's live performance only as they appeared on stage, not before or after. A pre-recorded show would have benefited from the automation interface, but the live show required manual operation to keep the voting and artist data dynamically updated. By their very nature, these kind of dynamic data updates – regardless of whether they are initiated by a manual or automatic process – need to be broadcast by a system that suffers from the absolute minimum latency (the time it takes for the data to get to viewers). In some critical cases, this should be no more than a couple of seconds.

So with data updates under control, the other major operational issue was how to deal with all of those responses. With a typical telephone network return path, there are four particularly important components: the set-top box modem, the point of presence, the authentication server and the application server that will manage responses once they arrive back at the headend. With these in mind, NDS set about creating a way to limit the potential load on the response processing system with the underlying intention of eliminating any risk of not being able to capture all the responses. We also needed to try not to use endless amounts of costly hardware. The answer was to randomise the callbacks from the set-top box back to the response processor at a calculated frequency.

As a result, the interactive routers at the headend were able to load balance the response data throughout the event and pass those data back through the data play-out system to display the latest voting trends back to the MTV viewer. This meant that the response data would first of all need to be analysed and secondly would need to be prepared for inclusion in the next data carousel.

NDS technology enables fast carousel generation because it only has to recompile the data that has been updated. What this meant for MTV was that only a small percentage of their entire data carousel required compilation before being broadcast with the latest voting trends. As a result, viewers could see quick and regular feedback throughout the show.

As a result of all of the hard work by both MTV and NDS, the whole experience was deemed a great success. The interactive application is credited with increasing viewing figures by 12 per cent, giving the European Music Awards their highest ever rating in the UK – MTV's most successful viewing night to date on the Sky Digital platform.

Case study: *Walking with Beasts* interactive on digital satellite

Sandra Gorel, producer, BBC New Media.

Walking with Beasts interactive consists of four parallel video streams and one additional audio stream, alongside a linear television programme, to provide one of the world's first truly interactive television documentaries. The service offered a great deal of additional content and interactive features, and as such the major challenge for BBC New Media was to invent an intuitive application to allow the viewer to navigate through the various options with ease.

Walking with Beasts interactive was based on a video switching model that BBCi had created for the multi-streaming *Wimbledon* application in 2001. *Walking with Beasts* took the functionality, designed a different template and produced a full screen rather than the mosaic effect that was seen in *Wimbledon*. Nevertheless, it was the audio/video switching from *Wimbledon* that was to provide the backbone for *Walking with Beasts*.

Walking with Beasts interactive was intended to be a linear experience, along with an additional audio stream. We could have reused the basic OpenTV code for *Wimbledon 2001* and made alterations to the navigation. Instead, it was decided that upon entering the service the viewer would be presented with a copy of the linear broadcast. The viewer then could navigate their way through the content using the colour (also known as fast-text) keys. The four colour keys were assigned to the four video streams: *Red* for Main Feature, *Green* for Facts, *Yellow* for Evidence and *Blue* for Making Of.

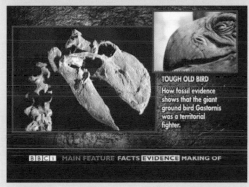

2.35 The BBC's *Walking with Beasts* was the first interactive documentary. *Courtesy of the BBC; Walking with Beasts*™ and © *BBC 2001.*

Each stream in the *Walking with Beasts* service is in reality one additional video channel. The *Beast* application allows the viewer to move between those streams, by pressing a colour key on the remote control, while at the same time giving the impression that they are staying within the *Beast* service.

Each stream, as well as containing the video and audio, has a data track. On that we broadcast the OpenTV application. When the viewer presses a colour key the application tunes them to the chosen channel. Before starting to display the stream it has to wait for the next service information (SI) to be broadcast. This causes a slight delay in jumping between the video streams. To maintain the feeling of continuity, all four streams contained a copy of the linear television programme either full screen or, in the case of Evidence and Making Of, as a small picture-in-picture television window. This meant that as the viewer changed television channel, they would still maintain a close association with the actual linear television show. To help the viewer find the best times to change channel, i.e. just before a new segment on Evidence and Making Of, we incorporated prompts into the Main Feature. This ensured that the narrative of the programme remained throughout.

The synchronisation of the video streams was possible via the multi-stream transmission area (MSA). The content was loaded onto the servers and time code locked. The additional audio for video streams one and two was delivered as a second audio track. The MSA would then continuously transmit the four video streams and additional audio stream on the BBC transponder set aside for inter-active services. The application was available 24 hours a day for the six-week duration and was updated once a week by the MSA at the start of each new episode.

For *Beasts* we decided to burn the navigation into the video rather than have the application display it (as an interactive overlay). As *Walking with Beasts* was shot in 16:9 we decided to convert the video to 4:3 and use the letterbox effect that this creates to brand the service and add the navigation. This meant that we could display the four colour-key options and the narration changer at the bottom of the screen without overlaying the actual *Walking with Beasts* video.

There are several benefits to including the navigation and design elements within the video wherever possible. The first is that it keeps the application small in size. *Beasts* was only a modest 45 kb. In comparison, *Wimbledon 2001* was around 90 kb as it contained more graphics than the *Beast* application, as well as dynamic content such as live updating scores and results. As *Beasts* did not have any dynamic content and it was a small application, the whole service was down-loaded into the set-top box when the application started. This download was fast in comparison to larger services. Building applications in which the majority of the navigation and interactive features are contained within the video also means that the application is very easy to reuse. The *Walking with Beasts* inter-active application was almost immediately reused for a *Top of the Pops* Christmas special, which again had all the navigation burnt into the video. The downsides, however, are that late changes to the navigation are not possible, as re-editing the video stream can be both timely and costly.

For *Walking with Beasts* we did, however, have to use the application to display the graphics for the Narration Changer. On Main Feature and the Facts video streams, the viewer could select an alternative commentary entitled In Depth. At the bottom of these two video streams, underneath the colour keys, the appli-cation displayed two graphics, one for the Original narration and one for the In Depth narration. At the beginning of the programme the Original narration was selected, and the Original narration graphic contained an orange highlighter around it. For the Narration Changer we wanted to create the illusion of a high-lighter bar moving between the two options to show which one was selected. There were four bitmaps to create this: each option in its selected state and each option in an unselected state. When the viewer changed narration, using the left/right arrow keys, the application would switch both of the graphics and then request that the screen is updated. The viewer would therefore see both graphics appear on-screen simultaneously, giving the effect of a highlighter mov-ing between the two options. Without changing video channels it is impossible to create this within the video streams.

As mentioned before, it was very important to create the impression that the viewer was changing narration and pulling up additional information/video con-tent all within one *Beasts* service – rather than show the reality: that the viewer is simply changing channels. To maintain this feeling of the viewer navigating around within the *Walking with Beasts* interactive environment, we wanted to make sure that any narration changes the viewer might make would be remembered if they changed channel. The application would store the viewers' last audio choice in the set-top box's memory and would then use that to select the appropriate audio stream when jumping between video streams. So if the viewer had chosen In Depth audio while watching the Main Show, we wanted to ensure they would still be listening to In Depth audio when moving over to view Facts.

Walking with Beasts interactive has been designed to offer a high level of additional content in a user-friendly, intuitive format. In total, *Walking with Beasts* interactive contained over four hours of additional video footage, three hours of alternative commentary and around 700 pop-up facts. By using a relatively simple video switching application, we enabled the viewers to explore the documentary at their leisure and in a format tailored to their interests.

Actions

- ✓ Visit the web sites of major interactive television technology companies, like www.liberate.com, www.opentv.com, www.canalplus-technologies.com, www.nds.com and so on. There's a full list of links at www.InteractiveTelevisionProduction.com.

- ✓ For thorough technical information on interactive television, read *The Essential Guide to Digital Set-top Boxes and Interactive Television* by Gerard O'Driscoll, *Interactive Television Demystified* by Jerry Whitaker and *Interactive Television Technology and Markets* by Hari Om Srivastava.

- ✓ For epicurean technical fun, go to www.etvcookbook.com.

- ✓ Test your interactive television technical IQ with the quiz on www.InteractiveTelevisionProduction.com.

Chapter **3**

Making money

Chapter 3 in 30 seconds . . .

▷ Interactive television has commercial promise: television is a trusted medium that impacts on people's lives and generates large revenues, while interactivity has proven its appeal on the internet and with analogue teletext.

▷ The commercial reality of interactive television does not always live up to the promise. However, there have been some successes that bode well for the future.

▷ Potential revenue sources include betting, interactive shopping linked to television programmes and channels, advertising and pay-per-use applications (particularly games).

▷ Interactive television applications can deliver benefits beyond cash.

“ While theoretically and technically television may be feasible, commercially and financially I consider it an impossibility, a development of which we need waste little time dreaming. ”

Lee DeForest, radio pioneer and inventor, 1926

M any interactive television services and companies have shut down. This is good. You can avoid making the same mistakes. This chapter takes a look at the business strategies, revenue sources and benefits of interactive television, with particular reference to the lessons learnt in the United Kingdom. But first: what's all the fuss about anyway?

The commercial attractions of television

Many of the largest companies in the world, and numerous smaller operators, have invested hundreds of millions of pounds to extend television's capability into interactivity. There are a number of reasons why they think this is a clever thing to do:

- Television already makes money – big money.
- Television is ubiquitous (at least in the industrialised world).
- Television has impact.
- Television is trusted.
- Television is in the home.
- The right types of interactivity look likely to be popular and likely to add to the money-making potential of television.

Television makes money

Television is big money. Very big. To service the world's 1400 million television sets there are over 21 000 television stations. In Europe, it's not unusual for 100 new television channels to be launched in a year. According to Pricewaterhouse-Coopers, the global television network market was worth £73 billion ($107 billion) in 2001. That's about the same as the gross domestic product of Finland.

Conventional television industry revenues primarily come from licence fees and advertising (for the broadcasters), customers' payments (for the platform operators), and commissions and licence agreements (for the production companies). The consumer electronics industry also benefits from selling television sets and related equipment.

Interactive television investors believe that there is an opportunity to add new revenue streams and to blur the lines between platform operators, broadcasters and production companies, enabling companies to move into new and profitable areas.

Television is ubiquitous

Investors in interactive television have another reason for pumping in money: television is everywhere. According to UNESCO, it's second only to radio as the most accessible and widespread communication technology in the world. What's more, nearly every household in industrialised countries has a television set – or two, or three or more. In lots of countries there are more televisions than people. This means that any new product or service designed for television has the chance to draw on a large existing user base.

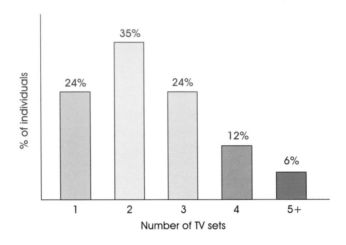

3.1 The average number of televisions in UK households. *Source: ITC, the Public's View (2001).*

Digital television, the main platform for interactive television, is also making an impact. Digital television is available in virtually every European country plus a number of other countries around the world and penetration is increasing. It's difficult to predict how quickly the digital market will grow and there is quite a lot of disagreement, but some commentators are optimistic. 'Consumers continue to demand better television, and demonstrate a clear willingness to pay for it', says Nick Griffiths, director, Strategy Analytics.

Furthermore, from 2006 onwards, a selection of European and other governments are hoping to switch off analogue television signals completely, freeing up more bandwidth for digital television channels and interactive services. Although the switch-off timetables in most countries are well behind expectations, it is possible that a number of countries will have switched off their analogue transmissions by 2010 – and it's not beyond the realms of imagination that nearly everyone in Europe and the United States will have digital television – and therefore interactive television – by 2015.

Television's ubiquity also makes it easier for interactive television companies to benefit from the economies of scale of operating globally. A successful interactive television service built in one country (like the United Kingdom or France) is – up to a point – straightforward to roll out with the same commercial formula and operational systems in other markets – even if the specifics of the technologies have to be different in each country.

Television has impact

Have you ever cried during a television drama? Been fascinated by a documentary? Or been unable to look at the screen because of the tension during a sports event? If so, you have experienced the impact of television. Even with hundreds of channels and thousands of programmes fragmenting audiences, the right programme can bring a population together, with perhaps 30, 40 or even 50 per cent of a nation crowding round boxes. This is part of the reason advertisers and sponsors like to be associated with television programmes, and it's another factor that makes any investment in interactive television look attractive. If interactive television can achieve just a fraction of the personal impact of regular television, then revenues should follow.

But we don't watch television just for emotionally charged events and entertainment. Television is part of our lives. Although people with the television on in the same room are not always paying as much attention as advertisers and programme makers might like and viewing figures have been dropping a little in recent years, television use is unquestionably part of our daily routine.

Table 3.1: Average television viewing per person in 2000 in European countries, Japan and the United States

Country	Average viewing per day (minutes)	Notes
United Kingdom	221	
Germany	193	Age 6+
France	196	
Spain	220	
Italy	239	
Finland	171	Age 10+
Denmark	151	
Netherlands	166	Age 6+
Sweden	153	Age 3+
Japan	214	1996
United States	227	

Ages 4+ except where noted. For other countries and statistics in full, see *European Audiovisual Observatory Statistical Yearbook 2001*.
(Sources: European Audiovisual Observatory Statistical Yearbook 2001, and Nielsen Media Research, 2001.)

According to the United Kingdom audience research body BARB (in 2002), the average British person watches television for more than 25 hours per week. According to Nielsen Media Research (2001), the average American person clocks up over 26 hours per week (that's four hours 45 minutes per day for women, four hours ten minutes for men and three hours for kids).

Television brands are trusted

After many hours and years of repeated viewing of particular programmes and particular channels, people become familiar with the brands they see on-screen. And they begin to trust these brands. According to a 2001 survey by PR consultants M Booth & Associates television is trusted above radio, the internet, advertising and direct mail, and is on a par with print. Also, Gallup research in 2001, for set-top box manufacturer Pace, showed that certain groups of people would prefer to buy goods via a television than a personal computer, mainly because they see it as more secure.

Interactive television can draw on existing television brands in a natural context. If interactive services can tap into the trust people have in television, there's commercial potential.

Television is in the home

Television, and therefore interactive television, gets to people when they are relaxed and receptive – in the home. 'The home has immense personal, social and cultural significance,' says environmental psychologist Jeanne Moore. 'Research has shown that the home has psychological meaning. It tends to include feelings of safety, security, warmth, comfort, belonging, identity, status and love.' Television is also predominantly used in the living room. This room is the heart of our day-to-day lives outside work, school or college. As broadcaster David Frost puts it, 'Television is an invention that permits you to be entertained in your living room by people you wouldn't have in your home.'

Television and interactivity

There's one final reason why interactive television should be a winner: the potential power of interactive information and entertainment.

Communication-focused interactivity using the PC-internet is already popular. Although a mere shadow of the hyped-up version some were predicting, the PC-internet services that have survived the bursting new media bubble look to be here for the foreseeable future: According to PricewaterhouseCoopers, global internet advertising and access spending was £33 billion (US $53 billion) in 2001. While at the beginning of 2003, there were estimated to be around 250 million regular users from home.

Furthermore, historically, the right kind of interactivity has been popular on television. For example, in the last few years of the 1990s, analogue teletext services available on United Kingdom television channels were used regularly by more than 40 per cent of the total population (80 per cent of households had teletext-equipped televisions), according to figures from the Independent Television Commission (2001). And according to TGI, in 2000, 22 million people every week used the analogue teletext service on ITV, a popular channel in the United Kingdom. That's more people than drank instant coffee or visited fast food restaurants in the same year. Teletext Ltd, the company running the service, effectively dominated the commercial analogue interactive television market – and, up until the introduction of digital television platforms and the increase in the number of interactive services, had a very lucrative advertising opportunity.

PC-internet versus television

It's possible that the PC-internet will become the medium of choice in the home, and that personal computers will move into living rooms, rather than being left in studies and bedrooms. In fact, some television audience research suggests that PC-internet usage already cuts into television viewing figures. A study from UCLA Centre for Communication Policy in 2001 claimed that American internet users watch 4.5 hours less television per week than non-internet users, while Forrester Research in 2002 found that online Europeans watch 8 per cent less television than those without access to the net. Meanwhile, Gallup Research in 2000 found that some people prefer to conduct certain interactive activities, like using email, on a personal computer rather than on a television. Some of the latest PCs are even starting to look and work like hybrid PC-TVs.

However, it looks unlikely that the PC-internet will take over in the living room in the near future, at least not until the experience of using the PC-internet includes more video. Personal computer penetration is peaking at around 50 per cent in many countries, limited by high cost and difficulty of use. Forrester Research also went on to establish that there is probably not a causal relationship between online usage and television viewing. The study suggested that online users are the kind of people who watch less television, not that online use results in less television viewing.

The amount of time people use the PC-internet also has a very long way to go before competing seriously with television viewing. Moderate to serious internet users typically surf for 5–12 hours per month from home. This is about the same as the television viewing many people clock up in two or three days.

There's more on the convergence of PCs and TVs in Chapter 6 (see section 'A social future').

What to do if you have an interactive television idea

If you want to make an interactive television idea happen, there are a number of different places you can start:

Broadcasters. Every broadcaster has a commissioning process. If your idea could work with an existing or new type of television programme, then a worthwhile port of call is the commissioning executive for the particular genre that the programme fits into. However, most commissioning executives are only prepared to deal with production companies, not individuals, so it may be best to link up with a production company first or, if you are confident, set up your own. Also, some commissioning executives are not interactive television savvy and your ideas may get a more sympathetic hearing with the new media or interactive department, who, if the idea is suitable, will be able to provide contacts within the station and at production companies. Most broadcasters have details of their commissioning executives and their new media departments on their web sites; see www.bbc.co.uk/commissioning and www.channel4.com/4producers/, for example.

Production companies. Production companies are constantly on the lookout for new ideas, particularly ones they can turn into formats that can be sold worldwide. Most production companies have a development department, who are worth contacting first. Some even have specific interactive development teams. If the production company likes the idea, they are likely to work on it for a bit (perhaps by creating a pilot) before trying to sell it on to broadcasters. One example of a production company with a large interactive department is Endemol (www.endemol.com/interactive/). There's also a list of independent production companies (those not owned by big broadcasters) available at www.pact.co.uk.

Platform operators. Platform operators will be interested in ideas that could give their platform a competitive advantage over other operators – perhaps by utilising technologies unique to the platform. They may also like to hear business plans for how to make more money from their customers using interactive television. However, platform operators are not usually set up very well for hearing ideas from individuals, or even production companies, and it might be difficult to get through to the right person. The business development or content team is probably the best bet.

Another option is to try retailers or other companies that can benefit from your idea. Most large multi-nationals will have a new media development executive. If not, someone in the marketing department may be able to handle the job. The government, EU organisations and other public bodies may also be interested in funding relevant interactive television ideas.

Bear in mind that it's unlikely that anyone will pay out money for the early stages of an interactive television idea. Payments are likely to be based on contributions to the project's development or on some kind of buy-out of the intellectual rights, once the idea is at a suitably well-defined stage. However, it's certainly worth taking measures to protect your idea before speaking to anyone. It is possible to establish ownership of the intellectual property rights for ideas that have been developed into a format or script. Media solicitors know how to do this. Extreme care should be taken when divulging less well-developed ideas though. Pure ideas are very difficult to protect and, at the very least, you should get a non-disclosure agreement signed before talking to someone. Firms like Shadbolt & Co (www.shadboltlaw.co.uk) and Olswang (www.olswang.com) specialise in these areas of media law and copyright.

Characteristics of commercially successful interactive television services

There are lots of interactive television companies positioning themselves to take a cut of what should, in theory, be a very lucrative business. Unfortunately, the first three years of the new millennium in Britain proved that, unless you get the formula spot on, interactive television money and other benefits do not come easily at all.

Companies involved with interactive television include broadcasters, platform operators, production companies, technology companies, retailers and advertisers. In the early 2000s, there was an explosion of activity and a number of new interactive television-specific companies were formed. But by the beginning of 2003, many of them had gone out of business. The United Kingdom alone has seen the closure or realignment of:

- Platform operator ITV Digital.
- Walled garden services Open . . . and brightBlue.
- Near-video-on-demand supplier U-Direct.
- E-commerce applications from Gameplay, Somerfield and others.
- Part-interactive broadcasters the Money Channel, Simply Money, Taste Network, Wellbeing Network and others.
- Specialist interactive television production company Smashed Atom and production companies with interactive television involvement, like Razorfish.
- Internet on television services from NTL and ITV Digital.

The ingredients for success simply weren't there.

The particular problem for broadcasters, production companies and advertisers is that the first version of an interactive television service can be expensive to produce: between £50 000 and several million pounds is not unusual. It is particularly expensive to launch on platforms that use proprietary technologies or have high tenancy fees, or to try and launch services on more than one platform. And it has often proved more difficult than expected to get a return on investment quickly.

Worryingly, the lack of expected revenues from interactive television and other sources has even put a question mark over the future of digital platforms themselves. Denis Olivennes, head of French pay-TV group Canal+, said of pay-TV terrestrial digital television, 'In the best case the service is not selling, as in Spain and Scandinavia. In the worst, it is a disaster, as in Britain. The time scale for return on investment is infinite, it is uneconomic.'

But it is possible to get interactive television right. There are examples of services that have been popular with viewers and resulted in revenues or other benefits being delivered back to the instigators. These imply that the commercial promise of interactive television will be realised. For example:

- Apart from the badly designed ones, electronic programme guides are incredibly popular. Canal Satellite in France says its EPG is used by 80 per cent of subscribers. Sky Digital in the United Kingdom reports a 90 per cent usage rate. In the United States, TV Guide Interactive says that its viewers return an average of three to four times per hour, looking at more than three screens per visit.

- The best interactive television services can be more popular than television channels. The United Kingdom-based PlayJam interactive games service regularly attracted 250 000 viewers per day on Sky Digital in 2002. It was reported by audience research company BARB to have been more popular in some months than MTV and Sky Sports One – ranking between the eighth and fifteenth most watched channel on Sky Digital. Sky's own games service, Gamestar, is equally popular.

- Some enhanced television services attract a very large proportion of the available viewers. In the United Kingdom, the video switching services that the BBC provided for *Wimbledon* viewers in 2001 and 2002, were both used by around 50 per cent of people who had access to them.

- Although the commercial models are far from proven, some interactive television services are generating significant revenues. Domino's Pizza achieved more than £2 million in sales via interactive television in the United Kingdom in 2001 (there's more on this in the e-commerce section later), while Channel 4's *Big Brother* 2002 programme is reported to have made more than £1 million in revenue from interactive television voting (there's more on this in the telephone payments section). Meanwhile, interactive bingo channel Avago claimed to be running at break-even within 2 months of its 2002 launch.

It's possible to look at these and other successes and identify some common characteristics. When producing an interactive service, these are all worth considering. The common characteristics include:

- A large enough group of viewers (to realise significant revenues or other benefits).
- Alignment with existing viewer behaviour.
- A clear proposition.
- Effective marketing and promotion (particularly using television programmes and channels).
- Flexibility, so elements can be added and dropped, depending on how they are received by viewers.
- If necessary, the involvement of partners in development.
- If necessary, the use of other media as part of the package (the internet and mobile phones, for example).

A large enough group of viewers

One mistake that many early United Kingdom interactive television services made was to base their financial and other projections on over-optimistic expectations of how many people were likely to use a particular interactive service. Just because a digital platform has six million customers doesn't mean that millions are likely to use a given interactive application on that platform.

For instance, half the people in the United Kingdom who had access to it used analogue teletext on a regular basis. But it took many years to get to this point – and there was relatively little competition. Modern interactive television applications often need to be able to sustain themselves on reasonably small numbers of users, while people get used to the interactive offerings. According to an ITC survey in 2001, less than 40 per cent of digital viewers in the United Kingdom ever use interactive services. Although this figure is likely to increase as more compelling applications are developed, it does suggest that the average interactive television application has to fight for a share of just a slice of a platform's total customer base – not for a share of the whole pie.

Alignment with existing viewer behaviour

A consideration for producers trying to formulate a well-directed offering is that it is usually much easier to redirect existing consumer behaviour than generate new behaviours. The best example of this is pay-per-view movies. These, in the main, have been a success on digital and analogue television platforms. This is partly because they provide a mechanism for viewers to watch a movie that is cheaper and easier than going to the video shop – an existing behaviour. There are a number of other examples: digital teletext builds on existing analogue teletext behaviour and television games build on existing console-game and quiz show usage and viewing.

Ease of use is also worth considering with regard to existing television viewer behaviours. Televisions are generally pretty easy to use. If an interactive television service is harder to use than switching channel or, at the other extreme, using analogue teletext, then it will have difficulty getting viewers on-board. There's more on this in Chapter 5.

Persuading viewers to do something completely new on television is possible – but more difficult. It may require lots of educational and promotional work. For example, Sky Digital has to run lots of on-air promotions to teach people about the benefits of pressing the red button to visit the interactive services.

A clear proposition

Most of the popular interactive television services are based on research work into the viewers' needs and time spent honing the product. With successful interactive television services, it is usually possible to tell very quickly what they are offering and who they are aimed at. For example:

- Interactive Wimbledon from the BBC: the opportunity to choose between video coverage on different courts. Aimed at anyone likely to be watching Wimbledon tennis.
- PlayJam: the opportunity to play games and enter competitions. Aimed at 16- to 34-year-olds.

Quite a few interactive television services fall into one of two categories: mass market (like BBC Wimbledon) or niche (like PlayJam games). Mass-market interactive television services sometimes aim for a small amount of usage from a considerable number of people; niche products are often after heavy usage by a small amount of people. The revenue sources and designs are likely to be different depending on the focus.

Whether mass market or niche, interactive television services that don't offer clear and tangible benefits to viewers are likely to fail: particularly anything that makes viewers think, 'Why do I want to do this?'

3.2 Play or win: PlayJam is clearly for playing games and entering competitions (with a few mobile phone ring tones thrown in for good measure). © *Static2358*.

Marketing and promotion

Many of the most popular and commercially lucrative interactive television services have close ties with a television programme or channel. Without this, it's more expensive and difficult to promote the service. This is illustrated by the experience of Sky Digital in the United Kingdom.

In 1999, Sky and its partners hoped that the Open . . . walled garden interactive television shopping environment would be more successful than shopping channels like QVC. Viewers accessed Open . . . by pressing the *Interactive* button on the remote control. The service was mainly focused on shopping via the television and had some information and games too. It contained a mix of a number of different retailers. Viewers could not watch their favourite television programmes while using Open . . . and the branding was very different from the branding Sky used on its television channels. Sky also eventually produced its own teletext and enhanced television services linked to its television channels, effectively in competition with Open . . . .

It became clear that a number of retailers weren't selling anywhere near enough to justify their existence on the platform. And after two years on air, the commercial situation became untenable and Open . . . was closed – effectively writing off a multi-million pound investment in the brand.

3.3 Sky Active front page. © *BSkyB.*

Its replacement was called Sky Active. Viewers access Sky Active by pressing the *Interactive* button on the remote control or by pressing the red button while watching a Sky Digital channel. An interactive icon that prompts viewers to press the red button is frequently displayed on-screen on Sky television channels, to encourage viewers to give the interactivity a go.

In the service itself, the television channel that the viewer was watching before pressing the red button is displayed in a small window (an advertising video is still displayed for people who arrive via the *Interactive* button). Sky television branding is also used throughout. The most prominent on-screen links lead to services like games, pizza delivery, betting and support for the television programme currently on air. Some shops are given less prominence and a number of the old Open . . . retailers have been removed.

Sky made these changes because viewers – unless they were highly motivated to do interactive television shopping or browsing – didn't bother to visit Open . . .. The broadcaster found that one of the most effective ways to promote interactive services is by using television programmes and channels: convincing viewers that they will get something useful or relevant to the programme they are watching. Sky now produces a regular stream of television programmes and associated enhanced television services to promote revenue-generating interactivity linked to programming. They have produced a shopping television programme to drive e-commerce, enhanced sports events to train viewers to bet, and many different enhanced television shows offering access to voting, competitions and the purchase of programme-related goods.

The reason that television is such an effective promotional device for interactive television is that it is possible to set up the link between the two in such a way that there are very few barriers for viewers between watching regular television and using interactive television. Television channels and programmes are available on the same device (the television), and viewers barely have to move a muscle to make the jump between television and interactive television – it's all operated from the same familiar remote control. Other promotional media (magazine adverts, junk mail, posters, telephone calls, even interactive walled gardens) can't compete with this.

The easier the interactive television producer makes it for viewers to jump across from television to interactive television – like letting them continue to watch the television programme in a small window or offering them some information or interactivity relevant to the programme they are watching – the more interactive usage there is likely to be. Evidence of this comes from news organisation ITN, which was able to track the effectiveness of different types of promotions for its interactive television news services in 2001. There were three different types of promotion that were tried:

- Promotions using banner adverts on the platform operator's walled garden menu pages. These resulted in a reasonable uplift in interactive usage.

- Promotions using on-air television graphics on the channel itself (for example, a line at the bottom of the television sports-results graphic that said 'Press red for more sports results'). These resulted in bigger jumps in traffic than the banner adverts.

- Presenters talking direct to camera, promoting interactive television information relevant to the particular story being covered on air. For example, the presenter might say, 'To see an up-to-date list of train services that are running during the strike, press red.' This kind of promotion resulted in by far the biggest increase in traffic to the interactive television application. The more useful the information, the more people used it. The promotion by the presenter of the interactive election results during an election programme resulted in a phenomenal jump in interactive usage.

Perhaps the ultimate use of television to promote interactivity is seen in television channels that work symbiotically with interactivity, with specific support for the television channel's programmes being an integral part of the interactive service and vice versa. This is the direction that shopping channels and quiz-show channels like Flextech's Challenge TV are heading, although interactive bingo channel Avago is perhaps the best example. With this channel, the bingo numbers are read out on-screen by a presenter, but viewers can only really enjoy the channel by participating using the iTV service. As mentioned previously, Avago is reported to have been running at break-even within two months of its 2002 launch. It is also said to gen-erate £20 000 per day in revenue.

Any interactive television service without a television programme or channel to provide promotion is at a disadvantage compared to those that have one. That's not to say that it's necessarily worth building a whole television channel to support an interactive proposition. Both the Boots WellBeing Network and Sainsbury's Taste Network in the United Kingdom found to their cost that a television channel isn't much good for driving interactive usage if the programming isn't good enough to get people to watch it in the first place. And some services are good enough to succeed without television support: a number of games and information services have succeeded without a link to a television channel. The PlayJam games service on Sky Digital, for example, doesn't have a television channel to support it, but it is still very popular. Promotions on a television channel or programme just make it easier to build up the number of users.

There's more on the kinds of content that work well with interactivity in the 'Lean forward versus lean back' section of Chapter 5.

Flexibility

If there's one thing that's certain about the interactive television industry, it's that there's a lot of uncertainty. Interactive television services could be heralding an enormous change in the way we use television. But, as with the move from radio to television and the move from black and white to colour, no one is certain how long it will take and exactly how things will turn out. Consequently, many successful interactive television practitioners try to recognise this uncertainty in the way that they go about doing business. Most interactive television contracts, for example, are for reasonably short periods, like one or two years, with 30-day or three-month get-out clauses. This protects companies against the incredible pace of change. And most interactive television technology companies try to avoid contracts that impose fines for missed launch dates. A number of interactive television technology pioneers in the United Kingdom made the mistake of contractually committing to launch deadlines – then went on to miss the dates again and again. This cost them not only goodwill, but also cost them money for breaking contracts. They made the mistake of thinking that contractual dates would motivate their technology teams – true, perhaps, but only up to a point.

The fast-changing nature of the interactive television industry can be recognised in other ways too. Interactive television production is often undertaken very quickly or in phases, to allow for changes in direction. Pilot schemes are common, giving interactive television companies the opportunity to dip their toes into new areas without committing too much. Pilot schemes involving external partners have the double advantage of helping to build relationships with companies that may be useful later. Whatever the methodology, the ability to change the direction of an interactive television product or strategy quickly, as opportunities arise or models are proved or disproved, reduces the risk of financial disaster. There's more on this in Chapter 4.

Partners

Interactive television is a new and difficult business. Big operators who own content, platforms and technology, like BSkyB, Canal+ and AOL TimeWarner, dominate large parts of the market. These vertically integrated firms have a wide range of resources that they can call upon quickly and easily, at cost price. They also benefit from considerable economies of scale (by reusing interactive programming code, for example) and can draw on large reserves of cash for investment.

To remain competitive, smaller interactive television companies often have to specialise or, for ambitious projects, find partners. For example, if the only way an interactive television service will work is if a popular television channel promotes it, a television channel would be a good partner. If tenancy fees could destroy the business case of a walled garden product, a platform would be a logical partner.

If a product will bring in money quickly enough to justify paying other companies upfront, rather than entering into partnership agreements, then that may be the best route. However, interactive television services can often take a number of years to pay back and there may be limited venture capital available. In this case, informal or formal partnerships are a common interactive television industry solution. Partnerships make interactive television products possible that would otherwise not have got off the ground.

The use of other media

Companies in very competitive environments often have to use multiple media channels to make sure that their product or service is available to customers whenever and however they want to access it – be it by telephone, the web, interactive television or the high street. (The word channel here defines a route to market rather than a television channel.) A PricewaterhouseCoopers survey in 2001 showed that nearly a third of people believe that having a choice of means to interact is the most important aspect of dealing with a company.

Companies dealing with multiple channels are often trying to build a ubiquitous brand with high levels of customer loyalty. The full approach to doing this encompasses advertising, e-commerce and customer communication across all available media – making sure the branding and quality of service that the customer encounters is the same, and that the services available on each channel or platform complement each other and build on the strengths of each medium.

With the multiple channel approach, the benefit of any particular channel is not judged by the revenue it brings alone, but by its contribution to the whole. An interactive television service that loses £1 million per year may be kept going on the basis that it adds to the total proposition. A car buyer may not make a purchase via interactive television, for example. However, if an interactive television advertisement helps them book a test drive then, taking the overall view, the interactive television part of the operation has done its job.

There's more on the multiple-channel approach in the iTV banking case study at the end of this chapter.

The problem with the multiple channel approach is that it can be expensive to build services on a number of platforms. Any company that does not already have a strong revenue stream from an existing channel to market could find that costs outweigh total revenues very quickly. Another problem is that to get full value out of having customers using your product or services across lots of different media, it is necessary to track what they are doing and quickly take action based on this information. This is where customer relationship management comes in.

Customer relationship management

Customer relationship management (CRM) is a business strategy that focuses on building close relationships with customers and making sure all parts of a business work together to build that relationship. Volvo North America's manager of CRM, Phil Biernet, says, 'From the first digital launch of a car in 2000 to the first multi-platform interactive television promotion in 2001, Volvo is dedicated to harnessing new technology. The aim is to continue building relationships with customers by giving them information and experiences they can't find elsewhere and letting them react to it.'

To further CRM strategies, a number of vendors have developed CRM technologies. A basic level of CRM technology is a registration system that covers all the sales channels. For example, if a customer registers for a bank account on the PC-internet from work, they will be able to use the same password to access the account on an interactive television service at home. More advanced CRM technologies can collate data about how customers are behaving across platforms, making it possible to customise the offering to them. Different types of viewers could be shown different interactive television screens depending on the information that is built up about them. For example, a customer goes into a bank in the high street and asks for some information about mortgages. The teller enters this information into the CRM system at the bank branch. The CRM technology then makes sure that when a new mortgage product is launched later that month, it is promoted to the customer when they log into their TV-banking service.

The problem with CRM technologies is that they can be very expensive to build – the software has to be flexible enough to work across the different technologies on the different platforms. Also, a complete CRM strategy arguably involves not just building technologies, but changing working processes and management styles too. The company has to concentrate on communication between its different arms as well as serving and understanding the customer, however they want to interact with the company – not just via the main sales channel. For this reason, companies that have a vested interest in understanding lots about their customers and that are in a position to make large technology investments, like banks and big retailers, tend to have extensive CRM operations; others do the best they can without it.

Revenue sources

Assuming you are confident that your interactive television idea has the ingredients required to be successful, what sources of revenue and other benefits are worth targeting? There are several possibilities, including:

- Advertising revenue.
- E-commerce revenue.
- Pay-per-view and pay-per-use revenue.
- Subscription revenues.
- Betting revenues.
- Marketing benefits.
- Hardware sales revenues.
- Tenancy fees and commission payment revenues.
- Soft benefits – beyond cash, such as brand development.
- Public-service benefits.

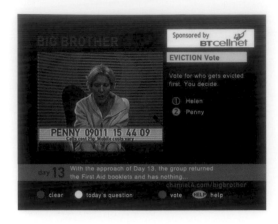

3.4 Pay-per-use voting was just one of the revenues sources targeted by iTV *Big Brother* in 2002. There was also advertising, betting and text messaging. © *Channel 4* (© *Endemol*, © *Two Way TV*).

Advertising

Interactive television advertising has the potential to combine the wide reach, contextual relevance and impact of television with the direct response and focused targeting aspects of PC-internet advertising.

'The beauty of digital interactive television is that it combines the strengths of television (mass reach) and the web's interactivity (one to one),' says Andrew Howells of interactive consultancy AH Associates. 'Television brings a strong proven awareness-building medium with strong impact (see, hear, remember) while interactivity provides consumers control, convenience, personalisation, transactions and allows us marketers to gather data and extend our brand bonding with interaction and experience.'

Interactive advertising comes in three main forms:

- Banner advertising. Just like banner adverts on web sites, interactive television banner adverts occupy a set portion of the screen and are usually carried on pages that have content or services that viewers want to use. Banner adverts appear almost anywhere – in walled gardens, on internet on television services, on electronic programme guides and in enhanced television services. Viewers are usually directed to press a button on the remote control to get further information on a product, get taken to a retailer's service or use some other kind of interactivity, like a quiz or survey.

- Interstitial adverts. These appear between pages or as applications are loaded, interrupting the user experience in the same way that television adverts do. As with banners, interstitial adverts often aim to get viewers to perform specific actions (like press the blue button for more information).

- Enhanced television advertising. This works by overlaying graphics on the television adverts that are shown between and during programmes. Typically, an icon appears on the screen during the advert, prompting viewers to press a button. The carrot used to get viewers to press the button can be anything – free vouchers, a competition or more information. For example, the interactive icon may say, 'Press *Red* for more about BT.' After pressing the button on the remote in response to the advert, viewers are sometimes taken away from the

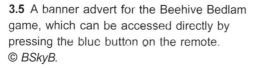

3.5 A banner advert for the Beehive Bedlam game, which can be accessed directly by pressing the blue button on the remote. © BSkyB.

3.6 An interstitial advert, while the main service loads. © BSkyB/Comet.

full-screen television channel to take part in whatever interactivity is on offer. Taking viewers away from the subsequent advertising and programmes isn't ideal, however (especially for subsequent advertisers), so to get round this, some adverts are designed so the interactivity can be completed before the video spot is over (quite tricky if it is only 30 seconds long) and/or using overlays rather than full-screen interactivity. Some platforms are also working on book-marking systems (so the viewer can store the advert, along with other interesting services, for later use).

Unfortunately, the interactive television advertising industry in the United Kingdom had a tough start between 1999 and early 2003. Some advertisers complained that platform providers were unwilling or technically unable to provide them with the kind of detailed customer-profile information that they were used to from the PC-internet. Others thought that the audiences for interactive television services were too small and the costs far too expensive. Early interactive television advertisers in the United Kingdom were asked to pay very high fees (sometimes hundreds of thousands of pounds), often without a clear idea of the return on investment.

The drop in internet advertising revenues, which hit companies from 2000, also affected the fledgling interactive television advertising market, and resulted in projects being cut. In particular, walled garden operators in the United Kingdom had to throw out projections for banner advertising revenues and start again, with much lower expectations.

There are, however, a number of examples of types of interactive television advert that have driven sales and provided other tangible benefits.

One is direct-response interactive television advertising. Direct-response advertising attempts to get viewers to take a very specific action, during or shortly after viewing the advert, usually the purchase of a product or the registration of an address (that can be used as a sales lead). Direct-response advertisers are not

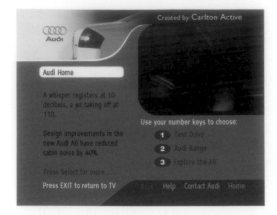

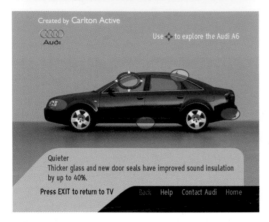

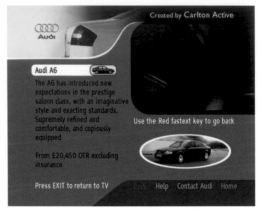

3.7 After pressing the red button during an Audi television advert, viewers are taken to screens with information and promotions about the product. *Courtesy of Carlton Active.*

really interested in the brand value of their advert; they just want to see a figure for the number of purchases or other actions. Interactive television is particularly attractive to direct-response advertisers because it can be used to help build a two-way dialogue with customers, helping make the advertising more targeted and responsive.

The United Kingdom's first interactive television advertising campaign, back in 2000, was for Chicken Tonight cooking sauce. A small icon was put on-screen during a Chicken Tonight television commercial on Sky Digital. The icon prompted viewers to press a button to jump to interactive screens offering information and a voucher. Ogilvy, the agency responsible, reported that the campaign was 70 per cent more effective than the average direct-response television campaign (which has a phone number that viewers can call) and the rate of redemption from the voucher was four times higher than average. Ian Kenny, digital communications director at Ogilvy, says: 'That [rate of response] could be put down to novelty value but further campaigns have achieved similar results.'

Another successful production was Virgin Mobile's 2001 interactive advertising campaign linked to the Brit awards interactive television application on ITV. The advertising achieved a 91 per cent brand recall rate with viewers and an unusually high 0.4 per cent response rate to competitions within the service. Alison Pye, brand manager for Virgin Mobile, says, 'In addition to the high advertiser-recall rate, research showed that users of the interactive service were ideally matched, demographically, to Virgin Mobile's target audience.'

Other examples of successful direct-response adverts come from Wink and RespondTV in the United States. They claim response rates up to 50 per cent, depending on the offer and the type of response required. Both companies have technologies that allow advertisers to run interactive television campaigns across a number of different interactive television platforms.

There's more on direct-response advertising in the interactive advertising case study at the end of this chapter.

Another success story for interactive television advertising is sponsorship. There are two types of sponsorship that look particularly promising. The first is sponsorship that is very closely integrated with a particular interactive television service, beyond simply putting the brand name in a prominent position. These are often aimed at niche markets. One example of this is Glaxo Smith Kline's Aquafresh toothpaste sponsorship in 2001 of the *Push My Button* quiz game on the United Kingdom-based PlayJam games service on Sky Digital. The Aquafresh name was incorporated into the quiz, as you would expect with traditional sponsorship. More cleverly though, around 10 per cent of the quiz questions became dental questions and the toothpaste brand colours were humorously incorporated into the on-screen graphics, by changing the colours of the virtual quiz-host's jackets and giving him an extra-wide toothy smile. Because the quiz offered a prize that viewers had to register for, Glaxo Smith Kline could also follow up the sponsorship using post and email, helping make the promotion more targeted and responsive. PlayJam called this type of sponsorship 'advergaming'. The game was played around 16 million times for six to seven minutes. Follow-up research suggested there was also a 5 per cent increase, among game players, in their stated propensity to buy Aquafresh toothpaste.

This kind of integrated sponsorship offers companies the opportunity to sidestep traditional advertising channels and effectively become media owners themselves. The danger of this power is that advertisers will produce services that nobody uses. The advantage is that services can be customised to the sponsors' needs and marketing strategy (within the bounds of the advertising regulations).

The other type of sponsorship that looks promising is cross-media or multiple channel sponsorship. With this, the interactive television advertisement is just one part of a bigger campaign that makes sure the brand is associated with a service, wherever it appears. For example, a news service might be available on television, the web, interactive television and via personal organisers. The sponsor would make sure its brand appears on the news service across all those media channels. What interactive television sponsorship brings to the mix is its unique ability to support traditional television content on the same device. An advertiser can sponsor a regular television programme and, by sponsoring the interactive television component of the programme too, can make sure the brand stays in viewers' minds as they move from passive viewing to interaction

Littlewoods Leisure, a gambling company, struck what it claims to be the biggest deal in British interactive television history on the basis of a multiple channel

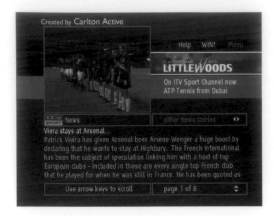

3.8 The Littlewoods sponsorship deal. The company name appeared on a number of services. *Courtesy of Carlton Active.*

approach. The deal with ITV consisted of sponsorship of interactive television sports news and games services, plus promotions on ITV's television channels and programmes. It was simultaneously supported with a Littlewoods web offering. Mobile phone company O_2 sponsored *Big Brother* in a similar, multiple channel, way.

E-commerce

Lots of people involved in interactive television in the early days thought retailing through the television would make them millionaires. It hasn't happened. In fact, some retailers are having more trouble selling via the television than they do on the web – quite the reverse of expectations. According to a Forrester Research survey in 2001, the average interactive television retailer in the United Kingdom is very disappointed with sales and less than impressed with the high costs and lack of information about customer behaviour.

Moreover, in the last six months of 2000, Open...the walled garden shopping service, received 655 000 orders from 30 million unique visits – a visit to purchase ratio of only 2 per cent. Even worse, some of the retailers in early versions of the digital cable walled gardens complained that they could count weekly sales on the fingers of

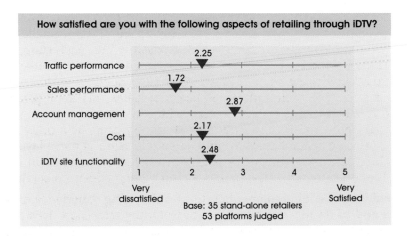

3.9 Forrester Research satisfaction survey. *Source: Forrester Research (2001).*

one hand. So, Open...closed down and a number of retailers on digital platforms have pulled the plug. Others have simply pulled back on the level of investment in interactive television, while they wait to see what happens.

There are, however, some retailers who claim to be on the road to making money. Domino's Pizza in the United Kingdom drove 60 per cent of all its e-commerce transactions via interactive television in 2001. Total sales via e-commerce were £3.6 million, with the interactive television component generating more than £2 million. 'There's a massive synergy between television viewing and pizza eating,' says Chris Moore, sales and marketing director for Domino's United Kingdom. Other retailers also claim to be making headway with iTV, particularly shopping channels like QVC.

What are the common characteristics of these, at least semi-successful, e-commerce on iTV operators?

- They all have an infrastructure that is suitable for interactive television. While digital interactive platforms are still building customer numbers, e-commerce on television companies have to sustain themselves on relatively small markets. Consequently, successful interactive television shops tend to find ways of generating high turnovers, high margins and low costs of sale. In particular, they can easily cover the cost of delivery of every sale, or persuade the viewer to pay for it, while having a fulfilment infrastructure that can accommodate the additional interactive television customers at very low cost. Having to buy extra warehouses and delivery vans just for interactive television customers will put a big strain on any company's cost-benefit equation.

- The products most likely to succeed on television seem to be ones which customers are prepared to buy on impulse. Books, certain types of food, holidays and plane tickets are likely to work well for direct sales – expensive and luxury items less so.

- Successful interactive television retailers tend to work in close co-operation with platform operators. Platforms can give retailers better positioning on their menus, they can run promotions and agree flexible commercial terms. One of the factors that limited the early growth of e-commerce on interactive television in the United Kingdom was that platforms tried to wrestle very high upfront tenancy fees and very high commissions from all their retailers, while squeezing as many competitor companies as possible into each shopping category. The extortionate fees combined with fierce competition made it almost impossible for retailers to make a profit. The success of Domino's on Sky Active is due, at least in part, to the fact that it has very good placing on the menus. It is alone in the pizza section, which is accessible direct from the first screen. Domino's also runs a number of affinity deals with other companies, offering special deals to interactive television games players, for example. The company claims these deals have led to an increase in the average value of customer orders across its interactive television services.

- Commercially successful retailers often tie the shopping experience in with the compelling and mass-market experience of watching television. This can be achieved using advertising and sponsorship slots or through programmes. Sky Digital is developing a number of programmes to drive e-commerce sales.

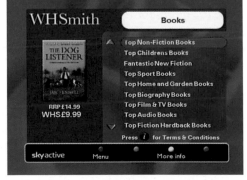

3.10 A glimpse of the interactive television shopping experience. © BSkyB, Asda, Comet and WH Smith.

Also, there's the opportunity to extend the model that shopping channels like QVC have used to build up enormous and profitable businesses. The benefit that interactive television brings to shopping channels is that it can dramatically reduce costs, by replacing telephone call-centre operators with interactive television e-commerce facilities. It can also make it even easier for viewers to make impulse purchases. Research by TechTrends Inc in 2000 found that 82 per cent of United States consumers who purchase from shopping channels are interested in e-commerce via the television, twice as many as those who have never bought anything from a shopping channel.

Pay-per-view and pay-per-use

Another way to bring in money is to charge viewers each time they use a service – be it watching a film, playing a game or looking up a piece of information. Pay-per-view (PPV) movies and sporting events, particularly boxing, football and wrestling, have done very well on analogue and digital television platforms. Canal Satellite in France said in 2002 that its two million subscribers bought 11 million pay-per-view and video-on-demand events per year. An SRI study of the United States market in 2001 found that 73 per cent of those with pay-per-view access said they buy movies using it.

To access pay-per-view video, viewers type in a pin number or ring a telephone line to get permission to watch the event. The programmes are delivered using near-video-on-demand or video-on-demand technologies and are encrypted to prevent unauthorised access (the conditional access system in the set-top box manages access to each event in conjunction with the smart card slotted in the front).

Regarding the potential of pay-per-use revenues from interactive applications, as opposed to pay-per-view revenues for video, games have been one success story, consistently topping the popularity and revenue tables across platforms. In the United Kingdom, games companies Two Way TV and PlayJam both generate significant revenues from viewers paying to play prize games. And Sky Digital charges viewers to play some of its interactive television versions of console and other games. Its version of Tetris took 1.5 million pay-per-plays in the first three months after launch.

Interactive television service providers can work with the platform operators to put payments on customers' monthly television bills. This can be technically and operationally complicated though, so most iTV service providers charge viewers using other methods.

Credit card or debit payments

A popular method of charging for pay-per-use interactivity is to get the viewer to type in their credit card or debit number using the remote control. The card number can then be stored permanently or used for one transaction. The main problem with pay-per-use by credit card is that charges levied by the banks can easily outweigh the maximum price an interactive service can get away with. Games and other interactive services are often priced at 50p (72 cents) per go – not enough to cover the 50p or £1 fee banks often require for processing a transaction. One way that interactive television producers have found to get around this is to take bigger payments, less often. For example, it's possible to set up a system where viewers deposit money to buy credits. Each time a viewer uses an interactive service that requires payment, a set amount is removed from the balance. In this way, the charge by the merchant bank will only be applied to a large and occasional deposit made by the viewer (say £10). This is the method that iTV bingo channel Avago uses. The deposited money can even be converted into some kind of virtual money, which can be freely transferred in the interactive world. This does mean, though, that the viewer has to make a reasonably large commitment to the service in advance, which is a significant barrier to usage.

Another option is the use of special cards into which customers can deposit money. Although not in widespread use (by viewers or platforms), in theory, these can then be slotted into the set-top box. Operators with appropriate licences can then remove money from this card, incurring minimal charges.

A final alternative using the bank route is to agree some kind of micro-payment system, where the fees paid per transaction are much smaller than normal. This makes it possible to charge customers 25p (36 cents), 10p or even 5p per go. To date though, banks have been reluctant to develop anything other than experimental micro-payment systems.

Telephone payments

If a phone line is attached to the interactive television set-top box, the easiest way to charge on a pay-per-use basis is to tell the box to ring a premium rate telephone number. The interactive television service, using the modem in the set-top box, dials a telephone number to complete a task, be it registering a vote, sending a text message, entering a competition or buying a product. Using this method, there's no need to pay a merchant bank 50p, £1 or more for every transaction, as the companies that run premium rate telephone lines accept fees based on a percentage of call revenues.

In the United Kingdom, Channel 4's *Big Brother* in 2002, the reality-TV series where contestants are voted off by viewers, managed to get 5.2 million votes by interactive television at 25p (36 cents) per go. This amounted to revenues of more than £1 million. Sky News also claims to generate thousands of interactive television votes, at 25p each time, based on current affairs issues.

The problem with taking payments using phone lines is that the revenues have to be shared with others. Typically, around 50 per cent of the call cost goes back to the telephone company and the company running the call-answering systems and modems (not including any upfront set-up charges, which are normally a few hundred pounds). Some platform operators also have the right to charge for any use of the modem in the set-top box or to specify which numbers it dials. In this case, the platform operator will probably want 20–50 per cent of call revenues too. Once revenues have been split two, three or four ways like this, even the money from millions of calls starts to look modest. This is the reason that some interactive television producers have foregone incorporating interactive telephone calls via the set-top box modem into their services. In preference, they try to get television viewers to pick up the phone and call premium rate numbers directly instead. This way, although the viewers actually have to make the extra effort of picking up the phone, the interactive television producer keeps more of the revenue. An alternative in the same vein is to use SMS text message numbers (by charging people to either send or receive messages related to the programme or interactivity). Some shows, such as Channel 4's *Ri:se* and a number of programmes on MTV, have made text messaging an integral part of their output. *Big Brother* in 2002 got 5.4 million votes by SMS, beating the iTV voting by 200 000 (although both are less than the regular telephone voting, which registered 12 million).

Digital cable companies in the United Kingdom missed a revenue opportunity by not incorporating premium rate telephony into their set-top boxes. Because they had super-fast cable modems, it wasn't thought necessary to include a plain old telephone system modem. However, the companies neglected to develop a pay-per-use payments mechanism for the cable modem. This meant they missed out on the significant premium rate telephony revenues enjoyed by their slower-speed modem rivals like Sky Digital.

Subscriptions

If someone likes something enough, they'll be prepared to pay a monthly fee for it. Indeed, there is a well-established subscription model for multi-channel television, which brings in billions in revenues around the world. Unfortunately, it seems that viewers do not want most interactive television services enough to pay an extra subscription.

The interactive television services that have tried to charge subscription fees have struggled. Internet on television is one example. Although the idea appeals to some viewers (around 10 per cent of pay-TV digital terrestrial subscribers in the United Kingdom signed up, along with some digital cable subscribers), the number of users came in well below predictions even though the subscription rates were relatively low, typically £5 per month. NTL in the United Kingdom closed down its analogue

Table 3.2: Desirable features of digital television

Desirable feature	Total %
Better quality sound and pictures	27
More choice of channels	24
Type of programming offered	22
Email access via television	5
Home shopping and banking	2
Don't know/refused	20
Total	100

(Source: The Pace Report 2001, United States market survey section)

TV-internet service, because so few people were prepared to pay the subscription. As discussed in Chapter 1, in the United States, Microsoft has refocused and relaunched its internet on television service several times due to lack of interest. Even with interactive television services that have obvious benefits, like personal video recorders, the willingness of viewers to pay monthly subscriptions is far from proven. Certainly, in the United States and Europe, PVR services that charge monthly payments have been struggling to find market share.

The reason that viewers are reluctant to pay subscriptions for iTV services is, perhaps, because they rarely know what to expect. An Independent Television Commission survey in the United Kingdom in 2001 revealed that, although respondents placed a certain amount of value on interactive services, such as email and games, just one in four was prepared to pay anything for them. Meanwhile, a report by research company SRI Consulting in 2001 found that 72 per cent of United States consumers were interested in nothing more than watching television. While a report from set-top box manufacturer Pace the same year showed that most Americans put better quality pictures well ahead of interactive services when considering the main attraction of digital television.

Most platform operators and broadcasters know that interactive television is not at the top of every customer's must-have list when they first get digital television – but they also know that interactive services can be successful once people are exposed to them. Therefore, they focus on ways of generating revenue that don't involve a monthly commitment before the viewers have had a chance to understand the benefits of the service. For example, some operators take a two-tiered approach: viewers can try large parts of a service for free or on a pay-per-use basis, but can also upgrade to a subscription for more advanced services or to avoid paying per-use fees. This model is being used by Two Way TV for its games, Avago for bingo and Yo-Yo for its chat and community services.

Betting

Betting might be the killer commercial application for interactive television. 'The only two things that people are making money from on the internet at the moment are pornography and gambling,' says Andrew Burnet, an analyst at Merrill Lynch. 'The same could be true of interactive television.'

3.11 Interactive television betting on Sky Active. © *BSkyB*.

Sky Digital is hoping to lift its revenue per subscriber up from under £300 ($430) to £400 ($580) by 2005, largely off the back of interactive television and telephone betting. And its 2002 partnership with Channel 4, called attheraces, has committed £300 ($430) million over ten years, in a deal to broadcast horse racing and associated interactive television betting.

The reason Channel 4, Sky and companies globally think that interactive television betting is worth the risk is that it could eventually draw in people who would not otherwise visit a betting shop. According to a survey from Orbis, the betting software division of iTV technology company NDS, 40 per cent of people feel uncomfortable entering a betting shop. It's this 40 per cent, plus the numerous others who are happy to enter a betting shop but don't normally make the effort, that the interactive television companies hope to serve.

As with many parts of the interactive television industry though, the reality has yet to live up to the hype. Most companies are quite secretive about their interactive television betting revenues, no doubt because they are low (especially once commissions and other payments to platform operators have been taken off). Even BSkyB (owner of Sky Digital), which is usually at the vanguard of United Kingdom interactive television publicity, has released betting revenues that combine interactive television, internet and telephone orders – making it difficult see how the iTV component is performing. There's also the question of whether sport betting will ever be attractive to people who only ever play the lottery and bet on the Grand National once a year. It may be that the games industry, rather than the betting industry, has more to gain from interactive television gambling – although there will be a number of regulatory hurdles to overcome.

The reality is also that betting companies have tended to concentrate their initial interactive television efforts on attracting existing experienced punters – to try to encourage them to transfer from betting shops, or from the web to television. Although betting companies are very much aware of future mass-market opportunities, experienced punters are more lucrative to begin with, because they complete many more transactions than the average customer. The average person is likely to be tempted by crazy high-odds bets (which make the bookies more money), but the quantity and monetary value of the bets will be much lower. This is one of the reasons why interactive television betting services often offer horse racing (the most popular betting shop sport) and a whole gamut of complicated betting options – many of which beginners won't understand. The bookies want to make the services work for the high-spending connoisseurs.

Whether interactive television betting will eventually generate the super profits that have been promised remains to be seen.

There's a case study on iTV betting at the end of this chapter.

Marketing benefits

Many interactive television services are built without any expectation of making money. Rather, they are designed to help another service, be it a television programme, television channel or digital platform, to make money or build ratings.

Sports coverage, an important driver of the uptake of digital television, is a good example. There's not much to choose between digital platforms that all show the same sports channels and the same games. However, a platform that offers a sports channel with a choice of different commentators, enhanced television betting and instant video highlights has a competitive advantage over the ones that don't. Although the direct revenues from the interactive component may not cover costs, if the interactive television service is good enough to prevent, for example, 1 per cent of customers from moving to another platform, it may be justified. (Losing 1 per cent of customers could be 100 000 people, each expected to bring £500 ($720) in revenues to the platform each year – that is, a loss of £50 million ($72 million) per year.) It is certainly the case that digital cable platforms in the United Kingdom are worried about sports fans moving across to digital satellite, because the interactive sport offering is more compelling.

The problem is the same for channel owners and programme makers. The competition can be so fierce that any channel that does not offer the most advanced and most compelling service is likely to lose viewers to one that does. In the past few years in Europe, digital systems have heralded the introduction of hundreds of new television channels – fragmenting the audience of existing channels (to nearly the same level as the United States, where there have been large numbers of channels for years). This means that established channels have to work harder to keep viewers. (See Table 3.3.)

Table 3.3: Television audience fragmentation: market share of the main channels in the United Kingdom, 1996 to 2000

Channels	Daily share %				
	1996	1997	1998	1999	2000 (Jan–Jun)
BBC 1	32.5	30.8	29.7	28.4	27.3
BBC 2	11.6	11.6	11.1	10.8	10.8
ITV	35.1	32.9	32.4	31.2	29.9
C4	10.8	10.6	10.2	10.3	10.5
Channel 5	–	2.3	3.8	5.4	5.8
Others	10	11.8	12.7	14	15.6

(Source: European Audiovisual Observatory, Statistical Yearbook, 2001)

Take news channels. In the United Kingdom these are fiercely competitive, with a number of channels offering broadly the same service. Of course, there are ways for these channels to differentiate themselves through graphics, journalistic style and format but, at the end of the day, the news is the news. Consequently, all the news channels in the UK have invested heavily in different types of interactive content to stay competitive. By doing this, they are not so much attempting to build revenues from interactive television (which can be very difficult with news content), but are attempting to protect and build their core television audience, maintain the core television advertising income and help promote the service as a whole. They worry that not having an interactive television service will result in 5, 10 or even 20 per cent of viewers eventually drifting over to other more cutting-edge and interactive services.

Another example is Discovery Channel, who remade and relaunched the United Kingdom's version of the classic television quiz *Mastermind* with a new presenter. To differentiate the show further and to provide a marketing boost, Discovery UK also added an enhanced television quiz, so viewers could play along with the contestants. This type of re-versioning of existing programmes and formats using interactivity is particularly useful for channels that have a back catalogue of programmes or formats. Interactive television offers them the opportunity to give a familiar television programme or format a new lease of life, attracting more viewers than would otherwise be expected.

Hardware sales revenues

Hardware sales are at the core of the business of set-top box manufacturers like Motorola, Scientific Atlanta and Pace. Set-top boxes are usually sold direct to platforms in bulk, who then rent, give or sell them to their customers, or let shops sell them on. As the standards for digital transmission and interactivity are developed and installation becomes easier, there are likely to be more set-top boxes sold by manufacturers direct to consumers, particularly boxes with advanced functionality (like PVRs).

Furthermore, consumer electronics retailers, like Dixons in the United Kingdom, make a large part of their income from selling the peripherals that come with multimedia systems. Peripherals (like keyboards, joysticks, printers and digital cameras) are particularly attractive to retailers because they are not subject to the same intense competition that affects larger price-ticket items, like televisions and personal computers, and therefore have higher margins. Platform operators and interactive television producers have also taken advantage of this opportunity. They sell keyboards and game controllers direct to consumers, sometimes adding their own branding to the devices.

Tenancy fees and commission payments

Platform operators and companies that are big enough to aggregate other suppliers within their own interactive television service enjoy another revenue source. The money here is from tenancy fees and cuts of revenues, taken from companies that appear in the operator's walled garden, portal or other interactive service. Tenancy fees on major United Kingdom platforms can range from a few thousand to several hundred thousand pounds, although aggregators sometimes pay companies that have valuable content or services – reversing the normal flow of money.

As discussed, in the early days of digital interactive television in the United Kingdom (1999 to early 2003), a number of platform operators tried to get the highest possible tenancy fees from companies, without caring too much about whether the companies would see a return on investment. The banks were particularly hard hit, investing millions of pounds in developing security systems for interactive television transactions as well as paying the platform operators' enormous fees. The banks hoped to bring interactive banking to new groups of customers that didn't have access to the PC-internet. Unfortunately, they found that the users of interactive television banking services tended to be the same high-tech early adopters that used the first PC-internet banking services. It was an expensive mistake, although one that is gradually being corrected with changes to the interactive television banking offerings.

Platform operators, walled garden operators and portal owners are now more likely to try to work in much closer co-operation with their tenants. The terminology is of partnerships and the commercial models are often based around revenue shares, rather than upfront fees, although Sky Digital in the UK has a reputation for being a tough negotiator.

Soft benefits

A number of interactive television services that have made it through start-up phases have done so because they have been able to justify their existence to investors, not just in revenue terms but also from the value they bring beyond cash. Non-cash value can come from a number of sources, including brand value, training staff and building relationships with other companies.

The problem is that benefits beyond cash are often difficult to measure. There are techniques, however, even for rather nebulous concepts like brand value (customer surveys and usage analysis, for example).

Public-service benefits

In the midst of the capitalist frenzy that is much of interactive television, there are also benefits beyond the acquisition of cash or the protection of existing revenues. Services like home banking and shopping can transform the lives of the elderly and disabled. Information via interactive television can reach people on the wrong side of the digital divide, who do not have access to the PC-internet. The United Kingdom government has been experimenting with providing health and other information via interactive television. One service even allowed viewers to consult a nurse using live video (see the health case study at the end of this chapter).

Others services have focused on the chat and email capabilities of interactive television, to bring local communities together, providing opportunities for schools to post information and for parents and community groups to disperse messages. A Manchester school was one of the first interactive television services on digital cable in the United Kingdom.

Meanwhile, the BBC and public broadcasting stations in the United States have looked at providing services that commercial operators are unlikely to be able to justify in financial terms, including educational interactivity for children and alternative audio streams with translations of programmes into minority languages.

Ultimately, even interactive television services with public-service objectives may end up being able to justify their costs in hard commercial terms. For example, the total cost for the government of communicating complex information to citizens will potentially be much lower once everyone has access to interactive television (see the local government case study at the end of this chapter). And any platform that can claim to be the medium for community participation and local information will have a competitive advantage.

The best business strategy in the world, unfortunately, counts for nothing if the service takes forever to launch and runs over budget. Next: production techniques for interactive television.

Case study: The commercial experience of interactive television advertising

Andrew Howells, former director, OMDtvi. OMDtvi is an interactive television advertising agency and consultancy. Andrew Howells became managing director of the iTV consultancy AH Associates towards the end of 2002.

Television is undergoing the biggest change since the launch of multi-channel television. Digital television transmission allows viewers with an intelligent box the chance to interact with content. Interactive television, in all its various forms, is set to change the way viewers use television. It can be viewed as both a threat and an opportunity. Uptake is already impressive and new routes to consumers for advertisers and broadcasters are already available and proving valuable.

Fundamentally, digital transmission just allows for more channels to be broadcast with better quality pictures and sound. Digital television is attractive across a broad scale. Consumers get a better quality service as well as more choice. Advertisers have new and better routes to their markets. Broadcasters believe they can make more money. The government can sell off the existing analogue bandwidth, although a replication of the 3G bonanza is unlikely. Digital television has had the fastest growth for any new technology. Admittedly, this has been driven by the platforms stimulating consumer demand. As soon as BSkyB started giving away set-top boxes, the other platforms had to follow suit. The platforms were prepared to invest heavily in digital television for a variety of reasons. Interactivity increases revenue for the platforms from many sources, such as telephony, betting, home shopping and pay-per-view services. The platforms also increase their share of advertising revenue as penetration levels increase. From our point of view, digital television offers a new take on a trusted advertising medium.

The growth of television as an advertising medium has been driven by the ability to deliver huge mass audiences quickly and cost-efficiently. The proliferation of channels and the relative strength of the BBC have affected the commercial broadcasters and viewing has become more diverse and fragmented than ever before. Interactive television can offer a panacea for this. Interactive television can deepen brand involvement and increase impact.

Television viewing habits are changing. A whole generation of viewers are now accustomed to multi-channel, 24/7 television, text services, five terrestrial channels, television on demand, subscription services, electronic programme guides, channel surfing, the internet and games consoles. In other words, multi-functionality from their television sets. This multi-functionality will ultimately affect viewing behaviour, but also provide potential for greater depth of relationship and interaction between advertiser and viewer. Television viewing is increasingly becoming an active, rather than a passive, experience.

Interactive television will play a significant part in our future both as consumers and marketing professionals. Understanding interactive television, its developments and the ramifications for the marketing industry is crucial. But there comes a time when the theory has to be put into practice. The following case studies illustrate the challenges and commercial benefits of two real-life interactive television advertising campaigns.

The Rimmel campaign

Coty's Rimmel brand was launching their new Exaggerate Hydracolour range of lipsticks. As part of the launch, Rimmel wanted to sample the new product. The company had not used interactive television before. The aim was to increase the awareness of the Exaggerate Hydracolour lipstick amongst women aged 16–44 as well as recruit new users via product sampling. In order to do this, Coty decided to use interactive television as an extension to their traditional television campaign. Other benefits included increased brand exposure from the interactive content and the opportunity to capture data, creating a targeted database of women for future use.

Creative

JWT created the television campaign featuring Kate Moss 'experimenting' with the lipstick in a nightclub. OMDtvi managed the production of the interactive content on the Sky Active channel. The call to action was the opportunity to have a free Hydracolour lipstick plus the chance of winning one of 30 Rimmel cosmetic sets. The interactive site was kept purposely simple and featured the voice-over, music and imagery from the television advertisement, creating a powerful link for viewers who jumped to the site from the television execution.

3.12 The Rimmel interactive television advertisement. © JWT (© *OMDtvi and Rimmel*).

Execution

A single-screen 'poster' site was created which used a close-up of Kate Moss taken from the original television advert. A new script was produced to explain how the viewer could claim their free lipstick. Interaction was limited to answering a question about Rimmel's competitor products and opting in or out of future marketing activity. Because of the simplicity of approach, viewers were not expected to visit the poster for much more than 30 seconds.

Media used

Some of the planned television campaign was adapted to provide an interactive link or jump to the interactive content. Interactive advertisements or i-Ads are restricted to the last advertisement in the break. For viewers already in the Sky Active channel, traffic was delivered from top-level menu video banners.

Results

The campaign ran from 30 October to 26 November 2001 and is considered to be the most successful interactive poster campaign ever run on the Sky Digital platform. Total responses reached 52 000, which was in line with expectation. What was more extraordinary was the rate of response. The interactive advertisements (i-Ads) delivered a 3.2 per cent response rate. (This is counted as viewers who interacted with the broadcast advertisement through to the completion of their request for a Rimmel lipstick.) This compares favourably with typical response rates averaging 1.5 per cent.

Data value

Post-campaign, the Rimmel respondents were then analysed against the Sky Digital base using Claritas' lifestyle and demographic database. Claritas, who own and compile the data, were able to examine the Rimmel respondents in more detail looking at gender, age, income, children at home and lifestyles. This provided new evidence of how well targeted the campaign had been against a defined core Rimmel customer. Furthermore, 68 per cent of all respondents also opted-in for further marketing activity by Coty. Over 30 000 permission-based names and addresses is a useful addition for Coty, who can now use this data for future retail promotions, new product launches and other cross-marketing activity.

The Finish campaign

Finish Powerball 3in1 had a television campaign planned, and wished to test interactive television in collaboration with Whirlpool Dishwashers. They had coupons, samples and a dishwasher to give away. The campaign objective was to learn as much about interactive television as possible. Reckitt Benckiser (RB) wished to test different incentives/media placements in order to understand what compels users to interact with their television. Bearing in mind the fact that 70 per cent of the United Kingdom population don't have dishwashers, there were three areas of particular interest:

1. Traffic generation – broadcast stream versus walled garden banners.

3.13 The Finish/Whirlpool interactive advertisement on Sky Active. To start with, viewers were asked if they owned a dishwasher. © *JWT* (© *OMDtvi and Rimmel*).

3.14 Non-dishwasher owners were offered the opportunity to win a dishwasher. © *JWT* (© *OMDtvi and Rimmel*).

2. Call to action – sample versus coupon versus prize draw.
3. Offer (to dishwasher owners) – freshener sample versus 75p ($1.15) coupon.

Creative

The advertisement used copy provided by RB and presented a clean and simple site designed to enable viewers to respond with minimum complications and fuss. The voice-over used the same artist as the 30-second advertisement for continuity, and explained the benefits of Whirlpool 6th Sense dishwashers and Finish Powerball 3in1's 'intelligent solution'.

The banners were also simple, and designed to get the message across as clearly as possible. From previous experience the word 'free' has proven to be a big draw, and the call to action centred around the three offers: a free 75p Finish coupon, a free mint dishwasher freshener sample, and a prize draw to win a free Whirlpool 6th Sense dishwasher.

Execution

The split of dishwasher owners and non-dishwasher owners in the audience (3:7 respectively) posed a problem. We did not want to offer samples and coupons for Finish to people who didn't own a dishwasher! The first page avoided this problem by asking the viewer to declare whether they owned a dishwasher or not.

Dishwasher owners were then offered the choice between a free 75p Finish coupon and a free mint dishwasher freshener sample, before being entered into a prize draw for a Whirlpool 6th Sense dishwasher. Non-dishwasher owners were offered the chance to enter the prize draw. All respondents were asked whether they wanted to hear from RB in the future with news and offers.

Media used

Some of the planned television campaign was adapted to provide an interactive link or jump to the interactive content. Interactive advertisements or i-Ads are restricted to the last advertisement in the break. For viewers already in the Sky Active channel, traffic was delivered from top-level menu video banners, and from normal banner adverts in Beehive Bedlam on Gamestar (Sky Active's games channel).

3.15 Dishwasher owners were first offered a free sample and then the opportunity to win a new dishwasher. © *JWT* (© *OMDtvi and Rimmel*).

Results

The campaign ran for four weeks in January to February 2002. The number of responses exceeded the planned number of 35 000. The response rate from the airtime was 0.32 per cent of adults (0.2 per cent predicted). In addition, 54 per cent of responders also opted-in to being contacted in the future by RB.

Sky television channels provided around 50 per cent of the responses, with Flextech channels providing around 25 per cent, and iTV banners the remaining 25 per cent. The games banner performed particularly well, with around 66 per cent of the banner responses coming from Beehive Bedlam. As expected, 50 per cent of responders were dishwasher owners. The split between coupons and samples was around 27:73 respectively, showing that samples were a more popular offer to dishwasher owners. However, it was found that between 26 and 32 per cent of people who entered the site from coupon and sample banners did not own dishwashers – that is, they were timewasters (people who responded to sample/coupon banners, who then press 'no' when asked if they own a dishwasher). Applying this data to particular channels, dayparts and media placements enables RB to highlight where timewasters arise, and to plan future campaigns to avoid them.

Case study: The business model for interactive television platforms and service providers

Mervyn Metcalf, vice president, media investment banking, Merrill Lynch International.

To assess whether interactive television providers and platforms have viable business models, it is important to understand both the revenue and the cost model of the industry. The revenue model is founded upon providing the consumer with a range of services including, but not limited to, enhanced television, telephony, fast internet access and interactive applications, such as games and educational content. The cost model is largely driven by infrastructure costs (including upfront capital investment, network and connection costs) and the cost of content and other services. Excluding execution risks, which should be factored into any analysis, one important part of the analysis in considering the returns on an investment in an interactive television platform is to look closely at the relationship between revenues and costs.

The cost and revenue considerations highlighted below refer primarily to interactive television providers who provide full end-to-end consumer service offerings, not broadcasters or companies that provide single applications or particular technology solutions.

Revenue model

Despite the superior functionality an interactive television provider or platform can offer, in my view, the consumer is unlikely to pay a significant premium for what may be perceived as broadly similar services to ones he or she can receive today. Hence the pricing of an interactive television service will need to compete with the pricing of equivalent services. This is particularly true with regard to traditional entertainment services, such as broadcast television channels, video-on-demand and so on.

However, an interactive television provider competes on many more levels than just traditional television entertainment and consequently has the ability to generate revenues from a number of alternative offerings. For example, in its provision of interactive games, the interactive television provider is a player in a significant global market, where games retail for, say, £50 each. The interactive television provider has the option of charging per hour of gaming or renting a game for a single play. The same rule applies for other interactive services.

Consequently, when examining an interactive television service provider from an investment perspective, it is important to understand the full extent of revenue-generating opportunities.

Cost model

Turning to costs, an interactive television provider's basic cost structure can be broken into infrastructure and content.

In the context of launching satellites or laying fibre-optic cable, an interactive television platform can be cost-effective in terms of developing an infrastructure. For example, if the technology utilises an existing infrastructure (such as the existing copper wire infrastructure of a telephone network), the provider can create a 'virtual' network at relatively low cost. The costs associated with this are primarily driven by advances in technology and the cost structure of the network provider (often the incumbent national telephone network provider). Other costs will relate to establishing an operational infrastructure, such as establishing a head office, call-centres, billing facilities etc., in addition to developing a brand through marketing.

In terms of content, it is expected that costs will ultimately be charged in relation to usage. Taken together, the cost structure of the industry is more variable than fixed, with the result that in order to generate an acceptable return, the interactive television provider will need significant scale (that is, millions of connected and active subscribers).

Consequently, when examining an interactive television service provider's cost structure, it is critical to understand the long-term cost assumptions and the associated execution risks. This is likely to include that ability of the service provider to attract sufficient subscriber numbers.

Execution risks

A word on execution risks. Given that there are a number of major established pay-TV networks in the world, the launch of a new, mass-market product will prove a challenge. This is particularly the case as the incumbents begin to layer near-interactive television functionality onto their service offering, such as hard disk drive recorders. Ultimately, the challenge for an interactive television provider is to demonstrate a superior product offering; even so, as the VHS–Betamax war proved, the superior product does not always win.

Summary

An interactive television provider or platform will have a viable business model if an appropriate balance can be made between revenues and costs, even if it is in the longer run or after only achieving a certain minimum level of subscribers. But the risk remains that, for whatever reason, true interactive television never becomes a reality as a consequence of a perceived weak investment case and an inability to attract funding.

(Note: the views expressed in this article are the author's own and not necessarily those of Merrill Lynch.)

Case study: The benefits of banking services on interactive television

Mike Constantine, head of electronic services, HSBC Bank. HSBC launched the world's first nationally available digital interactive television banking service.

As an international provider of financial services, HSBC needs to ensure that customers can bank whenever, wherever and however they choose. This means putting the customer at the centre of everything and delivering innovative products and services in a way that suits them; it is about choice – not about forcing customers down the newest, or cheapest, delivery channel.

New developments in e-commerce have been harnessed to ensure that the bank can deliver the highest quality customer service in the most efficient manner. HSBC has rolled out a global system, enabling the bank to connect any device customers may have (such as their internet-enabled personal computer or their digital television) to its internal systems. This provides customers with a seamless service; when a transaction is made on one channel it will immediately show up on any other.

What customers really care about is how technology makes it easier for them to manage their financial affairs – often it's the little things that make the difference; for example, checking their transactions or paying a bill during the commercial break of a favourite television programme.

Benefits

- HSBC's Television Banking empowers customers to do their banking whenever they want, from the comfort of their own homes.

- HSBC customers do not have to open a special account to use the television service; it is an integral part of HSBC's multi-channel approach and customers use the same security number as the one they use for HSBC's internet or telephone banking services.

- A high level of functionality enables satellite digital TV subscribers to access many of the products and services that HSBC offers, as well as allowing HSBC customers to transact with their accounts via the television.

- The only equipment required for HSBC Television Banking through Sky Digital's Sky Active service is a digital satellite system linked to an existing telephone line.

- There are no subscription charges for HSBC Television Banking and customers pay just the cost of a local rate phone call when accessing their accounts.

- Television banking is particularly appealing to people with mobility difficulties, shift workers and people living in rural communities.

- Customers can check their balances and transactions, pay bills, make payments to family and friends, view credit card information, transfer money, and view their standing orders and direct debits.

3.16 The HSBC banking service on Sky Active allows customers a range of banking services. *Reproduced courtesy of HSBC.*

Security

HSBC's Television Banking service meets industry standards of security. The system is protected by sophisticated secure gateways, including firewalls and monitoring devices. In addition to strong data encryption, where sensitive information is scrambled in transit, customers need to input a security number to access the service.

Developments

HSBC is continually learning how best to use the power of television and the service has been adapted accordingly. Television is an entertainment medium

3.17 HSBC customers use the same security number as the one they use for HSBC's telephone or internet banking services. *Reproduced courtesy of HSBC.*

and HSBC has been very successful in making television banking fun, engaging customers by use of video clips, humour, voice-overs and music. The service is updated regularly to maintain customer interest and in keeping with seasonal and sporting events, such as Easter and Wimbledon. On-screen promotions are run to attract customers, using existing sponsorship partnerships, such as a coaching session with Tim Henman during Wimbledon and a trip to the British Grand Prix (using HSBC-sponsored Jaguar cars as the visual image).

3.18 HSBC's interactive television banking service includes on-screen promotions to engage the viewer. *Reproduced courtesy of HSBC.*

Case study: Bringing betting home

Ismail Vali, head of interactive development, Ladbrokes e-Gaming. Ladbrokes is the betting and gaming division of the global Hilton Group and has nearly 2000 retail locations.

The internet created the expectation that services could be accessed at any time, from anywhere. But Ladbrokes was cautious in launching new media services due to mistakes made by other market entrants and the wish not to alienate any of the potential customer base. Taking the view that it was not good enough to have a new media presence unless it was a compelling one, Ladbrokes embarked on the challenge of making available technology work effectively for our customers and us.

The company launched its first new media service in 2000 and has innovated rapidly on several platforms since that time, launching interactive betting services on the internet, on mobile phones (WAP and SMS), and on digital interactive television on the Sky, NTL and Telewest platforms, as well as on Web TV.

New Media = new audiences?

Opinion across the web, phones and digital interactive television industry suggested that services on each new platform would deliver a raft of new customers, averse to entering a betting shop, but who would happily bet through new, available methods. It is certainly true that Ladbrokes has seen a huge number of new

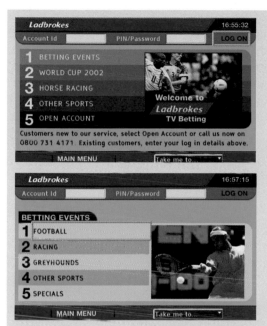

3.19 Ladbrokes on digital cable.
© *Ladbrokes.*

customers who favour betting through new media devices, but the increasing penetration of these devices is fast muddying the distinction between a new and traditional customer. Additionally, gaming presents a positive 'Pareto effect', where 80 per cent of your business tends to come from only 20 per cent of your customers – building a service for one group within a broad spectrum is then bound to alienate other customers who may bet if the service was presented more to their liking.

Since launching our e-Gaming operation, we are ceasing to view interactive gambling as that removed from traditional gambling – the technology simply allows another way of serving our customers when and where they demand our services. Whether those customers are novices or experienced, Ladbrokes would seek to offer an accessible service without alienating any customer group. Just as the shop estate adapts to reflect changes in our customer base, equally our new media services evolve in light of the platform, available technology and regular feedback from all our customers. Keeping everyone happy all of the time, though, can often be difficult and positioning a service to satisfy the Pareto effect and draw in interested novices (who may only bet on popular events like the Grand National) is one of the key challenges of a betting service on digital interactive television.

The initial thinking behind launching on digital interactive television had centred on the need to build a betting service accessible to novice punters – those who would be watching sporting events and wish to increase their enjoyment of an event by placing a bet on it within easy reach of the broadcast. Usage, however, was found to come from moderate to experienced customers who, typically, learnt how to use one service and stayed with it, despite flaws in how it might operate. The Ladbrokes Best Bets application for digital cable featured chronological bet selection and the ability to bet up to a treble – key customer complaints were the time-ordered menu necessitating lots of clicks if you entered the service in the afternoon and wanted to place a bet on an evening event, and the inability to place any bet over a treble. Despite these flaws, the service was very well received for its perceived convenience – problems with slow load and refresh times, common to digital interactive television, meant that many customers did not venture into opening multiple accounts, as they might on the web, as they did not want to endure a laborious registration process.

As one of few betting companies who have innovated their service since initial launch on digital interactive television, Ladbrokes are proud to have learnt from our mistakes, and those of competitors, and churned services in light of customer feedback. New services will present a faster, more intuitive betting application that increases audience accessibility and is focused on speed and ease of bet selection and placement – more able to deliver the transaction engine, 'get me to my bet fast' functionality that customers expect.

Furthermore, early ideas of how the interactive walled garden area would function anticipated easy linkage from normal broadcast to an interactive service, but the reality was often very different. Platforms experimented with a range of services that consumers might have wished to access in the interactive space, but a lack of context, heavy menu structures and slow load times conspired to create portal areas from where it was often difficult or time-consuming for a user to find the service and opportunity they required. Moving away from contained services that sit within a contained portal environment is one of the key issues for interactive betting services in coming years – access from the broadcast stream, whether from live events or advertising, will be one of the key drivers for new usage of betting services; more focused use of the walled garden area by platforms will also increase uptake and, since betting is one of the few revenue drivers on interactive television, it would make sense for the platforms to accept that betting companies should be provided more and better linkage in menu structures.

Digital interactive television – looking to the future

Given the fragmented digital interactive television market in the United Kingdom, presence on all major platforms is essential to long-term success, and Ladbrokes' ability to effectively market a television betting service has been improved since launching a service on Sky Active in 2002. The presence of millions more subscribers and Sky Active's intuitive menu structure, with betting flagged up clearly on main pages, has been a great success since launch, and both Ladbrokes and Sky have been encouraged by the results to date.

Good relationships with platform providers are only possible when both parties are realistic about the real status of interactive television services, including betting. They are embryonic and require an acceptance that unlocking potential comes with work on both sides, rather than simply demanding large fixed fee payments to enable access. Building for divergent software platforms and retaining consistency in usability and the product mix adds to the costs of running a digital interactive television service, and realistic negotiations with platforms are key to a long-term vision for betting on television. Linkage agreements from broadcast content, as with the development of affiliate agreements on the internet, will become increasingly relevant as betting services strive for multi-applicability and the need to offer services to customers in the most logical places rather than just within the walled garden. In this regard, betting and gaming services on digital interactive television will probably act as the drivers for early adoption of new technologies that improve the user experience across the interactive space.

Ultimately, future success will depend on how customers respond to betting services and the mix of products offered within them – just as Ladbrokes innovated a fixed odds sports betting service on the internet to include a casino, fantasy and numbers products, we would aim to approach the future adapting the digital interactive television proposition in light of customer feedback and demands, service performance, a broad product base and commercial opportunities. Most importantly in this new market, we aim to offer a secure, trustworthy operation that values traditional customer service above all else and that delivers what the customer demands, where they demand it.

Case study: Television and healthcare – possible bedfellows?

Ronnette Lucraft, general manager, Living Health, Flextech. Flextech is the content division of Telewest Communications, provider of multi-channel television, telephone and internet services to United Kingdom households, and voice and data telecommunications services to business customers. Flextech is one of the biggest providers of television channels to the United Kingdom pay-TV market.

Television plays a central part in people's lives in the United Kingdom – and television is changing. Digital television offers more choice, more services and more opportunities. It is also potentially a socially inclusive device that can, if used effectively, help to bridge the 'digital divide'. Television is non-threatening to those parts of the population who would not think to use the internet – many more people can drive a remote control than have mastered a mouse.

So when the Department of Health (DoH) was looking for new ways to widen public access to health information and services, an obvious method was through the television. In order to better understand this medium, the DoH made some research funding available and looked to the private sector for inspiration and expertise.

One of the pilot projects the DoH funded was Living Health, which gave 50 000 Telewest broadband cable television homes in Birmingham the ability to browse and search over 22 000 pages of National Health Service (NHS) accredited information. Selected users also had the facility to book appointments with their family doctor from the comfort of their living room. Furthermore, patients were able to talk to an NHS Direct nurse and see them on their television screen. In addition to being able to get the added reassurance of seeing a friendly face, the nurse had the

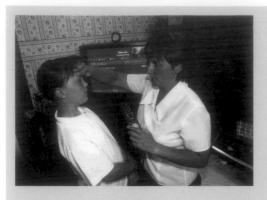

3.20 The Living Health project gave viewers access to NHS Direct information. © *Living Health* (© *Flextech*).

ability to show specially commissioned images and video clips to aid the consultation. This was the first deployment of this type of technology through the television anywhere in the world. Truly groundbreaking stuff.

How did it all begin?

Living Health began its life in 1998 when Flextech Television was planning its digital strategy. It was becoming clear at the time that the possibilities offered by hugely increased bandwidth, and the convergence of the internet and broadcasting, meant new types of niche, rich, interactive television would soon be possible.

Flextech already operated some significant brands within the pay-TV industry. Its stable of wholly owned channels – Living, Bravo, Challenge and Trouble – are among the most popular in multi-channel homes, and its successful joint venture with the BBC, UKTV, is a demonstration of public/private partnership. When looking for inspiration to expand the portfolio, Flextech executives looked to the internet. Health presented itself as something that many people were interested in, but could it work on television? Flextech felt that what was needed was the backing of a really strong brand, and few are stronger in the United Kingdom than the NHS. Also, the economics of the channel concept would not add up – it needed to be free-to-air to reach the widest population possible, but the advertising revenues forecasts were too low to sustain the high production values necessary to do justice to the subject matter.

The DoH faced a different set of challenges. The last few years have seen an explosion in demand for health information, caused in part by the demands of patients and consumers to be better informed about healthcare and the latest innovations in treatment and drugs. The concept of the empowered patient was beginning to emerge, and extra pressure was being put on an already overstretched NHS to cope with these extra demands.

The NHS had begun to explore new forms of access to care and information. NHS Direct provides nurse-led support to patients via the telephone and NHS Direct Online offers access to health information over the internet. Both had proven hugely popular with the public. The Living Health concept was presented to officials and ministers – there was great synergy between the government's objectives and Living Health's capabilities. Healthcare television had a new purpose.

What do the public think?

Since its launch in June 2001, the Living Health pilot has generated masses of information. Usage has exceeded all expectations – in the first month, over 500 000 pages of information were accessed. On average, people spent 20 minutes per visit looking at over 30 pages of information. The most popular type of information sought was on illness and treatment, closely followed by information on NHS Direct. By the end of the six-month pilot period, 44 per cent of households had used it, with 41 per cent making a return visit. This made Living Health the most popular part of Telewest's interactive service, after games. Indeed, extrapolated across the digital universe, usage would be an estimated four million pages of health information per day, comparable to an internet search engine.

The demographics prove interesting too. Market research shows that Living Health has twice as many users who are from the C2DE demographic group than from the ABC1 category. Compared against the profile of the internet (where there is almost three times the usage from ABC1s), Living Health is up to five times more effective at reaching the less well-off demographic groups than the internet.

Living Health has shown itself to be an effective way of bringing quality information to the masses. The public has embraced this new, but old, communications medium. It is too early to tell whether people are doing anything differently because of this – but access to information is usually the first step in any change process. This could also be a new model for the rest of government – instead of public-service broadcasting, this is more like broadcasting public services. Whatever its use, the principles underlying future development remain the same; television is a unique medium and cannot be treated in the same way as the internet. While broadcasters have much to learn from government, equally government can learn much about how to reach their citizens through the latest form of new media. Perhaps watching television can seriously improve your health.

Case study: The benefits of public-service interactive television

Richard Steel, head of information and communication, Newham Council. Newham is a borough of London.

In Newham, interactive digital television is a real alternative to the home personal computer and internet. Only about 37 per cent of Newham residents have internet access and, of these, many people are reliant on access through public locations, such as libraries. Contrast this with leafy Surrey, where about 83 per cent of people now have a personal computer in the home. Yet Newham is known as a council that is among the leaders in its exploitation of information and communication technology (ICT), and, for Newham, ICT offers significant potential to make the council and public services more accessible for people who, currently, may be socially excluded because of their circumstances.

Newham therefore had two quite different iTV projects, each of which is demonstrating the potential of the medium in service delivery and community engagement.

DKTV (a Different Kind of TeleVision) was established to provide a platform-independent, national programme that is locally customised and free to consumers. It therefore aimed to work with all the existing distribution channels. A pilot was run in several hundred Newham households, working with Video Networks Ltd's HomeChoice service, throughout the second half of 2001. Interactive services included consultation, housing repairs and booking services. The project also involved Newham's translation service to provide support for people who do not speak English. (About 50 per cent of Newham's population are from communities that do not speak English as their first language.) The service was delivered through a rich televisual medium – video based, and with minimal text – which proved very popular and accessible for those with low literacy skills.

Carpenters Connect was funded by the government Department for Education and Skills (DfES) through its Wired-up Communities programme. It started from the premise that, for some services, it is essential that the service provider can access its customer directly, rather than through an intermediary. For example, if a customer reserves a library book online, a copy of that book has immediately to be reserved and become unavailable for further bookings – a difficult nut to crack when working through intermediaries. The service was therefore based on making Carpenters Connect homes part of the borough's wide area network. It did this by installing local area network cabling at the same time as upgrading the aerial cabling in its social housing to enable digital television reception.

Since the project was funded by the DfES, it is hardly surprising that the main content development was educational and the local Carpenters Primary School was a key partner. Through iDTV parents and kids can access homework online and access a wealth of material. But Carpenters Connect included some other unique features. The set-top boxes provided to residents enabled thin-client computer applications, including email, Microsoft Word and Excel and a browser, to be run on the television. While Newham was not persuaded that the television can yet provide a fully effective substitute for the personal computer, the medium can help to introduce consumers to ICT, and raise awareness of its potential. The network provided by the Council included two points for each home. If residents felt motivated to graduate to the real thing they could therefore install their own personal computers and continue to benefit from free network access.

The project was actually run by the Carpenters Tenants Management Organisation and the community itself, supported by the Council. It was therefore in charge of determining its own acceptable usage policy and walled garden approach. It also had its own community television channel and programme making ability, assisted by the Media Trust.

Newham Council sees its participation in these two different projects as spreading and mitigating the known risks of pioneering, but they are also quite complementary. DKTV has, for example, developed a range of short community interest films that have been licensed to Carpenters Connect. Although the DKTV project ended in 2002, the experience and learning that has come from these projects has been invaluable, and the public reaction has been overwhelmingly positive.

Case study: The regulation of interactive television services in the United Kingdom

Martin Hart, the Independent Television Commission. The Independent Television Commission (ITC) is responsible for licensing and regulating commercial television in the United Kingdom.

The ITC published guidance on its approach to the regulation of interactive television services in 2001. This followed a period of consultation with its licensees and others involved in the interactive television industry.

The ITC's key objective was to ensure that regulation would be as simple and light touch as possible. In the regulator's eyes, viewers come first and must be allowed to benefit from an innovative and emerging market. Two key safeguards from current programme standards were identified:

- The separation of advertising from editorial content.
- The protection of children.

Furthermore, as the industry was at the early stages of development, both the regulator and the industry would need to adapt their approach as the market developed.

The ITC's approach

The ITC's approach is set out below:

- Interactive services invite viewers to make positive choices in selecting options. They are, by definition, exercising their own control and, consequently, expectations will be different from those of traditional television.
- Viewers should be clear about the material they are selecting; they should know when it is supporting the programme and when it is a selling opportunity.
- Television programmes should remain free of all commercial interference. This applies to all programmes, but special safeguards apply to news, current

affairs, consumer advice and children's programmes. Interactivity must not blur the fundamental separation of programmes and advertising.

There are two main categories of interactive services: dedicated services (such as shopping malls, games, betting and gaming services) and enhanced programming (such as editorial and advertising enhancements to programmes and advertisements). As these two types of service differ quite fundamentally, the ITC's regulatory approach also differs, as summarised below.

Dedicated interactive services

These include electronic shopping malls, games and entertainment services. They may be reached via an interactive menu or occasionally as an option from an enhanced programme service (see below). The services are mostly standalone and their content is not usually linked to a specific programme. The ITC has made it clear that its regulatory role in this area will be very limited. It does not propose to regulate the content of such services, beyond that provided by the broadcasters themselves. The ITC's only other requirement is that viewers should not be misled about which content is subject to ITC rules and which is not. Content on dedicated interactive services will still be subject to national laws where relevant but will not be covered by the ITC's own codes.

Enhanced programme services

These services start from conventional programming such as interactive editorial from programmes, interactive adverts, and mixed editorial and advertising content in the margins of programmes.

The ITC recognised that the financing of interactive enhancements is likely to depend in large measure on the use of the commercial opportunities the new technology provides. Its prime concern has been to ensure that these opportunities do not lead to any confusion amongst viewers about when they are being sold to, and that programme content remains effectively safeguarded from commercial influences.

A set of simplified rules has been developed setting out a range of general requirements, coupled with more specific safeguards for news and current affairs, consumer advice and children's programmes. Among the key requirements are that the interactive icons present during the course of a programme should not be commercially branded, and that when a viewer first interacts with a programme the destination must offer some editorial programme enhancements and not just commercial content (the 'two clicks' rule).

The ITC recognises that the interactive industry is fast changing and that, as a result, its guidance will need revising as the market develops.

Actions

⊘ Take a look at the web sites of the major research companies and check for the latest predictions and papers on the interactive television markct. A good start is with the broadband entries in the research section of www.marketspace.org.uk. There is also a list of links regarding the commercial and benefits side of iTV at www.InteractiveTelevisionProduction.com.

⊘ Look at the news sections of sites like www.broadbandbananas.com and www.itvt.com for new interactive television launches.

⊘ Read the detailed guidelines regarding interactive television regulation in the UK at www.itc.org.uk.

⊘ Test your memory on material introduced in this chapter with the rib-tickling quiz on www.InteractiveTelevisionProduction.com.

Chapter **4**

Production

Chapter 4 in 30 seconds . . .

▷ Interactive television production is more like software development than television production.

▷ Interactive television production can be split into four stages: development; specification; production and testing; and launch and operation.

▷ A typical interactive television production team has people that deal with production, technical work, content and operations, and marketing and business development.

▷ There are a variety of interactive television production tools for use with different middleware systems; some can be used by non-technical people, others are for computer programmers.

> " Interactive television is like having a baby – easier to conceive than deliver. "

John Enser, media lawyer

Good interactive television productions perfectly marry the spontaneity of programme making with the precision of software development. There's the chance to practise innovative ways of working, learn new skills and create something that has never been done before. If you get the opportunity to be involved with producing interactive television, do so with gusto. It's fantastic fun.

This chapter outlines, step by step, how to take the twinkle in somcone's eye and turn it into a working interactive television application. The first step: get the right attitude.

Overview of television, software and web site production

People involved with interactive television usually bring attitudes and ways of working from their previous jobs, which – more often than not – are in television, software or web site production. But these industries all have very different practices – and some are more relevant to interactive television than others.

Television production

There are typically fives stages to a television production:

- In development, ideas are developed, defined, researched and pitched to commissioning executives.
- In pre-production, the programme structure is defined, the production team recruited, budgets finalised, plans written up, participants located, and the script and storyboard completed.
- In production, all the material required for the programme is shot onto videotape.
- In post-production, the finished programme is put together in an edit suite, and graphics or special effects are added.

There's also a broadcast stage, but most people involved in the production of television programmes don't worry about this. From the production team's point of view, they hand over a tape and there are almost always people and technologies in place that automate the whole process from then on.

Table 4.1: Television production stages

	Development	Pre-production	Production	Post-production	Broadcast
Examples of what gets done	• Opportunities spotted • Idea development • The pitch • Research around the idea	• Production schedule • Recruitment • Budget • Storyboard • Script • Research for the programme	• Filming	• Editing • Graphics	• Play-out • Marketing and promotion

The television production process has been refined over the last 50 years. Refined to make production technologies easier to use and refined to make it possible to show programmes around the world. But, most of all, refined to facilitate creative changes at any point.

In television production, major changes can be made during development, pre-production, production and post-production. Programmes are often restructured and re-invented in the edit suite – sections can be moved, live action can be replaced with graphics, voices re-dubbed and video effects used to correct mistakes or change meanings.

That's not to say that television producers always throw out their plans once they get into post-production, it's just that they have a considerable arsenal at their disposal should they want to make improvements.

Software development

Everyone uses different terminology for the stages involved in software development, but broadly they are: research and development; specification and design; production and testing; and launch.

Table 4.2: Software development stages

	Research and Development	Specification and design	Production and testing	Launch
Examples of what gets done	• Opportunities spotted • Idea developed • Concept testing (including market and user research) • Business case	• Requirements • Specification • Project management tools specified • Project plan • Budget • Recruitment	• Graphic design • Coding • Change management • Deadline management • Testing	• Launch (including marketing and promotion) • Technical support

Where software development differs from television production is that, once the specification is determined, any changes that take place in the production and testing phase risk having a detrimental impact on the schedule, costs or scope of the project. Therefore, software project managers tend to focus a lot of their time on clarifying and communicating the impact of change.

All this is necessary with software work because unexpected changes can mean that large parts of the computer code will need to be rewritten – a waste of expensive programming time. Programmers (developers) usually work by looking at the specification then assembling the code, step by step. It's a bit like building a house. The foundations are laid first, then the walls, roof and windows added. There's no problem if someone wants to change the programming equivalent of the colour of a window frame. Unfortunately, the changes that people want to make are often more fundamental – like the functionality available to the user or the structure of a database. These kinds of thing are often much more part of the programming foundation than the decoration – and can mean rebuilding large parts of the computer code.

Web site production

A looser version of software development practice is used on web site projects. Web sites are usually produced in HTML and JavaScript, which deal primarily with the layout of information on screen. This makes it much easier to make changes. Nevertheless, the more complex the web site, the more interlocking systems there are likely to be. The inclusion of back-end systems for e-commerce and other functions can also increase the complexity dramatically. With most of the bigger web sites, last minute changes can have all sorts of unexpected impacts. Therefore, bigger web projects are usually run using rigorous practices much more akin to software development.

What's the right attitude to producing interactive television: the creative impulsiveness of television or the rigorous change control of software development?

Interactive television production

Interactive television applications are built using software programming code – and are often large-scale and complex. They can require months of work from multiple programmers.

Anyone charged with producing an interactive television application will have problems if they expect to be able to make changes right up to the last minute – television production style. Television production attitudes will quickly result in arguments with the software programming team – and deadlines will be missed. 'Digital television, and the interactive part of it, is complicated,' says Mark Rock, founder of interactive television games company Static. 'The traditional broadcast model of "shoot it and sort it out in the edit suite" doesn't work. Unfortunately, the process is more akin to software production, with all the checks, compromises and order that it brings with it.'

The majority of interactive television projects will benefit from the application of techniques used to manage software projects. This chapter outlines some of those techniques. Television and web production methods are by no means irrelevant to iTV, however, and this chapter contains pointers for the use of these when appropriate.

The real world

The software production methodology espoused in this chapter is not the way that everyone produces interactive television. In the real world, things are often done differently, for all sorts of reasons. These include:

- The drive to save money by reusing elements of existing interactive television applications. Almost all the companies regularly involved in the production of interactive television applications will reuse code, reuse graphic design templates and make sure that all new interactive television services fit into an existing infrastructure. These factory-style production operations can cut the length and the cost of all their productions after the first by 75 per cent or more. Several of the stages outlined in this chapter can be omitted, since lots of the work will have been done already.

- The drive to save money by using interactive television production tools that make it possible for non-programmers to create applications. These tools aim to provide easy-to-use graphical interfaces for producing interactive television applications. Although much less flexible than programming from the ground up, non-technical users can, in theory at least, build applications by dragging and dropping elements on-screen. Some of the production stages outlined in this chapter can be bypassed completely. There's more on tools (both for non-technical operators and programmers) later.

- The drive to save money by cutting corners. In the real world of interactive television production – as teams buckle under time or budget pressures or lack of experience – stages are dropped and best practice goes out of the window. User testing, in particular, is often given much less time and money than it deserves, and many applications are built without any reference to users at all. Clear documentation and communication is often sacrificed as well, in an attempt to save time. The danger of cutting corners is that the final application will actually take more time and cost more money as a result.

- People have different views about what works best and therefore do things differently. This chapter contains just one view, to help you get started.

The production process step by step

This is one possible step-by-step process for producing interactive television applications from the ground up. Like television production and software development, interactive television production can be divided into distinct stages, although everyone involved in interactive television has different names for these stages and may break them up in different ways or change the order around as they see fit. The stages are: development; specification; production and testing; and launch and operation.

Each of the stages can be subdivided again into a number of specific tasks. Depending on the size of team, the whole process typically takes anywhere between

Stage	Development	Specification	Production and testing	Launch and operation
Table 4.3: Interactive television production stages				
What gets done	• Opportunities spotted • Idea development • Concept testing (including market and user research) • The brief	• Decision on project approach • Project management tools specified • Identification of stakeholders • Requirements • Specification • Project plan • Budget • Recruitment	• Graphic design • Technical architecture • Coding • Change management • Deadline management • Testing	• Launch (including marketing) • Operation and development

two and nine months, unless the application is very simple or the production team is able to draw on pre-existing code or interactive television production tools that remove the need for computer programming.

Stage 1: Development

The job of development is to identify opportunities, cultivate ideas and predict whether an end-product will work in the real world. This all needs to be done as quickly and cost effectively as possible, since a number of different opportunities and ideas may need to be examined before the right one is found. The development stage can be divided into the following specific tasks:

- Spotting the opportunities.
- Developing the idea.
- Testing the concept.
- Writing the brief.

Spotting the opportunities

There are a number of methods for making sure that opportunities are captured – such as empowering everyone involved to come up with ideas, monitoring market trends, running creative workshops aimed at spotting opportunities and so on. In particular, it's worth:

- Closely monitoring changes to technology. Interactive television is constantly pushing technology boundaries – and each advance creates new opportunities. For example, improvements to compression technology have started to make video-on-demand a viable business proposition, after many years of failed attempts.

- Thinking mixed media. People involved in interactive television can draw inspiration from almost any medium – television and the web in particular, but also CD-ROMs, DVDs, arcade machines, radio, bank auto-teller machines, telephones and so on. It's possible to replicate and mix aspects of these in one interactive television production. There's the opportunity, for example, for customised video news, personalised advertising, radio-on-demand and so on. In the early 1990s, a group of television executives saw the opportunity for mixing console games with television programmes, and enhanced television games operator Two Way TV was born.

- Thinking about different types of interactivity. Interactive television applications can work in a sequence-based, narrative form (like a television programme), using one-to-one interactivity (like a web site), by drawing on community participation (like a multiplayer game) and so on.

- Looking very closely at people's needs and wants. This is best done through user research and observation.

Developing the concept

Once someone has spotted an opportunity, the first step is to do some thinking about ways of making the most of it. Again, brainstorming and the many other techniques that facilitate creative thinking can be useful here. The aim of concept development is to generate different ideas around the opportunity and generate some firm concepts or approaches that can be tested objectively before going into production. For example, let's imagine you've identified an opportunity to sell alcohol via the television, specific approaches to this could involve building a walled garden version of an off-licence, running an auction channel for cases of wine or using late-night enhanced television quiz shows to attract drunken buyers.

Testing the concept

Once there's a firm concept, it's time to get serious. Will people use it? Is there a need? Is there a market? Is it possible technically?

Concept prototyping

One of the best ways to get to grips with the issues associated with an application in development is to build prototypes. Prototypes help everyone understand what the application is trying to achieve and can also be exploited in market and user research.

Animated prototypes can be created using web tools like Dreamweaver and FrontPage, using video editing software like Avid and Final Cut Pro, or using animation tools like Macromedia Director and Flash. Alternatively, still versions can be created using graphics programs like Photoshop or – even faster and cheaper – sketched on paper. Prototypes don't need to be super high-quality work. The aim of prototyping is to help get a clearer idea of the options available and to facilitate discussion – preferably as quickly and cheaply as possible. Prototypes that are too well designed risk distracting people with their glitzy graphics and prototypes that take too long to build risk delaying the launch of the actual application.

Concept market and user research

Market and user research is about attempting to predict how successful the interactive television service will be in the real world and how it will fit into people's lives. There are several different approaches, including formal surveys, in-depth inter-

Table 4.4: A selection of market and user research techniques

Research type	Pros	Cons
In-depth personal interviews	Targeted, qualitative information	Can be expensive, people sometimes overly positive
Focus groups	People's qualitative reactions can be interesting and useful particularly for sparking ideas in the production team	Needs proper facilitation, can lack direction, too small a sample to draw quantitative conclusions
Surveys: email and mail	Cheap, quantitative data	May get response only from people who like responding to surveys
Surveys: telephone	Cheap, quantitative data	Can't show prototypes
Usability testing techniques (including those focused on helping develop and define a concept, such as card sorting and ethnographic observation). There's more on usability testing in Chapter 5.	Can be close to real usage situation	Can be expensive; certain types of observation will require a reasonably well-formed prototype

views, focus groups and usability testing. It's surprising how much hearing people say how and whether they would use an interactive television application can help coalesce thinking and generate more ideas around a concept. Even just observing and talking to colleagues or very small numbers of customers can be illuminating. If the skills to do market and user research aren't available in-house, there are a number of specialist agencies that can perform the work to order. There's more on usability testing in Chapter 5.

Preliminary financial forecasting and analysis

At this stage, some preliminary work on the financial side can help kill off no-hope concepts and highlight important issues. Financial forecasting work relevant to interactive television includes:

● Reading research papers that predict the value of the target markets.
● Performing competitor analysis.
● Completing outline cost and benefit investigations.

It may also be necessary to do a preliminary budget, outlining the likely costs for moving the interactive television project through the specification stage.

Technical assessment

The aim of technical assessment is to work out whether the planned application can be built and, more importantly, whether it can be built with a reasonable amount of money. The technical assessment flags up areas of particular risk, so the production can be structured to circumvent them. If, for example, the concept is based on using a brand new search engine technology, some extra work may need to be done during the specification phase on fall-back options, should the technology not work as hoped.

Writing the brief or pitch

Once the concept has been tested, it should be possible to write down a definition of the application. Known as the brief or outline, this is a statement of the central aims and aspirations – preferably on less than one side of A4 paper (much longer and people aren't likely to read it). These also sometimes draw on a key insight about the potential viewers or on a clearly identified need that the viewers have.

Interactive television briefs are sometimes worked into pitches. Pitches explain the application and define, in an easy to understand way, what the investor or commissioner is likely to get out of the proposed interactive television service – and roughly what it will cost. Interactive television pitches often go hand in hand with regular television programme pitches.

The person or team in control of the money decides at this point whether the interactive television application can go onto the next stage – specification.

Stage 2: Specification

The pitch or brief has been accepted and permission has been given for the application to be specified in detail. Now a company or individual involved in interactive television production will have a range of options for going forward. The brief can be sent to an interactive television production agency to work on. Or some work can be done in-house and the rest completed by outsiders. Or everything can be done in-house. The various routes all have their advantages and disadvantages.

Production agencies, like Wheel and AKQA, can pass on the benefits of economies of scale by reusing work done for other clients. They also take responsibility for managing risks, like the use of cutting-edge technology. But using agencies keeps all the experience of building interactive television outside the company that initiated the project and could end up being more expensive if more applications need to be produced later.

With a hybrid approach, companies with particular areas of expertise can be bought in for particular elements of the production. For example: the project could be managed in-house; a specialist agency like Di3 could be used for the technology implementation; a branding agency, like Lambie-Nairn, used for the artwork; and a usability agency, like Serco Usability Services, used for the navigation design. One problem with this approach is that involving multiple companies can easily make production more complicated and, if deadlines start being missed, it can be difficult to establish which company is responsible. (This problem should never be underestimated on complex interactive television projects – it occurs frequently.)

Going it alone, on the other hand, keeps expertise within the company that initiated the project and provides a foundation for future interactive television development.

In particular, code can be used on other services later. It does, however, mean that recruitment may be necessary and people may have to venture outside their normal experience and skills (although, because most interactive television technologies are quite new, everyone has had to do this to some degree).

Whatever decision is taken about whom will be involved, it needs to be clear at this point who is in charge. Whether it's a producer, a project manager or someone else is not important, as long as there is someone who is driving the project forward.

Step one for this person: start the specification process. The more time and effort spent on specification, the more likely the production stage will deliver the right application on time. Some interactive television productions allocate much more time to specification than to production and testing. Although this can be difficult to justify to the bosses or clients, who are waiting to see something on-screen, it can pay off if problems are identified and dealt with before they arise. Also, the time spent on specification should reduce the amount of time spent on production – thereby saving money. The tasks involved in specification include:

- Deciding the project approach.
- Getting hold of project management tools.
- Identifying stakeholders.
- Collating requirements.
- Specifying the service.
- Producing the project plan.
- Producing the budget.
- Recruiting the staff.

The following pages cover each of these in detail.

Deciding the project approach

There are a number of different ways of managing projects. Two popular options, often used for interactive television applications, are the waterfall (also known as the staircase) approach and rapid application development.

Waterfall (staircase) projects

The waterfall approach splits the task into several key stages. The idea then is that each stage is pretty much complete before the next one is started. Presented graphically, as time against the stage of development, it looks like a waterfall or staircase.

The waterfall approach works well if the definition of the final product is unlikely to change during the course of the project and if the technology is likely to work as expected. The approach provides a great deal of clarity regarding expectations and deadlines, which can easily be communicated and understood across an organisation.

The system breaks down a little if the production team isn't quite sure what viewers are going to want and how they are going to use the interactive television service. Or if it's not entirely certain whether a given piece of technology will be able to deliver all the desired functionality.

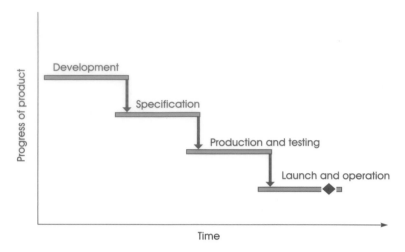

4.1 A waterfall project approach.

One variation of the waterfall model adds a prototyping stage to the beginning of the process, to help lock down the correct specification before production work kicks off. Another, called rapid application development, takes this even further by making prototyping and continuous iteration a core part of the project process.

Rapid application development

Rapid application development is ideal for interactive television applications where it's not entirely clear how and whether people will use the service or if there are uncertainties with any aspects of production. It follows exactly the same path as the waterfall model. But, rather than attempting to define the specification at the begin-ning and then have the whole product working before launch, it aims to deliver the core functionality in the first iteration and then continuously evolves it from there. It

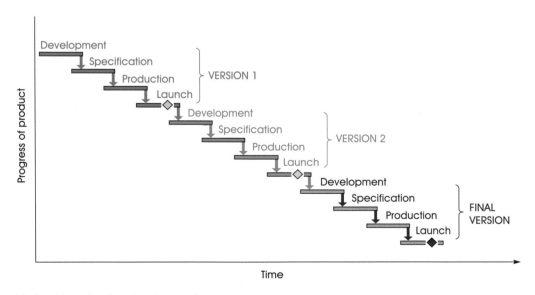

4.2 Rapid application development.

works by repeating all the stages of the staircase model many times, each time adding new functionality.

As each version is completed, features are added or removed depending on what is learnt about the usage and the technology involved.

Rapid application development requires a high level of feedback between viewers and the specification-setting process for each version. As each version is completed, viewer's reactions are checked – and used to help define the next iteration's functionality. It's not always necessary to launch the end-product of a stage into a live environment, as user testing can be done on prototypes.

The disadvantage of rapid application development is that the coding can be more complicated. Programmers are expected to add and remove functionality with each version, rather than just creating one final version.

The first cable company in the United Kingdom to launch digital cable television services used a form of rapid application development. In 1999, Cable & Wireless Communications started with a version of its digital television platform that only had a simple electronic programme guide. The next version extended the EPG functions and added a walled garden. In contrast, rival United Kingdom cable operator NTL attempted to launch a fully functional enhanced service all in one go. It never managed to get it to market with its initial specification – wasting millions of pounds in the process.

Closely linked to the rapid application development methodology is user-centred design. This is based on the idea that users need to be consulted all the way through the production process, and that the more prototypes and designs that are tested with users, the better. There's more on this in Chapter 5.

Getting hold of project management tools

Bigger interactive television projects can benefit from software tools designed to help manage deadlines and responsibilities. The ubiquitous Microsoft Project is a popular choice and it can be used for lots of different styles of project. Alternatively, there are specific project methodologies, like Prince and Rational Unified Process. These come with software tools, training and support. For small interactive television projects, or for project managers who want to avoid spending all their time updating the software tools, it's not unheard of for people to rely on whiteboards and Post-it notes as project management tools. It's best to use whatever you feel most comfortable with.

Identifying the stakeholders

It's big companies or agencies working for big companies that often produce interactive television. Producers in big companies in particular need to spend time identifying the parties from within and outside the company that could have an interest in the application.

'I always make sure that I involve all the key people early on in a project,' says Innes Ballantyne, senior producer in the BBC's interactive television production team. 'It prevents trouble happening further down the line, when things are expensive to change.'

Not consulting early on can result in someone, who later proves to be crucial, either not co-operating or, even worse, actively trying to sabotage the launch. Actual sabotage may sound a little difficult to believe. However, just think about how you would react if you were a brand manager who had just spent millions building the company brand and you saw a completely off-brand interactive television application about to be launched. Or if you were a technology team manager receiving a last minute request to use one of your busy specialists on an interactive television application you've never heard of. This kind of thing can and frequently does trip up interactive television projects.

Likely stakeholders in interactive television applications include:

- The business development team.
- The marketing department.
- The television production team (if the interactive television application supports a television programme).
- Brand guardians.
- Customer service and call-centres.
- IT support.
- Technology.
- Operations.
- The team that deals with regulators (particularly if betting or overlays to television are involved).
- The legal team (if, for example, certain EPG or other technologies are involved that may be covered by patents).
- The various parties involved in the chain from the originator of the project to the viewer – including TV channel owners and platform operators.

Collating requirements

It's easier and faster to work with fewer stakeholders – but there are ways of avoiding committee thinking even with lots of stakeholders. The first step is to get everyone involved in the collation of requirements.

A requirements list is a collection of everyone's view of what they think the service should, in an ideal world, deliver. It will, among other things, cover which interactive television platforms the service needs to work on and how many viewers it will need to support.

Requirements lists are generally broken down into several sections, such as commercial requirements, technical requirements, usability requirements and so on. It's also worth specifying the requirements for how the success (or otherwise) of the application will be judged – that is, deciding what needs to be measured to prove the application was worthwhile. This could be revenue, page views, numbers of users and so on.

The requirements should not specify any aspect of the solution, just what the application should be able to do. It can be helpful to do some more directed creative work, such as brainstorming, on the requirements and to try to think ahead about what the product will need to do when it is launched (which could be several months away), not what it needs to do at the time the requirements are being set. The requirements, of course, should always be created with reference to the end-users.

Collating a requirements list gives everyone involved the chance to make a contribution – and will, hopefully, highlight any mismatched expectations.

Specifying the service

Once the requirements are understood, the next step is to define the functionality that will be delivered and how this will be done – the specification. Unless there is an infinite budget and infinite time available, it's quite likely that it won't be possible to deliver all the requirements straightaway. Therefore, ruthless decisions need to be made about which of the requirements will be incorporated in the first version of the product and which won't.

In most companies, this can be a reasonably fraught process, as everyone has a slightly different view of what the service should be about. Also, if it's been used, user research can sometimes be interpreted in different ways. Heated argument can ensue.

With this in mind, it's useful if there's one person who has the final say on what will be in the specification and what won't – ideally the interactive television producer or project manager in charge of delivering the finished product. Research on team structures for complex projects has shown that those with strong leaders, who take the ultimate decision-making responsibility, perform better. Having a strong leader also avoids endless meetings arguing about specification – the leader can make decisions there and then, after consulting his or her team.

There are other ways to ease the process:

- It helps if everyone has a reasonable understanding of the technical potential of the different platforms for which the service is intended. Requirements that are clearly not possible or outrageously difficult (like putting true video-on-demand on the United Kingdom's terrestrial television transmission network) need to be removed straightaway, or creative work needs to be done on alternative ways of framing the request. For example, is it really video-on-demand that is required or is it just that information needs to be accessible by viewers quickly and easily? Training sessions can be held explaining what's technically straightforward and what isn't.
- It helps if everyone feels involved in the decision making. One classic way of doing this is to have stakeholders rate each of their requirements as either 'must have' or 'like to have'. This immediately gives the people responsible for implementing the service an idea of the relative importance of each request, as well as transferring some of the responsibility for decision making to the people setting the requirements.
- Use, as much as possible, user research data to help make decisions about requirements.

The output of all this work honing the requirements is a functional specification.

Functional specification

The functional specification is an expression of, in the clearest and simplest language possible, what the application will be able to do. It's a bit like what you would produce if you had to explain the application to an alien.

The functional specification is used as the primary reference point for building the application. If it's not in the functional specification, it won't be done. As with the requirements, functional specifications do not define any aspect of the technical solution, only what the end result is. For example, a functional specification item for a car is not that it has four wheels; it is that it should be stable and move along near the ground. If the people building the service come up with a better way of doing it – anti-gravity jet boosters in a car, for example – they should have the flexibility to build it that way. The person writing the functional specification also doesn't need to have an in-depth technical understanding and can concentrate on what the service is meant to do.

Table 4.5: Extract from a functional specification list

Number	Description
4.1	Viewers will be able to purchase goods using Visa, Amex, MasterCard and Switch.
4.2	Viewers will be able to view the progress of their order/s at any time on-screen.
4.3	Viewer credit card and personal information will be encrypted during all stages of transmission, to the same level as web-based banking transactions.
4.4	It will be possible for two or more members of the same household to be independently identifiable as users.

Television production and project management cultures don't always mix

Functional specifications in some companies come with reams of extra tables, including distribution records, glossaries, version control lists and more. Be warned: functional specifications are not generally used in television production environments, except for big engineering projects – and they can cause bemusement or even negative reactions. If the document is going to be viewed by television production executives, it's worth keeping the overheads to an absolute minimum and, perhaps, even changing the name to something less formal and intimidating (like service outline).

Conversely, it can be tempting to dispense with functional specifications completely and brief everyone in person (this is especially tempting for interactive television producers from television backgrounds). However, because computer programmers need to have absolute clarity about what to build and be confident that this will not change unexpectedly, dispensing with the functional specification risks costing much more time later on.

Ideally, each element of the functional specification should be discrete, to make it easy to add and remove specifications as necessary. Having said this, some people write functional specifications using prose paragraphs, rather than in a list format.

Functional specifications can run to hundreds of pages and thousands of items – especially if the service is very complex or if the person writing the specification doesn't trust the person building it (which is often the case if one is paying the other). However, it's possible to keep functional specification lists short by repeatedly rewriting and reducing to the bare bones. It should be possible to describe most interactive television services in less than 100 functional specification items, even less if a rapid application development approach is being used.

Functional specifications cover every aspect of the application, everything from the type and frequency of advertising it will need to support, to the number of content updates required, to the granularity of viewer usage measurement that is needed.

Storyboard and graphic design brief

A functional specification is often accompanied by a storyboard. This is a pictorial representation of the navigation and functionality of each screen. It does not include any graphic design work and does not define the exact positioning of elements on the page. Storyboards can be sketched on paper or created using the graphics options in programs like Word, PowerPoint, PhotoShop or Illustrator. A specialist program, called Visio, is also excellent for creating storyboards, although it can take a little while to learn. Usability research work and prototyping can be used to help define the best storyboard (see Chapter 5).

Along with the storyboard come the design brief and a navigation map. The design team use the design brief as a guide for creating the graphics for the application. It specifies the objectives that the designers will need to address and has details about the target viewers. The navigation map is a high level representation of all the screens within the application and how each is connected.

4.3 One page of a storyboard for the lottery section of a digital teletext service.

A producer or specialist in user-interface design usually creates the storyboards, navigation map and design brief with as close reference as possible to the end-users.

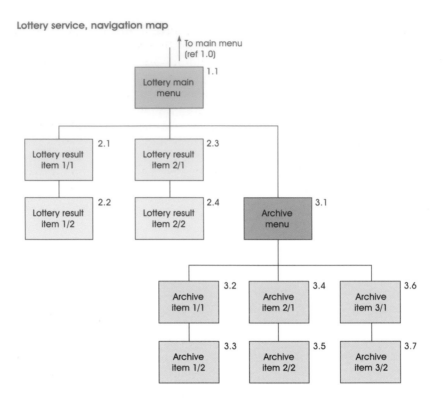

4.4 A navigation map for one section of a digital teletext service.

Technical specification

Once most of the functional specification and storyboard has been completed, it's time for a technical expert to define the technical specification. This describes exactly how the application will be built.

The main part of the technical specification is the technical architecture. This outlines, usually pictorially with supporting text, how the various bits of technology, including all the major pieces of hardware and software, will work together.

The complexity of the technical architecture depends on a number of factors, such as:

- The middleware system being used.
- The type of interactive television (enhanced television and channel switching, because they involve video channels, are often much more complicated than walled garden services).
- The back-end functionality required (transactional capability and multi-player gaming both add to the complexity).

• The infrastructure already in place (some walled garden services will fit into an existing infrastructure, so may need a relatively small amount of work on technical architecture).

In addition to the technical architecture, the technical specification will include documents that detail the types of computers, mutliplexers and other electronics, the technical details of the set-top boxes and middleware systems, and details of the security systems. There may also be guidelines for the structure of the computer code and the way it should be marked up by the programmers, with rules for version control. Version control helps programmers share files without mixing up their work (there are off-the-shelf products that manage version control by forcing programmers to formally check code in and out of a central storage area, just like a library).

Finally, the technical specification will define the content management system (the software that shifts content around platforms and manages advertising) and any customer relationship management system (used to keep track of customer information).

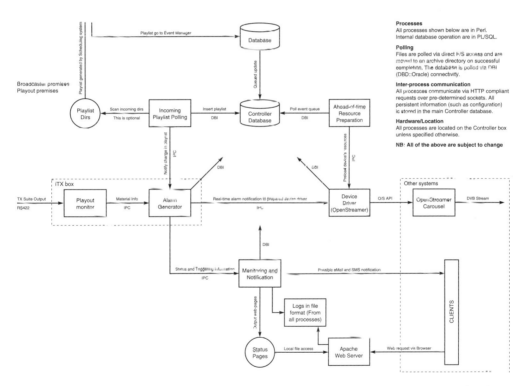

4.5 A technical architecture diagram for an iTV service (only needs to be understood by the technical team). © *CentricView Software.*

Producing the project plan

The project manager can now work out exactly how long each stage of production should take. It's usually better to have people define their own work schedules. This makes it much more likely that they will buy into the deadlines. For certain interactive television applications, parallel development may be possible. For example, it might be possible for work on the back-end functionality (such as customer data-bases) to take place at the same time as the coding of the application, rather than waiting for the coding to be finished. Parallel working is common when coding in HTML and JavaScript.

Watch out for underestimating particular stages of production in the project plan. In particular:

- Graphic design invariably takes longer than expected, particularly if the designers are new to interactive television.

- Plenty of time needs to be allocated to integrating finished chunks of code with each other and integrating the finished application with the back-end system and platform.

- Getting the application to work on different types of set-top box can be enormously time-consuming, even if the middleware is the same. Middleware is not always perfect at making differences between set-top boxes invisible to applications – and some tweaking may be required.

- The implementation of systems to manage multiple video streams can take much more time and effort than the coding of the application itself.

The project plan should also be used to plan for slippage. Contingency options can be placed around the parts of the schedule that look uncertain. These include putting buffers in the schedule, allocating time to set up alternative staffing options, and allocating time to locate and brief alternative suppliers. Do not fall into the trap of secretly planning for slippage by mentally preparing to squeeze the time available for the last stage of production – testing. Testing is crucial for interactive television (see the testing section later in this chapter).

Producing the budget

Once the functional and technical specifications have been completed, it's money time – the budget. There are lots of questions to be resolved during the budget process, all of which can make a dramatic difference to the final figure:

- Should computers and other equipment be leased or purchased outright? It's easy to lease computers but using them for a few months can cost more than buying them.

- Is the production eligible for tax breaks or grants? Television and film productions sometimes get tax breaks that may also apply to interactive television, while various European governments and universities have helped pay for some pioneering interactive television work.

- What contingencies should be added to the budget? It sometimes makes it easier to manage the finances if the budget has contingencies rather than overestimated costs.

- Are there any economies associated with using the same technology for multiple applications or reusing programming code – or even going into partnership with another interactive television producer? Almost every company involved in interactive television reuses code between applications and most new interactive television applications are designed to be reusable and extendable (the costs of subsequent services based on the same code will then be much lower).

- Are all the costs covered? Often forgotten are the costs of a content management system (used to update and develop the service after launch), administration costs (like phones and office stationery) and post-launch costs (like a project review and tweaks to the code).

Ideally, each part of the team that will be spending money should come up with budget figures for their area and be held to account for under- and overspends.

After the project plan and budget are complete, it's worth reviewing the work so far. Is the project still viable? Are the costs appropriate? Will the benefits be delivered quickly enough? If not, it might be that the functional specification will need to be simplified or the technical specification reworked. If everything still looks good, then there's one last job to be done before production begins – assembling the team.

Recruiting staff

A large part of the cost of interactive television productions goes on human beings. It is theoretically possible for one person working from home to produce a credible interactive television service. However, applications that need to be high quality, compelling and launched to a strict deadline often require a range of people with different skills. Platform operators usually have the largest production teams – 200 people or more is not unusual – especially during the early phases of development. Companies involved in developing a single application for the first time will typically need anywhere between three and 30 people, depending on the complexity of the application and target platforms.

Staff with interactive television experience can be recruited using intermediaries, like Tara West Recruiting and Recruit Media, or directly using advertising in trade publications such as, in the United Kingdom, *Broadcast*, *New Media Age* and the *Guardian Media Supplement*. Another option is to place advertisements on interactive television discussion groups (like www.broadbandbananas.com).

Although roles will be broadly the same across companies, interactive television job titles can vary dramatically. It's also not unusual for people to cover web, mobile phone and television production duties, along with their interactive television work.

In-depth: An example interactive television budget

Interactive television budgets can vary wildly – from less than £15k for a simple internet on television redesign, to several million for a brand new channel switching service. Here is a hypothetical ballpark budget for an enhanced television service to support a music video television channel on a digital cable platform, running the TV Navigator middleware.

This budget assumes that the television channel is already in existence. It also assumes the iTV service aims to include a feature for viewers to chat with each other while watching the channel, some games, regularly updated in-depth information relevant to the music on the channel and a basic system for users to request videos using their credit cards for payment (the videos to be played out in order of request by the channel, jukebox style). The costs outlined here are for launch, not operation. The budget also assumes that the service will require contract staff, all working for six months, and all code will be created from the ground up in a London-based office. In this respect, it is a generous budget.

The production team is also expected to conduct most of the user research – with some help from an outside agency.

Table 4.6: An example budget

Budget item	Headcount/ quantity of full-time employees	Cost per item/ head (£)	Total cost (£k)
Contract staff			
Senior producer/project manager	1.0	50k pa	25
Technical director	1.0	50k pa	25
Developers (programmers) (client side – HTML/JavaScript with TV Navigator expertise)	2.0	35k pa	35
Developers (back-end)	2.0	40k pa	40
Assistant producer (user-interface specialist)	1.0	28k pa	14
Assistant producer (project administrator)	1.0	26k pa	13
In-house tester	1.0	26k pa	13
Creative director	20 days	300 per day	6
Senior designer	1.0	28k pa	14
System administrator	1.0	40k pa	20
Broadcast/network engineer	0.5	40k pa	10
Copywriter	20 days	150 per day	3

Budget item	Headcount/ quantity of full-time employees	Cost per item/ head (£)	Total cost (£k)
Testing and research			
Market research and user testing	External company	15k	15
Functional and integration testing (in addition to that provided by in-house resource)	External company	5k	5
Tools and equipment			
Programming tools (including version control software)			1
Interactive television production tools			1
Test environment (set-top box etc.)	1.0		1
Project management software and tools (Microsoft Project etc.)		Various	1
Content management system	1.0	Various	20
Servers (hosting, including backup systems)		Various	5
High speed connectivity to platform operator (including backup, launch and 3 months operation)		Various	5
E-commerce system (for video requests)			10
Integration with broadcast systems (for video requests – assumes video serving systems are already suitable for external input)			20
Admin			
Legal costs			5
Recruitment (agency and advertising)			5
Office space			5
Office administration (stationery, phones etc.)			3

Budget item	Headcount/ quantity of full-time employees	Cost per item/ head (£)	Total cost (£k)
Desk-top personal computers (to buy or rent)	15.0	1k	15
Training for operational and content staff			10
Platform operator set-up fees (not including on-going commissions)			50
Content costs			
Content and copyright fees (for example, for photographic images)			2
Marketing and promotion (including cost of producing on-air promotions)			10
Miscellaneous			
Cost of development stage (prior to budget)			5
A web site for project management information and design reviews			1
Photo research			1
Travel and entertainment			2
Manuals and documentation			1
Senior management time			5
		TOTAL:	**422k**

Note: headcount costs do not include overheads for pension, health benefits etc. Operational costs would need to cover operational and editorial staff, maintenance, customer support, connectivity, content development, business development, advertising sales, connectivity etc. The actual costs would be much lower for most companies, as staff would be used instead of contract resources, not all staff would be required for the whole project period, and some equipment and resources would already be available in-house. Advanced or multi-platform authoring tools and code reuse could also bring down the cost (although this may reduce the scope; see the production tools section later in this chapter). It should be noted that fees for testing, carriage and bandwidth for United Kingdom cable platforms are usually much less than for United Kingdom satellite. It's not unusual for a United Kingdom satellite interactive television production to cost £200–600k more than the same service on cable. Multiply by 1.6 to get the approximate figures in dollars.

In-depth: The interactive television production team

Interactive television teams can be divided into a number of key functions:

- Production, responsible for definition, storyboard, design brief and delivery of the final application.
- Design, responsible for graphic design.
- Technical, responsible for the technical specification and building the application.
- Content and operations, responsible for running the application after launch.
- Marketing and commercial, responsible for realising the benefits and promoting the application to viewers.

The production team

The production team makes sure the application does the job it is meant to do and is built on time. They also often manage, at a project level, the work of all the other teams involved.

The person in charge of the production team is usually responsible for producing the finished working service. The role can be split between two people: a project manager in charge of deadlines and delivery, and a producer in charge of content and design briefs. Splitting the role, however, can lead to confusion if it's not clear who has ultimate responsibility.

Assistant producers are either generalists or specialists in charge of a particular aspect of the application, such as user-interface design, the e-commerce system, content partners or community.

The best interactive television producers and assistant producers have good technical understanding, project management skills, communication skills and are very creative. They can come from any work background but, more often than not, learnt their trade in games, DVD, web or television production. For interactive television applications that involve video, it's not unusual for video professionals to be bought in to produce only that part of the service.

The production team sometimes also takes responsibility for delivering commercial revenues and for programming the code.

In terms of an office environment, the production team are best placed in open-plan offices (to enable creative and collaborative working) and in close proximity to the design and technical teams.

Table 4.7: The production team

Job title	Responsible for	Typical United Kingdom pay	Skills and experience
Producer and/or project manager	Delivery of the service, creative decisions, project management, managing production team	£20–50k per annum	• Editorial and design experience and good judgement • Lateral thinking skills • Technical knowledge • Experience of delivering projects on time • Communication skills – particularly motivating others • Experience and aptitude for user-interface design
Assistant producer and production assistant	Write design briefs, manage usability research, manage requirements, devise storyboards, administration	£18–40k per annum	• Editorial and design experience and good judgement • Technical knowledge • Experience and aptitude for user-interface design
Project assistant/ administrator	Update information into project management tools (like Microsoft Project), arrange meetings, track progress	£15–30k per annum	• Attention to detail • Communication skills • In-depth knowledge of project management tools

Multiply by 1.6 to get rough equivalent dollar salaries.

The design team

Designers create the images displayed on the interactive television screen. A creative director, or similar, usually leads a design team and makes sure the graphic design output keeps to a consistent style and ties in with any brand guidelines. Design teams either work to fixed templates previously created by the creative director or have more freedom. Some design teams are responsible for defining the navigation and functionality, as well as the graphic design. Design work is often collaborative, so an open-plan environment is best.

However, most designers also need time to concentrate on detailed work (and nearly all seem to have stereo headphones permanently attached to their skulls to help them get away from it all).

Producers need to be conscious of the fact that some designers are biased towards communicating visually. They are not always brilliant at justifying designs verbally or doing formal presentations. One result of this is the infamous 'that's just your opinion' argument that designers and producers get into. Each has his or her own view of what the design should be, but neither is able to articulate clearly the justification or rationale behind it. Later in this chapter, there are some tips for getting out of this loop by using collaborative design practices.

Good interactive television graphic designers can come from any background. Television designers have the advantage of being familiar with the design and technical requirements of television. Having said this, web and software user-interface designers are likely to have much more experience of interactive systems and usability. Console games designers probably have the most relevant experience – although the market they are used to designing for is quite different from the typical television audience.

Table 4.8: The design team

Job	Responsibilities	Typical United Kingdom pay	Skills/experience
Creative director	Design templates, brand guidelines, managing design team	£30–60k per annum	• Communication skills – particularly persuasion • Wide-ranging high-quality portfolio • Knowledge of design theory • Proven understanding of television viewers
Graphic designer	Design application screens, design icons, design protoypes	£18–40k per annum	• Portfolio of high-quality work • Ability to learn new software quickly • Thick skin
Design assistant	Scanning graphics, managing design versions, designing icons, copying and altering designs	£12–25k per annum	• Attention to detail • Ability to learn new software quickly

Multiply by 1.6 to get rough equivalent dollar salaries.

The technical team

The technical team is responsible for the construction of the computer code and back-end systems.

Working to the technical director are a number of different developers (also known as programmers or application engineers):

- Developers that write the computer code to build the application. They usually specialise in one or two languages, such as JavaScript, Java, C or C++.
- Developers that program interfaces and communication systems. They deal with, for example, ways of retrieving customer information from a database. They are experts in the computer languages used for this kind of work, such as Perl.
- Developers that deal with training and support. They look after, for example, the technical parts of the content management system. They also make sure the other members of the technical team aren't disturbed with day-to-day questions from operational staff and customers.

Working closely with the developers are staff with expertise in constructing and maintaining hardware

- System administrators who look after computer servers and the links to the internet or other external networks.
- Engineers who build and maintain transmission technologies, like video servers, satellite uplinks and mutliplexers.

Last, but not least, there's also a person or small group that specialise in testing. The testing team define and operate a whole series of test routines that will be used on the application. The testing team should have go/no-go authority on any part of the project – although testing scripts will need to be agreed with the rest of the technical team and the production team first. People working on testing need to maintain a dispassionate view of the project. This is because anyone who is emotionally involved in a piece of work is unlikely to be objective. After weeks of work invested on coding, it can be difficult to start looking for problems in your own work.

The technical team needs to work collaboratively, so an open-plan office can be helpful in this respect. However, programming and other technical work often requires a high level of concentration. Being disturbed by people asking questions or chatting is not great if you're trying to check thousands of lines of code for errors. Therefore, technical team members ideally should have access to private offices or, at least, open-plan offices with high-walled dividers.

Technical team members are often the kind of people who enjoy methodological ways of working. Therefore, interactive television producers working with developers need to be clear about specifying requirements, deadlines and expectations. Producers should particularly avoid moving the goalposts by constantly trying to change the specification during production. If there's no way round this (perhaps

Table 4.9: The technical team

Job	Responsible for	Typical United Kingdom salary	Skills/experience
Technical director	Technical specification and delivery, managing technical team	£40–80k per annum	• Communication skills • Wide-ranging technical skills • Experience of delivering technical projects on time • Lateral thinking ability
Developer	Tends to specialise in a particular programming language (e.g. JavaScript, C), database and interface programming, training or support	£25–60k per annum, £150–600 per day	• Attention to detail • Mathematical and logical mind (for most programming languages) • Lateral thinking ability • Ability to estimate and manage own work
System administrator	Build and maintain servers and back-end computer systems	£25–60k per annum	• Attention to detail • Mathematical and logical mind (for most programming languages) • Problem-solving ability • Cool under pressure
Engineer	Build and maintain broadcast systems	£25–60k per annum, £150–600 per day	• Attention to detail • Mathematical and logical mind • Problem-solving ability • Cool under pressure
Tester	Devising test scripts, running tests	£12–35k per annum, £100–500 per day	• Attention to detail • Confidence • Wide-ranging technical knowledge

Multiply by 1.6 to get rough equivalent dollar salaries.

because the viewer requirements are difficult to pin down), it's best to recognise this at the beginning and discuss it with the developers – code can sometimes be constructed to make certain types of change easier.

The content and operations team

Providing interesting content is one of the best ways of encouraging viewers to use an application. The content can be brought in from suppliers like Reuters (who offer a whole range of content as well as news – including sport, weather and features). It can be aggregated from different suppliers who want to get their brand or services on-screen (it's sometimes possible to get traffic information cheaply, for example, as long as the provider's brand is on display). Or it can be created in-house.

The in-house option for content will probably require a content production team. This could consist of an editor, working with journalists, producers or editorial assistants, who each cover particular times of day or particular topics. Even services that one wouldn't normally imagine needing content can benefit from it. For example, a shopping application is likely to be used by more people if it has interesting content, such as magazine articles, regularly updated quizzes and special offers.

The operations team is in charge of making sure that if something breaks, someone fixes it. They proactively put processes in place to support communication with viewers and to keep the application running smoothly from day to day. An operations manager, or similar, usually heads up the team, supported by people looking after customer services, technical support, content management systems and content partners. The operations team defines the daily checks that are required for the application, as well as processes for dealing with particular types of problems – a customer ringing in with a complaint, for example.

Table 4.10: Content and operations team

Job	Responsible for	Typical United Kingdom salary	Skills/experience
Content team	Creating and managing text, photos, interactive quizzes, special offers and so on	£12–50k per annum depending on position and experience	• Writing skills • Editorial and design experience and good judgement • Experience and aptitude for user-interface design
Operations manager	Managing operations team, design work processes, integrating company systems	£30–80k per annum	• Wide-ranging technical knowledge • Communication skills – particularly motivation and persuasion • Proven strategic abilities
Operations staff	Responsible for daily checks, managing content management and customer systems	£10–50k per annum	• Attention to detail • Customer focus

Multiply by 1.6 to get rough equivalent dollar salaries.

Marketing and commercial team

With interactive television applications there are often quite complex negotiations required with suppliers of content and technologies and with platform operators. There's also strategic work that needs to be done identifying markets and finding new revenues. A specialist commercial team can cover this kind of work, although the work is sometimes divested to the production team.

Effective promotion is crucial for interactive television applications. Specialist marketing teams can make the most of promotional channels, such as television programmes, advertising and viral marketing.

Table 4.11: The marketing and commercial team

Job	Responsible for	Typical United Kingdom salary	Skills/experience
Marketing manager	Design and implementation of marketing strategy, briefing agencies for advertising and promotional campaigns	£25–50k per annum	• Customer focus • Communication skills • Product design experience and good judgement
Commercial manager	Delivering revenue or other benefits	£20–55k per annum plus commission	• Negotiation experience • Proven entrepreneurial skills

Multiply by 1.6 to get rough equivalent dollar salaries.

Stage 3: Production and testing

Now the serious work begins:

- Designing the graphics.
- Building the technical architecture.
- Coding the application.
- Managing change.
- Managing deadlines.
- Performing rigorous tests.

Designing the graphics

Using the storyboard and design brief, the design team creates the graphics. For initial graphics work, most interactive television designers use a personal computer equipped with Adobe Photoshop, although some prefer the sketching freedoms of Illustrator. There's also the considerably cheaper PaintShop. Designers from a television background sometimes use television graphic design equipment, such as the systems from Quantel and Discreet. However, these are expensive to buy or hire and don't always output graphics in the right format for use in interactive television.

Whatever software is used, it should be connected up to a television as well as a personal computer monitor. A personal computer monitor provides a very poor reference point for television design and should not be used in isolation. PC-to-TV signal converters cost between £100 ($160) and £10 000 ($16 000) or more, depending on the quality and flexibility required.

It's worth bearing in mind that even viewing interactive television graphics on a television set connected to a personal computer is still only an approximation. The final design will be rendered by a set-top box for display on television, not via a personal computer – and set-top boxes sometimes work in different ways with graphics. To get round this problem, it's worth the design team or the developers periodically putting the graphics in a format that can be sent to a set-top box connected to a television for viewing. Most middleware suppliers provide set-top box kits that can be connected to personal computers for this purpose.

The designer can be left alone to produce the final design. However, a more collaborative approach improves the chances of the final design being spot on. One way of doing this is for the producer, in the first instance, to ask the design team to produce a number of different designs (known as mood boards). They can produce three to ten completely different designs, all of which fulfil the brief.

These mood designs or prototypes give the designer and producer a framework to discuss which approach works best – and can also be shown to other interested parties (potential users, for example). (Note for designers: make sure you like all the designs you come up with, because people will invariably want to use your least favourite.)

Once a decision has been reached, the design team can do the detailed work required to finalise the graphic design. Usability research will be useful to get the designs just right (see Chapter 5). Once the final design has been agreed, the graphics for each page can be cut up into constituent elements (such as the background, the titles and the different navigation icons), converted into a format that the middleware will support (for example, jpeg or gif) and then sent to the developers for incorporation into the application. The designer or developers should also optimise the graphics, using special compression software (provided with packages like PhotoShop and as part of the tool set provided by middleware suppliers). This software cuts out extraneous information in order to keep the file size down to an absolute minimum.

Building the technical architecture

One problem interactive television productions often have is that pieces of equipment take some time to be delivered or set up – or both. For example, leasing fibre-optic links for fast connectivity between an office and an interactive television platform operator can require two or three months lead-time. Similarly, the content management system is likely to need to be running as soon as possible, as the operations staff will need to be trained. And video feeds can also take several weeks

4.6 It can take a lot of work to build and run content management systems, particularly if you need to deal with complex video to interactivity synchronisation tasks. © *BSkyB.*

to build and test. The only way round this is to complete purchase orders and crucial technical work as early as possible in the project.

Content management systems that deal with synchronised enhanced television can be particularly complicated: both to build and use. With these, it's worth considering buying either off-the-shelf products, such as Two Way TV's synchronisation solution, called Ark, or multi-platform authoring tools, such as IDP from RegieLine, which includes components for dealing with enhanced television synchronisation on various platforms.

There's also the issue of installation and support. With interactive television lots of complex systems are involved and these may not have been used with each other before. For this reason, it can be worth considering outsourcing the installation and support of back-end systems. Just ask your friendly middleware supplier or platform operator.

Coding the application

This is usually one of the most time-consuming parts of the production. There are a wide variety of tools that can be used to help with the coding. See the production tools section later in this chapter.

It's important that the developers understand what is expected from them and that they can get on with their work without interference. However, the project manager will need to closely manage change and deadlines during the coding process.

Managing change

The biggest problem for most technical projects – from producing interactive television to building ships – is change. It's almost always the case that, after the specification is set, changes will be required. This could be because of: external factors, such as a competitor launching a similar service; technical problems; or because someone comes up with an unmissable idea for improving the application. Whatever the reason, changes need to be controlled by:

- Accepting and rejecting change requests with reference to all the people who will be affected. An efficient way of doing this is to set up a project change group. This will meet on a regular basis and should have representatives from each team involved in the project.

- Communicating changes to everyone involved. This can be done by making sure that everyone shares one functional specification document – perhaps by keeping it on a shared server. When it is changed, everyone can be informed by email.

- Recognising that some changes will have an impact on schedule, cost, scope or quality of the project (and it will not always be easy to predict the level of impact).

Managing deadlines

One of the key tasks of the project manager is to warn everyone if deadlines are going to be missed and identify the people who are likely to miss them. This requires good communication. The project manager should be in at least weekly contact with people working in the different project areas. Some people find it difficult to estimate how long their work will take, either because they are keen to please or through lack of experience of interactive television work. Progress can also be particularly difficult to fathom out if the project manager isn't familiar with the technologies. In both these cases, asking searching questions is good. For example, rather than asking 'will you meet your deadline?', it can be better to ask, 'what are the steps you have to go through to reach this deadline?' and 'what are the possible problems?', and so on.

Performing rigorous tests

Television programmes are usually viewed once to check for problems caused by damaged videotape, mismatched light levels or errors introduced in the edit suite (such as single frames missing from the programme, known as flash frames). That's more or less the extent of the testing process.

There's not much testing required for television programmes because the programme itself is very unlikely to cause any problems with the viewer's television set or with the television channel. And television production is so reliable that faults tend to arise only within the programmes themselves – sets falling down, presenters being attacked by animals or other amusing hitches – not with the delivery technologies.

In contrast, most personal computer software consists of a set of complex components that need to work in a range of circumstances, so software applications for personal computers are usually put through a barrage of tests. Despite these tests, personal computers still crash, software sometimes fails to work as expected and, even when working properly, some software is still very difficult to use. Personal computer users seem almost reconciled to these problems – at least for the moment.

The problem with interactive television applications is that they have all the complexity of personal computer applications but are working on a delivery platform that does not normally have technical or usability problems. Viewers' televisions don't crash, the remote control always works (unless the battery has run out) and, unlike the internet, the picture is unlikely to start running slowly at peak viewing times. Any interactive television service that causes problems with the television set or makes it do unexpected things is unlikely to be tolerated by viewers – especially if they are trying interactive television for the first time and are still learning about what it has to offer. They will not want to come back for more punishment.

What's more, as well as putting potential customers off, technical problems can result in hefty charges from platform operators. It's the platform operators that usually have to field complaint calls – even for interactive applications for which they are not directly responsible. It can cost a call centre £3–5 just to deal with a call. If an application causes a technical problem, the platform operators' call-centre may need to explain over the phone to thousands of viewers how to reboot the set-top box. They may even need to send maintenance engineers out. The costs of this may be passed on to the owner of the offending application. Sky Digital in the United Kingdom, for example, gets interactive application providers to agree to millions of pounds worth of cost liabilities, before they are allowed onto the platform. For these reasons, interactive television testing has to be comprehensive and formal.

For enhanced television services, it may be necessary to build a system to mimic the broadcast play-out architecture, so that synchronised triggers can be tested. Alternatively, testing can be completed live on the television channel that the enhanced television application is supporting. In this case, the graphics that prompt users to take part aren't displayed. Only the testing staff will know when to press the button on the remote control to start up the application.

Table 4.12: Various types of tests used in interactive television production

Tests	Description	Example
Functional	Checking that the application works as it is expected to	Pages link to each other correctly, the right information is on each page
Integration	Checking that the different elements of the service work together correctly	Customer information (from the customer database) is searched and displayed correctly
System	Verifies that the system as a whole (the application, back-end, platforms) functions as expected and 'does not do what it should not'	Making a purchase from a real viewer's home
Acceptance	Validating that the product meets the specification	Devising a measure for each of the items on the specification list, such as the speed of update of a page of information
Regression	Re-testing after changes	Re-testing after changes are made to the application that may invalidate previous tests
Ongoing code tests	Programmers' tests on their code as they are writing it	Does this code function as expected?
Performance/ load testing	Checking how the application performs in different circumstances	What happens if one million people request the same page at the same time (quite possible with an enhanced television application)
Usability	Checking how attractive and easy to use the application is	Observation in the home, interviews using prototypes (see Chapter 5 for more)
Proof reading	Checking for grammatical, legal, factual, typographical and other errors in the on-screen content	Is a consistent style of English used?

Stage 4: Launch and operation

Moving to the final stage:

- Launch.
- Operation and development.

Launch

Many interactive television services use soft launches. With these, the application is launched but not publicised. This allows a few days or weeks to iron out minor problems, with less people using the service than would be expected with a full (hard) launch.

With both soft and hard launches, it's best to avoid launching on Monday or Friday, as it can be difficult to sort out any last minute or post-launch problems over the weekend. It's also worth considering whether it's possible to launch during non-peak television viewing times, so that if something does go wrong, it's seen by less viewers (television is generally watched more in the evening and weekends than during office hours or late at night).

As part of the full launch, there will certainly need to be some kind of promotional work carried out. Direct promotion on-air by television presenters is one of the most effective techniques (see the marketing and promotion section in Chapter 3 for more on this).

Operation and development

After the launch party, it's easy to make the mistake of thinking that the job is done. Interactive television isn't like that. First, it's very rare that it's not possible to improve an application. Interactive television production is reasonably new territory for most people and producers rarely get it right first time. Second, there are always problems after launch. In terms of problems that crop up, the content and operations teams should feed customer complaints and other issues into a master list. It's usually worth arranging some more user testing of the live service, preferably in people's homes and with reference to competitors. Tweaks may be necessary – nasty surprises are possible. These could include:

- Viewers having difficulty finding the application. Electronic programme guides and interactive service menus have lots of entries and some are badly organised. The right kind of promotion is crucial. It may even be necessary to educate viewers about exactly which buttons to press by using television advertisements, direct mail or some other form of marketing communication.
- The application may fail to excite viewers in a real-world context. However good the market and user research, the competition from great movies, great television programmes and other exciting interactive television applications could prove too strong. In this case, some more work needs to be done on the proposition and how it ties in with people's daily lives and needs.

There should also be careful scrutiny after launch of the results of the measurement systems that have been put in place – be it to monitor revenue, viewer numbers, usage figures, or other criteria. Is the application fulfilling the original brief? How is it progressing over time (some interactive television applications get used once or twice, then never again)?

Whether tweaking or major revisions are required, the next phase of development should be approached with the same systematic process that applied to the launch. There needs to be an understanding of costs and benefits plus, if possible, market and user testing. In the fast-moving interactive television world, competitors will quickly usurp applications that aren't constantly looking to the next step forward.

Production tools

There are a variety of tools that can help with coding of interactive television applications. Some are effectively complex development environments, which are useful only for computer programmers. Others are designed to help non-technical people produce applications without the need to learn computer code.

As a rule, production tools for non-technical operators employ some kind of PC-based graphical interface to make production easier – for example, by allowing elements of the application to be dragged and dropped together on-screen. However, these tools usually have very limited functionality and the finished application is likely to run slower than if created by programmers from the ground up. Consequently, production tools for non-technical users are generally used to create very simple applications or to make minor adjustments to existing applications. Many companies don't use them at all.

It's also worth bearing in mind that even the production tools designed for non-technical people are not always very easy to use – and certainly not as easy to use as the internet production tools available in the high street. The usability of interactive television tools is likely to improve as more time and effort is spent on their development.

This section outlines the main tools that interactive television producers are likely to encounter. These can be pigeon-holed into three broad and overlapping categories:

- Middleware-specific tools.
- Virtual machine- and presentation engine-specific tools.
- Author once, publish-to-many tools – designed to produce services that will work on two or more interactive television platforms and, sometimes, across multiple media.

Middleware-specific tools

There are many different middleware systems. They come and go with changes to technology and as companies start up or go out of business. Outlined in detail here are the middleware-specific tools used for the three most important middleware systems in the United Kingdom, those used by the three main platforms: Sky Digital satellite, NTL and Telewest digital cable, and digital terrestrial. The middleware systems respectively are: OpenTV, TV Navigator and MediaHighway.

The official standard of digital terrestrial interactivity in the UK is actually an MHEG-5 engine, not MediaHighway. However, MediaHighway hosts the MHEG-5 engine in many digital terrestrial television (DTT) set-top boxes. Other DTT set-tops and televisions run the engine using other middleware systems or using specially written code.

Table 4.13: Examples of middleware-specific tools

Middleware	Programmers' tools	Non-technical producers' tools	Example deployments
OpenTV (from OpenTV)	Software Development Kit	OpenTV Publisher, OpenTV Author	United Kingdom digital satellite (Sky Digital), TPS and Via Digital in continental Europe
TV Navigator (from Liberate)	Off-the-shelf programmers' text-editing tools	Off-the-shelf web production tools with special extensions (for example, Dreamweaver extensions provided as part of Liberate TV Producer Studio toolset)	United Kingdom digital cable (NTL and Telewest), UPC in continental Europe
MediaHighway (from Canal+ Technologies)	Application Workshop	N/A (non-technical users will tend to write for a virtual machine or presentation engine, like MHEG-5, running in MediaHighway)	United Kingdom digital terrestrial (not all boxes and televisions), France Canal Satellite

OpenTV tools

Overview

American manufacturer OpenTV produces a middleware system that is popular with platform operators around the world. It is installed in millions of set-top boxes – including those owned by Sky Digital in the United Kingdom. Most OpenTV applications are created using a version of the computer language C, although the OpenTV middleware can also support various virtual machines and presentation engines.

There are three key methods for creating applications specifically for OpenTV:

- The Software Development Kit.
- OpenTV Publisher.
- OpenTV Author.

Using the Software Development Kit

For complex applications, like EPGs, games and enhanced television, it's necessary to have a high level of control of the C code. These applications need to draw on all the power of the set-top box, and programmers usually need to find clever ways of making them run as fast as possible in the smallest amount of memory possible. To expedite this, OpenTV provides a programming environment called the Software Development Kit (SDK).

The SDK helps programmers create the exact version of C that the middleware will understand. It has a user-interface to aid programming tasks (by colour coding commands, for example), a debugging tool (for identifying problems) and provides commands to access set-top box functions – such as manipulating video streams, managing encryption and communicating with other programs in the set-top box.

OpenTV's Target Decoder product is used to view applications in progress on a television screen attached to a set-top box and personal computer.

Using OpenTV Publisher

Some interactive television applications are straightforward. They don't need to run very fast, because they are performing simple operations, and they don't need to squeeze into a very small amount of memory, because more than enough is available anyway. Most walled garden applications and some digital text services fit into this category. To help create these applications, OpenTV has produced OpenTV Publisher.

Using OpenTV Publisher, non-technical staff can build services using tools normally used in web production. The application pages are built using OpenTV markup language (OML). This is based on extensible markup language (XML), a system for sharing different types of information between computers – anything from musical notation to the contents of an interactive television screen. OpenTV Publisher deals with the problem of converting this information into the C code that the middleware will understand.

Using OpenTV Author

OpenTV Author is modelled on television and multimedia authoring tools like Avid, Media 100 and Director. It provides a graphical user-interface for non-technical production staff to create interactive television services with a minimal fuss by dragging and dropping page elements on the screen.

Applications are defined in terms of scenes. Scenes are the equivalent of pages on a web site. They structure how viewers move around and experience different parts of the service. Each scene can contain a number of OpenTV Author gadgets. These perform functions like drawing a shape on-screen, animating a graphic, playing an audio file or putting up a timed icon on-screen.

Like OpenTV Publisher, applications written with OpenTV Author are less flexible and likely to run a bit slower than would be expected had they been written using the SDK.

TV Navigator tools

Overview

United States-based company Liberate (originally an offshoot of web browser company Netscape and database company Oracle) produces TV Navigator. Both the big digital cable operators in the United Kingdom (NTL and Telewest) use it.

TV Navigator was created with internet technologies very much in mind. By supporting internet standards, like HTML and JavaScript, Liberate hopes to make application development cheap and easy. This is because there is a large pool of people with knowledge of internet production and a whole range of production tools and resources. Some versions of TV Navigator, generally running on more powerful set-top boxes, also have the capability to support a version of the animation engine Flash. TV Navigator can also run a variety of virtual machines and presentation engines.

TV Navigator consists of two key parts: the TV Navigator client and the TV Navigator Connect Suite. The client sits on the set-top box and controls the hardware in the same way other middleware systems do. The TV Navigator Connect Suite sits on a server at the platform provider's office. The most important part of the TV Navigator Connect Suite is the transcoding server. This converts content into formats that the software on the set-top box can understand. It also caches data, improving the retrieval speeds and processes encrypted information. When it encounters web pages it converts them into formats better suited to television by, for example, lowering the level of colour saturation on graphics.

There are two key methods for producing Liberate applications:

- Using an off-the-shelf programmers' text-editing tool (like BBEdit or UltraEdit).
- Using an off-the-shelf graphical production tool designed for web sites, like Dreamweaver.

Using programmers' text-editing tools

Most complex TV Navigator applications are hand-coded, which means they are written into off-the-shelf text editors like BBEdit, UltraEdit or, even Notepad. These have functions to help programmers quickly identify, search and replace code.

Most TV Navigator applications in the United Kingdom are written in HTML and JavaScript. JavaScript is designed to help make web pages more interactive – anything from animating page elements to performing calculations. To complement the standard JavaScript functions, Liberate has developed special JavaScript extensions that can be used to control set-top-box-specific tasks like changing channels and displaying television-style graphics. For example, there's the TvChannel object, which can be manipulated to change channels. There's also a particularly useful JavaScript extension for manipulating on-screen content, called dynamic tables. This allows user-driven actions on one part of the screen to result in changes to other parts of the screen, using straightforward JavaScript commands – great for television-style animations, tickers and games. (Note: platform operators, to avoid applications breaking their customers' set-top boxes, sometimes restrict iTV producers' access to some of the TV Navigator functions, such as channel changing.)

To help producers and programmers check how an application in progress looks on-screen, Liberate has created the TV Navigator Emulator, known as Emmy. This reproduces all the elements of a typical TV Navigator interactive television system but on a personal computer. It does this by mimicking the TV Navigator client (which normally runs on a set-top box) on the personal computer. The computer is then connected, via the internet, to a mock TV Navigator Connect Suite and transcoding server held at Liberate's office or with a platform operator. Producers can then view applications in action on a personal computer, without the need for a set-top box. Emmy is available as part of TV Producer Studio from Liberate and from some platform operators (like NTL and UPC).

Liberate and platform operators also provide set-top boxes, which can be connected to the internet, to test applications.

Using off-the-shelf graphical-interface web production tools

Internet production tools like Dreamweaver and FrontPage are rarely used to create complicated TV Navigator applications. They risk adding superfluous code, which could slow down the speed of the application. They also do not offer the flexibility and control that most programmers require. However, they can be useful for simpler applications and prototypes. In fact, Liberate has worked with Macromedia to develop special additions to the Dreamweaver software so it can produce TV Navigator-compliant pages. These additions can be used to manipulate some of the JavaScript extensions that Liberate has written for TV Navigator. Liberate provides Dreamweaver as part of its TV Producer Studio package of authoring tools for TV Navigator.

Be warned: regular versions of Dreamweaver, without special extensions, are of limited use for creating TV Navigator applications. Also, platform operators often make changes to the parameters of the version of TV Navigator running on their systems – changing the size of the screen area or limiting the available functionality. If this is the case, even a TV Navigator-customised version of Dreamweaver may be of limited use – and it may be easier to hand-code the application.

MediaHighway tools

Overview

MediaHighway is used as the middleware in some of the digital terrestrial television set-top boxes and televisions in the United Kingdom (including the set-top boxes of the defunct ITV Digital) and on Canal Satellite, the French digital platform. French company Canal+ Technologies (part of Thomson) owns it. The middleware can support a number of different virtual machines and presentation engines.

Using the Application Workshop

The Application Workshop is a development environment for creating MediaHighway applications using the programming language Pantalk. The environment consists of tools for creating user-interfaces, editing graphics and debugging the programming code.

Tools for other middleware systems

As well as OpenTV, TV Navigator and MediaHighway, there are a variety of other middleware systems, each with its own tools.

Table 4.14: Other middleware systems

Middleware	Tools	Example deployment
Microsoft TV	Text-editing tools or off-the-shelf web production tools (like FrontPage and Dreamweaver with extensions)	United States cable (mainly analogue), TV Cabo (Portugal)
Power TV	Power TV Software Development Kit for C and C++, Power TV Content Development Kit and standard web tools for HTML, Java and JavaScript	United States cable (mainly analogue)
CableWare from Worldgate	CableWare Software Development Kit for C and C++, Content Development Kit and standard web tools for HTML, JavaScript and Flash	United States cable (mainly analogue)
NDS Core	Interactive Applications Development Kit and standard tools for HTML, JavaScript and Java	Chinese cable firms
Netgem	Text editors and standard off-the-shelf web production tools	Some web-on-television boxes and all-in-one web-on-television and digital television boxes (United Kingdom and Australia)

Virtual machine- and presentation engine-specific tools

The advantage of virtual machines and presentation engines is that applications written for them should be interoperable across platforms. The theory doesn't always live up to the reality, unfortunately, and applications often need to be tweaked to work on different platforms and set-top boxes.

Java for Multimedia Home Platform (MHP) tools

Overview

Depending on the version, MHP includes both HTML and JavaScript presentation engines as part of the standard. However, the core of MHP, known as DVB-J, specifies a virtual machine that supports a version of the Java programming language. Java is a powerful language designed to run on virtual machines and is ideal for creating interactive television applications.

Using the Java Development Kit

Java is typically created using programming environments, like the Java Development Kit or Visual Cafe. These help programmers write and debug code.

Using graphical-interface tools

There are a number of production tools designed to help non-technical people produce Java code for MHP-compliant middleware. One example is AltiComposer

Table 4.15: Virtual machine-specific tools

Virtual machine	Programmers' tools	Non-technical tools	Example deployment
Java for MHP	Java Development Kit and similar software	Alticast and similar software	Finish DTT
WML	Text editors	24X Rock Technology and similar software	Sky Digital UK
MHEG-5	Text editors	SmartStudio, SceneBuilder and similar software	United Kingdom DTT (not all set-top boxes and televisions)

from Alticast. This has a graphical user-interface where applications are created by dragging and dropping constituent elements together.

The basic unit in AltiComposer is called a scene. This contains all the pages and interactivity involved in the application. After the scene is created the shots and actors are added. A shot is comparable to a page on a web site, and is the basic unit for navigation. Within shots are objects and functions known as actors. Actors can be set to behave differently depending on what the viewer is doing. Examples of actors include animating a graphic or putting text on-screen after a set viewer action.

Expert programmers can also use Alticast to save time on Java coding tasks.

WML tools

Overview

A number of companies have written presentation engines that work with the mobile phone markup language WML. WML is based on XML (extensible markup language). It is particularly useful in the interactive television environment because it takes up very little bandwidth, which makes it relatively cheap to transmit alongside an existing television channel. Sky Digital in the United Kingdom has a WML browser running in OpenTV called WapTV (WAP is a phone data-transfer standard that utilises WML). Rather than having to broadcast code that the OpenTV middleware can understand, all the application producer has to do is send WML in the right format for the WapTV browser to understand.

Developers can use off-the-shelf WML management and editing tools or can work with specialised software, like that provided by 24X Rock Technology. This offers an easy to use graphical user-interface for creating WapTV services. Testing is done on specially adapted set-top boxes. Using WML makes it particularly easy to draw in content from existing web databases, particularly if the content is already in XML format.

MHEG-5

Overview

MHEG-5 is a standardised way for storing, exchanging and displaying multimedia content, sanctioned and developed by the Multimedia Hypermedia Experts Group – an organisation set up by the International Standards Association (ISO). The language focuses on the presentation and manipulation of on-screen elements (in this sense, it is similar to JavaScript, although the language itself is quite different). As previously mentioned, it is the standard for digital terrestrial television interactivity in the UK.

Using text-editing tools

Most development for MHEG-5 virtual machines is done using off-the-shelf computer code-editing tools, like UltraEdit. Developers can add their own customised debugging and coding functions to these. The code is sent to a set-top box running an MHEG-5 engine or engine emulator running on a personal computer for testing.

MHEG-5 applications are built by defining scenes. Scenes are similar to web pages, although they can also be set to exist for a period of time. Each scene contains elements known in MHEG-5 as ingredients. These define how the interactivity, text and graphics work on-screen.

Using graphical-interface tools

There are a number of products on the market that offer graphical-interfaces for building MHEG-5 applications. The market for these is quite small, however, and they are often used in conjunction with expert programming tools. Examples include SmartStudio from Samsung and SceneBuilder from Strategy and Technology.

Production tools for authoring once, publishing to many

Because there are lots of different types of middleware and lots of different tools, recruiting and deploying production staff that have expertise in enough tools to create an interactive television application for more than one platform can be very expensive. Consequently, there are a number of products on the market that attempt to take the pain out of interactive television production by offering a single tool or solution for authoring applications across platforms.

The main disadvantage of all these multi-platform tools and solutions is that they support a limited set of platforms and the applications can usually only perform a limited set of functions. Anyone wanting to produce an application that does something beyond the basic function set might as well commission or write his or her own application from the ground up. There's also the danger of having to drop to the lowest common denominator of functionality in an attempt to publish to multiple platforms – risky, since it may mean having to forego functionality that competitors will be only too happy to use.

These multi-platform tools can be split into three categories:

- Off-the-shelf systems designed specifically for interactive television.
- Extensions to existing television and internet production tools.
- Production companies' customised solutions.

Off-the-shelf systems designed specifically for interactive television

There are off-the-shelf multi-platform interactive television production tools available, including Regieline from IDP, Storyteller from Watchpoint, ITV Factory from NPTV, SCIP and Ensequence. (There are also advertising-specific solutions from companies like Wink, RespondTV and PressRed). These companies work with platform operators and middleware suppliers – usually to incorporate a special engine in the target platforms' set-top boxes. They then provide one central easy-to-use tool for creating applications for every platform.

Extensions to existing television and internet production tools

Some existing television and web production tools have been extended to deal with simple interactive television authoring for multiple platforms, including the Lyric range from television graphics company Chyron, extensions to Avid editing software and the SpinTV Studio Suite for Dreamweaver. As with the systems designed specifically for interactive television, they work only with a pre-defined set of platform operators.

Production companies' customised solutions

Production companies such as Go-Interact, Di3, NDS and Two Way TV have their own infrastructure and solutions for creating and running interactive television applications across a number of platforms. They can utilise and customise their existing solutions for a particular customer's needs. Some of these companies will also offer production technolgies that encompass publishing to the web, mobile phones and other media too. They tend to work with pre-defined platforms and it will cost much more to produce for a platform that isn't already covered by their infrastructure.

Case study: The production process for *Big Brother*

Andy Wyper, producer, Victoria Real. Victoria Real is a digital communications company specialising in the delivery of cross-platform solutions for blue-chip consumer brands.

Big Brother 2001 was the first truly multi-platform television-based project to be developed in Britain. Interactive television services were just one part of an overall project that also encompassed web, personal organisers, mobile phone and games development, together with the creation of a content management system (CMS) that would allow the editorial team easy access to all these platforms. These distinct services were tied to one another by virtue of a single source of content that originated them all, the television show. Since *Big Brother*, this kind of multiple media development has become more common in television with a number of companies emphasising the multiple points of access approach to viewing their content. The model has also been used to great effect on *Big Brother* 2002 in the UK and on other *Big Brother* shows around the world.

By their very nature, multi-platform developments are complex beasts. Over 27 companies were involved with the development of interactive services for *Big Brother* 2001, including Channel 4, Endemol UK, Victoria Real, Intel and BT Cellnet, to name but a few. Victoria Real provided the design and build of the web, interactive television, CMS, personal organiser and games elements. Intel supplied the hosting while BT Cellnet handled the various mobile phone services. Endemol UK and Channel 4 were, of course, the clients and ultimate owners of the content. Effective co-ordination between this array of companies was therefore paramount.

Furthermore, *Big Brother* had an immovable deadline, the launch of the linear television show. Any development had to guarantee completion by that date or not be done at all, it was as simple as that. Compounding this was the fact that, given *Big Brother*'s massive popularity, even the slightest delay or error would be noticed, and noticed by a huge amount of people. It was, therefore, not a project for the faint hearted.

The first and most critical task to be undertaken was the planning and creation of the overall project schedule. This set out what was needed and when it was needed by for every party involved in the project, and was managed by the core project team at Victoria Real, Channel 4 and Endemol UK. Every third party was required to sign up to the schedule and commit to the dates agreed.

Work started with the scoping of requirements for all services. A series of meetings over six weeks between Victoria Real, Endemol UK and Channel 4 resulted in a comprehensive design document that would serve as the development bible in the months to come. These meetings involved the three producers from each company, together with the project's art director and the two senior technical developers, reviewing the latest version of the design document, identifying the requirements both from a creative and technical perspective, brainstorming the solutions and applying liberal doses of pragmatism to make sure it was all achievable.

A helpful rule of thumb in any project's development is that time spent in the design phase is time saved during the build. This was certainly the case with *Big Brother* 2001. The extended period of design we undertook enabled us to be completely confident that we could deliver what we promised on time. At Victoria Real, workstreams were set up to handle sub-projects, with dedicated core teams for each.

Once the designs were agreed, work was started on the CMS and web site, as these were going to be the longest development phases. At the same time, hosting arrangements were organised at Intel, while BT handled the laying of the landlines and connections from the *Big Brother* house out to BT Tower and the United Kingdom's internet backbone.

A unified art direction and branding across all platforms, including offline media (such as print and billboards), was required for *Big Brother*, so once the main brand had been finalised this was propagated out to all third parties as a style guide, determining a consistent look and feel across the board. This was especially

Table 4.16: Workstreams for *Big Brother* 2001

Workstream	Team
Project management	Producer
	Account manager
	Senior developer
	Senior designer
Main design	Producer
	Senior developer
	Senior designer
Web site development	Senior developer
	Senior designer
	Three developers
	Three designers
Content management system development	Senior developer
	Two developers
Interactive television development	Two designers
PDA/wireless development	Senior developer
	Developer
	Designer
Testing	Four testers

important across the various third party web sites that were linked to from the main web site (such as sponsors and partners' sites), as they would be developing their own sites.

The main build phase of the project lasted eight weeks and included complete code and asset creation across all platforms. Testing was integrated into the build as an iterative process, with all testable elements being put through a rigorous test–fix–retest cycle. This was critical in the web site development, where browser and PC/Mac compatibility issues could often mean that a fix for one bug would cause another bug in another browser configuration. In addition, a full four weeks was scheduled at the end of the project to provide end-to-end testing.

Thankfully, the interactive television development was far simpler. Victoria Real handled the screen design over the course of two weeks, creating the user-interface based on the required functionality scoped out at the beginning of the project. Designs were prototyped and tested for television display then screen mock-ups, together with functional walkthroughs, were produced for delivery to Channel 4 and Sky for build and implementation.

Tying the various platforms together was the CMS. This was designed and built in Cold Fusion, allowing the editorial team at the house complete control over publishing and archiving. Any story created could be stored in the CMS in different platform-specific versions and channelled to the relevant outlet. Hence, SMS stories could be uploaded automatically to BT Cellnet for dissemination, while web stories would go via a staging server, directly to Intel's servers. The CMS staging server was crucial in the successful delivery of *Big Brother*. It worked by allowing versions of the site to be published statically at times of low load on the server. Normally, a CMS operates by dynamically fetching data from a server whenever a user requests them (for instance, by clicking on a link). If this had been the case on *Big Brother* the servers would have crashed repeatedly due to the enormous demand and therefore requests being generated. By implementing a dynamic staging server, which the CMS published data to then automatically copied across to the webheads, it allowed the main servers to remain static and not respond dynamically. The upshot of this was that the interactive services were guaranteed not to fail and fall over which, given the exposure it received, was vital.

The project was not without hitches and problems. For example, the timescales for end-to-end testing became compressed at the end of the schedule and constituted a sizeable risk to the successful operation and distribution of the live video streams. Fortunately, the streams worked perfectly from day one.

Big Brother 2001 went live to the world exactly on time at 9 a.m. on 25 May 2001, after the project team had worked straight through the previous 48 hours to accommodate last minute changes. Over the course of 16 weeks, the concept had gone from a ten-page brief to a true multi-platform interactive entertainment package. Whether on the sofa watching television, on the move with a phone or personal organiser, or using a personal computer or Apple Mac at work, *Big Brother* was finally there for the viewer anytime, anywhere, anyhow.

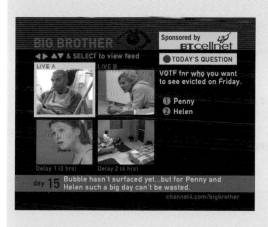

4.7 *Big Brother* – a massive production task across multiple iTV platforms and multiple media. © *Channel 4* (© *Victoria Real*).

Case study: Enhanced television production workflows – now and in the future

Humphrey Lau, senior technical manager, interactive television, BBC New Media and Technology.

Television production is generally a well-understood and mature process supported by mature tools. It will continue to evolve driven by advances in post-production technology and new formats for new distribution channels. But enhanced television (ETV) is rapidly establishing a new order with new work patterns. To some production teams it will feel like an imposition, while others will quickly embrace it. In either case, programme makers must learn to understand and accommodate the demands of its new sibling, as it is here to stay.

At the same time, ETV has a lot to learn from the television production process. Indeed, our experience at the BBC so far has shown that the two have much in common and should be more closely integrated – from commissioning through to production, play-out and distribution. This experience has been gained through the successful launch of a large number of interactive services since the introduction of digital television in the UK.

The journey so far

The BBC launched its first interactive service in 1998 on the digital terrestrial (DTT) platform. This is a media-rich version of its popular analogue Ceefax information service and shares much of the content and production systems with its analogue cousin. The DTT service was developed against a background of unproven receiver middleware and functionality, and the absence of commercially available production and play-out tools. The service was launched on digital cable in 2000 and on digital satellite in 2001.

The first daily ETV service with scheduled content was transmitted in 1999 on DTT. This provided supplementary information, which accompanied each BBC Knowledge programme. More enhanced programming for DTT followed in 2000, including the BAFTA-winning interactive coverage of Wimbledon and the Open Golf championships. In 2001, we launched several landmark enhanced television services on digital satellite and among them the multi-stream Wimbledon service and the BAFTA-winning *Walking with Beasts* service. We also broadcast our first return-path ETV service in support of the *Children In Need* event and viewers were able to pledge their donations using their set-top box modems.

Since the start of 2002, interactive television has been a regular feature of the BBC's transmission schedules on all the digital television platforms in the UK. These range from simple programme support applications, like walled garden sites on digital cable, to pre-recorded and live synchronised quizzes on DTT and digital satellite, to logistically complex live multi-stream sports services produced on-site for all the digital platforms. The provision of such an extreme mix of services for multiple platforms with different capabilities, coupled with immature production tools and the explosive demand for ETV services within the BBC, presents us with a unique set of challenges for the future of ETV production. But the experience and invaluable insight gleaned from producing ETV services over the last three years should hopefully stand us in good stead to meet these challenges.

ETV workflow

It may seem obvious but the BBC's experience so far has only served to reaffirm our early convictions that, to succeed, ETV must be considered as an integral part of the televisual experience and, what's more, be commissioned along with the television programme rather than as an afterthought. ETV production should be considered as part of the sequence of stages in television production, like video editing or subtitling. Until recently, ETV propositions have been conceived, commissioned and produced separately from the main programme. This has been necessary in the early days due to the specialist knowledge required and to help overcome natural inertia to change within programme departments. In future, both the ETV and television commissioning cycles will be linked to encourage a more integrated approach.

The level of production effort required is dictated by the complexity of the ETV proposition. It can range from providing simple programme support information to the provision of live multi-stream video and audio enhancements requiring a separate fully equipped production, editing and transmission gallery. Between these two extremes there is a vast middle ground, but a typical multi-platform ETV proposition will generally comprise video, audio, graphical and textural assets, and the software that controls the presentation of these assets on each platform.

The visual, aural and textural content is normally created by the same team producing the television programme, under the supervision of an ETV producer. This can sometimes place unwelcome additional demands on the existing production team, unless the resource requirements have been planned in from the start. On other occasions, a centralised ETV production team also creates assets. Once completed, these assets are delivered to a central ETV technical production team that is responsible for integrating these assets into the ETV application. The application is authored by a team of software engineers with intimate knowledge of the platforms. In the future, we envisage that the television production team, using ETV content-creation tools integrated within non-linear editing workstations, will create the majority of assets. But quality control, application authoring, play-out and monitoring are likely to remain centralised.

The ETV production process itself shares many similarities with television production. A typical television workflow will include commissioning, research and preparation, recording of content, digitisation of content, versioning for different markets, scheduling and play-out. The typical ETV workflow will similarly include commissioning, research and preparation, creation of content and the application, assembly and integration of content with the application, versioning for different platforms, scheduling and play-out. So it is conceivable that in future we will see the emergence of production tools that will allow a much more integrated approach to ETV and television production. However, before this can happen, we need to establish a set of interface standards to facilitate the interchange of assets between the different production stages, mirroring today's digital video and audio interfaces and tape formats.

Aside from interfaces, a number of other issues will also need to be addressed in future. Publishing to new and legacy platforms and the re-purposing of applications are important for driving digital uptake, as well as commercial exploitation. Rights management and tracking of usage are also important, as is archiving of applications for rebroadcast.

Interactive television is still in its infancy. We continue to learn from our experiences and to develop new ETV formats, so it is difficult to predict how production will evolve over the next few years. Its future shape and form will depend just as much on advances in technology as on the acceptance by programme makers that enhanced television is here to stay and will be a permanent feature of the television landscape in the coming years.

© *British Broadcasting Corporation 2002*

Case study: The development of BBCi, the BBC's digital text service – services, structure and processes

Vlad Cohen, head of design, and Damian Rafferty, executive producer, interactive television, BBC New Media.

Development work on new digital services has been a central commitment for the BBC over the past few years. As new technologies become available to British viewers, we hope to take advantage of them, and find new ways to entertain, inform and educate. The digital text service, known as BBCi, is the richest and most extensive service currently available. It has been in constant development since 1998, across all interactive television platforms, and over that time the service has faced a wide variety of challenges and obstacles.

The BBC interactive television department in 2002 is composed of over 80 people, comprising producers, project managers, applications engineers (computer programmers) and designers. Each of these disciplines has grown into a more specialised team and developed effective processes to manage the ever-increasing workload. On the editorial side, the producers have been organised into a hierarchical system similar to that in linear television production. An executive producer oversees the development of all '24/7 interactive television' services (meaning services that are not an integral enhancement to a particular television programme). These range from text services on all the platforms to return-path enhancements and video-on-demand services in Kingston upon Hull.

Senior producers take responsibility for particularly large projects or areas of development, while producers direct individual projects with the help of assistant producers and broadcast assistants. The technical team is also divided into large groups, each specialising in a distinct area, such as standalone services or programme enhancements, and led by a team leader. Project management, to co-ordinate technical resource and manage outside relationships, is also divided along similar lines. Design is somewhat of an exception, as the designers work with more flexibility than other teams, moving between projects and platforms as required. This structure allows us to be highly productive and flexible with a small team, rather than attaching permanent design resources to a long project, which may have only intermittent demand for new interface development. Additional functions such as legal and business affairs, finance, marketing, and publicity are not part of the central content production area, but are available at all times as resources.

As the digital text services have grown and developed, the department has had to change its structure and processes. We are developing propositions that involve very high risks in an environment that is constantly changing, and so, to cope with shifting priorities and the uncertainties of distribution and technology, we have had to become very flexible without losing the ability to innovate and identify opportunities.

4.8 Digital teletext on digital terrestrial television, entertainment section. *Courtesy of the BBC; images supplied by kind permission BBC/BBC Worldwide.*

In 1999, the project to develop digital text as a replacement for Ceefax (a teletext service available on analogue BBC channels) was already well underway. Two prototype applications had been developed and one system had proved superior. Simplified to reduce technical and editorial complexity, this service then became the first service for digital terrestrial television (DTT), launching in 1999. At the time, the prevailing feeling in the department was that anything too web-like would not work on television – a perspective that sometimes proved as unhelpful as the opposite view that the web could be transported wholesale onto television. In the early days every tiny detail, such as the precise functions of the colour keys on the remote control, provoked long and passionate discussions. Fortunately, over time, the service has matured to allow more flexibility within a broadly agreed overall framework.

While the first digital text service was being developed, the department was quite small and there was no dedicated technical resource for the text team. Everyone in the department worked on a range of new ideas and prototypes. While the text service was the most important product of the fledgling department, it was not such a problem, but later it became apparent that each major project would need to have sufficient technical resources to continue new development, and also a considerable amount of effort to maintain and optimise launched services. With additional technical resources and complexity came a requirement for detailed project management. These requirements have led, over time, to the development of our matrix management structure, in which expertise and skills are divided into groups by discipline (editorial, technical, design, project management), but in which individuals also take on long-term commitments to project teams (such as the text teams within 24/7 interactive television).

The business priority was to become the first broadcaster to launch a major text service. Although not an unreasonable goal, this rushed the release of the digital terrestrial television service and stifled the momentum to develop the service further; the process was additionally complicated by technical and commercial uncertainties with the platform itself. Had we known when the actual launch would have taken place we could have progressed the product by working an additional six months on it. As it was, we had to lock it down much too early to guarantee readiness.

By 2002, the digital terrestrial television service needed to be completely over-hauled in order to achieve editorial flexibility and technical stability. In retrospect, we needed a development system that would have enabled us to lock off a release version of the service and then continue improving it until public release became

4.9 Digital teletext on digital terrestrial television, main menu. *Courtesy of the BBC; images supplied by kind permission BBC/BBC Worldwide.*

4.10 Digital teletext (BBCi) on satellite. *Courtesy of the BBC; images supplied by kind permission BBC/BBC Worldwide.*

possible. That mechanism is now in place, but both the digital terrestrial television and satellite services were originally compromised by the focus on being first to market.

In contrast, the lessons we learned in the rush to launch the digital terrestrial television service had some positive impact on both the digital terrestrial television and satellite services later on. By the time the satellite service was ready to launch, early in 2001, we understood that essential functionality could not be abandoned to achieve aggressive, but arbitrary, launch dates. Several improvements were forced into the development of both services, including additional navigation with pop-up menus and an emphasis on the quarter screen television viewer, which allows text users to view any BBC channel while browsing the services. These service features proved to be crucial to the success of the product on both platforms and were well worth the effort.

Digital cable provided entirely new challenges. Unlike digital terrestrial and satellite, which essentially broadcast an entire service at once, cable provides an IP (internet protocol)-based or web-like environment, in which the viewer requests the desired pages directly from a server. Different sources of content were considered, although the same short form content as used by the other text services proved to be best for core areas such as news, sport and weather. Different navigational structures were also required, as the platform had entirely different controls from digital terrestrial and satellite, and different capabilities for inset video and pictures. The design process behind cable was a major leap forward from the earlier platforms in that decisions were made based on iterative testing. After the environment had been understood and analysed, various concepts of the service were mocked up and tested, both formally and informally. This was possible for the first time because basic questions about technology and content were

4.11 BBCi on cable television. *Courtesy of the BBC;© AP.*

4.12 News on digital cable television. *Courtesy of the BBC;© PA Photos.*

resolved earlier on, and resulted in truly user-centred decisions. The technical infrastructure of the cable service is also much more open to expansion and development, and it is the most dynamic of all of our live services, now including forums, message boards, games, revision material and teenage content, as well as more news and sport than text services on other platforms. Ever since its launch in 2000, it has been a hugely useful and popular service to viewers.

In terms of department structure, digital cable was set up as a separate technical development team from the beginning, because of the radical differences in its architecture. Over time it has grown to include dedicated editorial and project management teams as well. Because cable is constructed with HTML, content teams around the BBC have built large portions of the service, and this distributed development has required new processes for editorial and navigational sign-off that were never issues with previous text services developed entirely within interactive television. The cable service produced a need for style guides and templated production systems, which have since proved enormously useful to increase the speed and quality of our output.

Looking back, the constant change in our department has definitely led in the right direction. We still believe in many values that drove the department when it was a tiny development unit, such as keeping the viewer constantly in mind and getting editorial, design and technical to work together on projects right from the start. However, as the department matures, procedures and clarity have become increasingly important. With every project now, we make sure to produce a minimum proposition that could be launched, and only then continue on to more ambitious iterations. We also clearly identify a single individual who makes final editorial decisions, although proposals are invited from all involved. We have also learned that operating live services requires a great deal of time and energy, and this effort must not be underestimated. Some of these have been difficult lessons to learn, and the process of slowly evolving into a production department out of a blue-sky development team has been difficult at times, but we believe we are striking a workable balance between innovation and risk management.

© British Broadcasting Corporation 2002

Case study: The development and production of Sky NZ's weather channel

Michael Atherton, manager new media, Oktobor. Oktobor is a visual effects and animation company that produces digital design for television, web and film. They are also one of New Zealand's leading developers for OpenTV.

Oktobor created New Zealand's first interactive television application for Sky. This application, a weather channel, enables viewers to access up-to-the minute weather information on demand. Viewers can fast-track to a variety of services, including national and regional forecasts, satellite maps, and marine information.

Why weather?

When rolling out interactive television services on any platform, the hope is that supply is going to generate demand. Therefore, one of the first interactive applications usually chosen for deployment by a digital network is a weather service. Why? Essentially because weather is an inherently useful service, benefits greatly from interactivity and appeals to a broad range of viewers, thus kick-starting (in theory anyway) the everyday use of that little interactive button.

Weather is one of the uses of interactive television that consistently reaches that holy grail of improving on traditional broadcasting. Most television weather reports are seen in specific timeslots (usually after the news), although increasingly in multi-channel environments, dedicated 24/7 weather channels are available. However, if I want the weather in Bolton, or Rennes, or wherever I happen to be at the time, I have to wait for my chosen region to be covered in the report. Faced with this, the benefits of a viewer-controlled drill-down weather information service become immediately apparent.

4.13 Weather on Sky in New Zealand.
© *Oktobor and Sky NZ.*

4.14 On-demand information. © *Oktobor and Sky NZ.*

Challenges

So, armed with our value proposition, we can set about making the thing. Most interactive applications could be said to be stylistically and conceptually alien to the average television audience, thus allowing a certain perverse freedom in design. Conversely, when it comes to visualising an interactive weather channel, viewers have high expectations of a modern television weather report – replete with computer-generated map flythroughs and up-to-the-minute satellite imagery.

Also, depending on the size and shape of the country you live in, a national service has to offer a reasonably large range of information. This translates to a complex information architecture, that must remain broadcast-centric and easy to use by even the most computer illiterate.

Commercially, the opportunity for all interactive television developers is to create a universal application (for example, news, television-mail, chess game) once, then sell it virtually unchanged to networks around the world. Obviously, a weather service inherently requires considerable customisation for each country of sale. Our application architecture should therefore be sufficiently flexible to allow straightforward customisation.

To recap, we're looking for:

- A look and feel that meets the expectations set by modern weather reports.
- An information architecture that structures a large amount of content and supports a simplistic interface.
- An application architecture that allows us to make changes to our service quickly and easily.

The New Zealand story

Firstly, a quick overview: New Zealand is not a densely populated country. At the last count, just 3.5 million people were all present and correct. The country's only operating digital broadcaster, Sky New Zealand, has around 30 per cent digital penetration, yet this only equates to around 450 000 subscribers.

For the interactive television industry, this situation is both agony and ecstasy. Unfortunately, the more complex, sophisticated and consequently expensive services (for example, the Sky Sports Active application in the UK) just aren't commercially viable in such a small market. On the other hand, Sky NZ has the interactive television monopoly, so the multi-platform fragmentation that hinders other markets isn't present here.

Sky New Zealand launched interactivity on their OpenTV platform in December 2001 with Oktobor's weather application. However, Sky's interactive capabilities weren't born fully formed. Instead, they opted for a progressive infrastructure rollout, meaning that certain features of the platform, most notably two-way connectivity and programme-synchronous content, would not be available at launch.

As such, the weather channel was conceived as a 24/7 'virtual channel', as opposed to the interactive enhancement of an existing programme. This was particularly suitable, as the service would completely replace a linear weather channel in Sky's digital line-up. Our design brief was to match the presentation of the existing linear channel as far as possible. This meant that, unlike some other interactive television weather applications, ours had to be based around a national map with meteorological information superimposed over each region. Other mandatories included satellite and radar maps, marine conditions, and phases of the moon. In other words, to be able to generate dynamically the same level of graphic sophistication seen on a regular television channel. Some task!

Consequently, we chose to develop the service using the OpenTV SDK. This allowed us significantly greater flexibility than would be possible with visual authoring tools such as OpenTV Author, but at the expense of additional time and resource overheads. As with any project, the client had a penchant for requesting numerous revisions (both functional and aesthetic) during development. As OpenTV development can be fairly rigid and inflexible, it was clear that we needed a solution to allow rapid changes to the application as required. In answer to this, Oktobor's development team created GadgetMill, a customisable development framework, allowing OpenTV applications to be authored as an XML document. XML is a universal standard markup language (of which HTML is a derivative), and consequently XML developers are far more readily available than OpenTV SDK developers – in New Zealand anyway!

When designing a navigation system for interactive television, our team had to forget many of the paradigms ingrained through development of interactive media for the web or CD-ROM. Television viewers cannot be assumed to be computer literate, and all navigation must be done using the remote control. Concepts such as scrolling and multiple windows must also be kept to a minimum, as they take the viewer further away from the comfort of the familiar television experience.

One navigation decision every platform operator must face is whether to allow the use of the remote control's colour buttons within applications, or whether to reserve them for top-level consistent functions across all applications. Sky's initial policy was the latter, but eventually shifted to the former as they realised that removing such useful navigation devices would drastically impede the usability of a complex service.

The result

Oktobor's weather application is generally agreed to hit all its marks. It provides a logical interface that keeps navigation to a minimum by remembering your previously selected region of choice. It looks and feels like a television weather report, albeit without suited and smiley presenter. For us, the application's XML framework makes it easy to remodel for other networks around the world. From here, we are looking at the potential of customising our weather application to offer specialist reports for skiers, surfers, even farmers.

Interactive television should, wherever possible, look like standard television – the Weather Channel achieves this goal, while offering a higher level of service than the traditional television channel. Anyone considering the development of any interactive television service should first be asking: what makes this better for the viewer than regular television?

Actions

✓ Download and have a play with a TV Navigator emulator. There's one available at www.digitalcabletv.co.uk.

✓ Download and read *How to Start a Creative Revolution at Work*. This is a good introduction to some of the latest techniques for stimulating creativity during a production process and at work – and it's free. It's available at www.whatif.co.uk.

✓ Read *Managing Multimedia* by Elaine England and Andy Finney. This covers project management techniques for iTV and other multimedia projects in detail.

✓ Visit the web sites of as many middleware suppliers as you can find and read up on their production tools. For example: www.opentv.com, www.liberate.com, www.canalplus-technologies.com, www.microsoft.com/tv, www.powertv.com, www.worldgate.com, www.netgem.com.

✓ Visit the web sites of as many interactive television production tools and solutions companies as possible. For example: www.idp.fr, www.di3.com, www.twowaytv.com, www.nds.com, www.wink.com, www.respondtv.com.

✓ See the list of middleware systems at www.broadbandbananas.com/platforms1.html.

✓ Take the interactive television production quiz at www.InteractiveTelevisionProduction.com.

Usability
and design

Chapter 5 in 30 seconds . . .

▷ When thinking about usability and graphic design on any device, it's worth considering the needs and wants of the users, the speed of on-screen responses, the advantages of simplicity and the nature of the medium.

▷ Viewers tend to interact with their television in well-established ways. The set is viewed from a distance and controlled with a remote. Different programmes are watched with varying levels of involvement. Most activity is focused on entertainment and information.

▷ Television screens display graphics and text differently from computer monitors. Material needs to be designed specifically for the television screen in order to look good.

" Don't make me think. **"**

Steve Krug, usability consultant

It's a challenge to get people to take part in new and unusual behaviours – like using the remote control to buy pizza, or taking part in a programme rather than sitting back couch-potato style. To succeed, just like normal television programmes, interactive television applications need to offer viewers something they want or need in a way that keeps their attention. This chapter focuses on two key factors that help shape viewers' experience of interactive television services: the usability and the graphic design.

Usability is about whether it's easy to use a device or interface for the intended purpose. An application with great usability works well, is understandable and leaves a sense of satisfaction. This requires an appreciation of the different types of viewers that are likely to use the service, what they want, how they live their lives and what will be easy for them to understand on-screen.

Graphic and interface design, for the purpose of this chapter, is about creating meanings beyond the basic functionality by manipulating the style of the graphics. A great graphic design helps make a service emotionally engaging and aesthetically pleasing, helps signal how an application should be used, and helps boosts viewers' enjoyment. Think about the different reactions viewers would have to the same application designed in the style of a Japanese comic book, compared to the style of one of the early bank cash machines or the style of a kindergarten classroom. Each graphic design style would result in a completely different experience.

Usability and graphic design are symbiotic. An interactive television service designed purely for usability may allow viewers to perform tasks, but risks leaving them feeling disconnected, uninvolved and without a sense of allegiance. A service built only with graphic design in mind may look fantastic but be difficult and frustrating to use. The two must work together, not against each other.

How do you get the right mix? You wheedle your way inside viewers' heads – and stare right back out at the television set. This involves the application of common sense, experience, observation, technical knowledge and research. This chapter cherry-picks a little bit from each of these: first by looking at fundamental usability and design considerations for all devices, then by examining the experience of watching and using a television, and finally by suggesting a practical checklist for producing graphics that will work well on television screens.

Fundamentals of usability and design

There are some fundamental principles of usability and graphic design that apply to all devices, whether television, mobile phone or personal computer – any medium where human beings interact with a machine. These are well worth considering during interactive television production.

Users

Most successful user-interface designs have a common thread: they are built, as much as possible, with reference to users' needs and wants. For example, to help get the Palm Pilot personal organiser right, the inventor walked around for weeks with a small block of wood and a chopstick, pretending to enter information. Although the Palm Pilot wasn't the first hand-held computer, it was one of the

Table 5.1: Some overlapping examples of usability research tools and techniques	
Tool	**Explanation**
Card sorting	Can be used to help understand how viewers structure a topic or issue in their minds. Users categorise words or concepts written on cards. Results can be fed into the navigation design of a service and the requirements.
Paper prototyping	Quick and easy sketches of aspects of an application, aimed at helping clarify requirements and at highlighting issues.
Heuristic evaluation	Evaluating a service based on a specific set of principles (a technique known as expert evaluation is similar but more open-ended).
Walkthroughs	Predicting and testing the usability of a service by working through the experience of using it (asking what actions users would expect to take at various points, for example). It's very useful to watch videos of users doing walkthroughs.
Think aloud techniques	Users say what comes to mind during testing.
Journal studies	Asking users to keep journals of their daily experiences and use of a particular service.
Button hit records	Recording the number of button presses users take to perform particular tasks.
User surveys and checklists	Questions or items on particular issues or aspects of the design and navigation.
Contextual research and ethnographic research	Observing user behaviour in real-world contexts.
Eye tracking studies	Actually following how people's eyes move across the screen.
Scenario analysis	Examining how users perform different tasks in specific contexts and circumstances.

first really successful ones. It succeeded where others had failed because the inventor's research helped focus the specification and design towards the activities people actually wanted to perform – like looking up addresses and noting down phone messages.

There are tools and techniques that can be used to help observe and learn from users or to put yourself in their shoes. Some are informal and subjective; some are more formal and scientific – some are expensive to employ, others simply involve grabbing someone who happens to walk past your desk. Some common usability testing tools and techniques are described in Table 5.1 and in the case studies at the end of this chapter from Serco Usability Services and BBC Research and Development.

A production approach called user-centred design actively engages the target users in the production and design process. It involves asking questions, observing, testing and developing iteratively, building a product based on people's feedback, as well as producers' insights. The user-centred design methodology recognises that even the most visionary and brilliant producer of interactive systems will benefit from understanding that little bit more about the users he or she is trying to target.

Speed of response

There's a classic piece of user research from the late 1960s, which is still relevant today. Robert Miller looked at the effects on users of different response times with computer systems (response time being the time it takes for the desired result to happen after the user has pressed a button or key). He found that, on average, there needs to be:

- Less than about a 0.1-second response time, for users to feel that the system is reacting instantaneously and to feel that they are directly manipulating events.

- Less than about a one-second response time, for users' thought processes to remain uninterrupted. That is, the delay will be noticed but will not interfere with the feeling of working directly on the system.

- Less than about a ten-second response time, for the users to keep their attention on what is taking place. Anything longer and users are likely to do something else while they wait.

Response times are particularly relevant to interactive television, because screens often have to be downloaded or processed by the set-top box, and viewers have to wait for them to appear on-screen. Ideally, these response times should be kept to less than one second. Interactive television producers are in a position to reduce the response time of applications they are building by finding ways of reducing, among other things, the complexity of graphics and the amount of information that needs to be processed. Alternatively, content (an egg-timer graphic, for example) can be put on-screen to maintain or divert viewers' interest during the wait (see the remote control section later in this chapter) or the service can include a picture-in-picture television channel, so people can watch this.

Response times over ten seconds are particularly dangerous in a television environment, because there are so many other attractions that could draw the viewer away –

such as the pleasures of switching channel. Only the most compelling and valuable information will survive a response time greater than ten seconds.

Simplicity

Whatever the device, the simpler it is to use, the more people are likely to use it – as long as it still fulfils the core user needs. You don't have to look far for evidence of this. Video Plus sold millions, because video recorders were far too complicated to understand. The early success of the Apple Macintosh was partly due to the graphical user-interface, which was much easier to understand than command-based interfaces. The internet search engine Google has become a multi-million pound operation, by offering a fast-download front page, simple interface and effective responses to user requests. With all these examples of simplicity, users can get what they want, quickly, easily and without having to make cognitive leaps to decipher the interface.

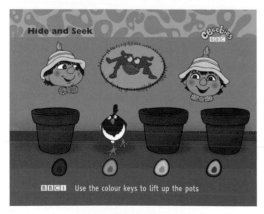

5.1 Keeping it simple. © *Fish4Homes*; © *Open TV; Courtesy of the BBC: images supplied by kind permission BBC/BBC Worldwide, Tweenies © BBC 1998 © BBC Worldwide 2003. Tweenies is a Tell Production for BBC Television. Bill and Ben logo and characters are trademarks of the British Broadcasting Corporation/Ben Productions LLC and are used under licence by BBC Worldwide Ltd. Bill and Ben logo and characters © BBC Worldwide Ltd/Ben Productions LLC 2000.*

The need for simplicity is doubly the case with interactive television. The control of television is an eminently straightforward experience already – and viewers seem to like it that way. Most people use just a few buttons on the remote – channel up and down, volume up and down, and the number keys. These always work as expected and aren't difficult to become familiar with. Similarly, television programmes tend to use on-screen graphics that are big, bold and to the point. And when voice-overs or on-screen presenters are used, they tend to speak clearly and keep the messages simple.

The challenge for interactive television is to work within this environment, where simplicity is the norm and where new ways of doing things may even be feared. A study from the United Kingdom Independent Television Commission in 2001 found that people see interactive television as more complex than computers and video recorders – even if, in reality, this is far from the case.

One good way to keep an interactive television application simple is to avoid extra features that the majority of people don't necessarily want or need. Consider what the core functionality is and make sure it is consistently presented and available throughout the application. Also, spend time thinking about how to help make that functionality as easy as possible to use. If advanced functionality for a minority of users needs to be included, it's worth finding ways of presenting it so that it doesn't get in the way of the core purpose of the application.

The medium is the message

The information in this book is presented in a certain way, to make the best use of a paper-based medium. It is broken down into chapters, there are long blocks of text that readers can digest at their own pace and there are lots of nice colour pictures. By building on the strengths of the delivery medium like this, it's possible to create an experience that is as engaging and as useful as possible.

To work well on a computer, *Interactive Television Production* would be delivered in a completely different way. The text would need to be broken into smaller chunks, to make it easier to read on a computer monitor. The illustrations would be a lower resolution, to make file transfer faster. And there could be on-demand interactivity, such as quizzes. To work well on a mobile phone, most of the content would probably need to be dropped. Reading lots of information on a small mobile-phone screen is tedious in the extreme. *Interactive Television Production* on a mobile phone might work best by concentrating on quick-access but useful interactive television production tips, perhaps sent to the phone each time the user arrives at the office in the morning.

Similarly, a service that has been designed for one medium then transferred directly to another is unlikely to be very successful. As discussed in Chapter 1, web sites that get plonked, unchanged, onto television screens are usually unmitigated disasters. They are strange and difficult to use on a television set. Most interactive television applications should be designed with the television experience in mind, not just moved across, unchanged, from other media.

Usability and design across media and platforms

Some producers work across a number of media and try to design services that make the most of the different features of each one. For example, Channel 4's *Big Brother* 2001 and 2002 used television for its video highlights programme; a channel switching enhanced television application, so viewers could monitor the goings on for most of the day and get information on demand; the web for in-depth news and games; and mobile phones for quick updates. Viewers could switch between the media, depending on what they wanted. For more on the use of multiple media channels with interactive television, see Chapter 3. There's also a case study on the production process for *Big Brother* at the end of Chapter 4.

The television experience

The television experience is very different from reading a book, sending a message on a mobile phone, or using a personal computer. Television itself necessarily affects the way interactive television services are designed. Unfortunately (or perhaps fortunately), there has not yet been a great deal of research carried out to determine the best way to design for interactive television. Current practices are often a mixture of opinion plus trial and error. The following are factors that are worth bearing in mind during design – not hard and fast rules.

Lean forward versus lean back

One distinction that is often referred to in relation to interactive television is between lean forward and lean back. Personal computers are thought to be lean-forward devices, because users sit near the screen and lean forward to actively engage in what they are doing. Television is thought to be lean back, because viewers sit back on the sofa to watch programmes – and expect everything to be delivered to them.

The premise is that people are in very different modes when leaning forward and leaning back, and that it is very difficult to persuade television viewers to sit up and lean forward to actively 'use' television. If any interactivity works at all, it will be interactivity that fits in with a very passive lean-back style.

It is the case that television is often less cognitively and physically demanding than using a personal computer or reading a newspaper. Televisions are frequently left on in the background, as just one of the many activities people are engaged in (vacuuming, reading, vigorous love-making and so on), and television is often used while viewers are in a very relaxed mode. Consequently, interactive television producers do need to recognise that it may well be more difficult to persuade television viewers to interact than it would be to persuade personal computer users. Nevertheless, the lean-forward, lean-back concept is, perhaps, an oversimplification. People already lean back and forward when watching regular television. Sports events and quiz shows, for example, are often far from lean-back experiences – with viewers shouting

5.2 Television viewing is often a group activity. *Courtesy of Telewest Broadband.*

out comments or arguing with the rest of the family. And console games on television are played actively rather than merely watched. Furthermore, United Kingdom and European viewers are familiar with switching instantly into a lean-forward information-retrieval mode when they use analogue teletext.

What this means for producers of interactive television applications is that the level of cognitive and physical activity that can be expected from viewers is likely to be dependent on the type of content on offer and the mode the viewer is in. 'Generalisation of mood experience when describing television consumption can be misleading', says Andrew Lowe, managing director of interactive television strategy company EnhanceTV. 'It is better to describe the lean-back and lean-forward postures around types of programming or activities, as opposed to a way that describes our posture for a particular content delivery mechanism.' For example, a viewer absorbed in a romantic movie is only likely to be prepared to engage in enhanced television interactivity that has a very low level of cognitive and physical effort, at least until the end of the show, and the reward on offer for interacting would probably need to be very high. Conversely, a viewer watching a quiz show may well be prepared to pick up the remote and get stuck in to the enhanced television, without needing too much persuasion at all.

Within interactive applications themselves, different types of content are also likely to be used in different ways. Viewers can reasonably be expected to proactively engage with a game, for example, but may only have a fleeting interest in a shopping or information application. Time should be spent working out how the usability and graphic design will tie in with the content and objectives of a given application.

Distance from screen

The distance between television viewers' faces and the television screen is typically 2–3.5 metres (children tend to sit the closest). This means that television screens generally take up much less area on the retina than personal computer monitors, which are viewed from less than a metre away. Activities in the rest of the room will easily distract television viewers and content on-screen will have to work harder to get attention, compared to content on a personal computer monitor. There are several tricks that can be used to sustain viewers' attention. These include:

- Using colour, sound, high-impact images and movement to attract and keep the viewers' attention – without getting in the way of the key functionality. Sound, in particular, can add tremendous impact to the interactive television experience.

- Making sure the screen is not cluttered. There should be one area of focus and/or a clear order for the viewers' eyes to follow. The number of elements on-screen should be kept to a minimum. Some producers try to have less than seven different elements on-screen at any time.

- Fonts and graphics should be clear and large. See the design checklist, later in this chapter.

- Written material should be broken up into small and easily digestible chunks, with plenty of spacing between lines of text.

5.3 Text is easier to read from a distance if it is broken up into small chunks. © *ITN*.

Remote control

Remotes control television; hence, interactive television applications need to be designed with the remote control in mind, not a mouse or joystick.

Navigation

Many television viewers will not have any understanding of the remote control beyond what the channel up and down and the number buttons generally do. It is

5.4

5.5

illuminating (and to be recommended) to watch the subjects of user tests struggling with even the simplest interactive applications – unable, for example, to make the connection between arrow keys on the remote control and the movement of a selector box on-screen.

To work well, interactive television navigation should pass the 'intra-ocular trauma test' – that is, it needs to be so obvious that it hits viewers right between the eyes. There are a number of ways of ensuring this happens:

- If there is an on-screen selector that viewers need to move around, it should be very prominent – perhaps it changes the colour and size of the selected element compared with the rest of the screen.

- Short text instructions can be put on the screen, explaining what the viewers need to do. (Don't expect viewers to navigate to a help section to find out this kind of information. They may not know how to select help unless that too is explained on-screen. And most people never make the effort to read help sections anyway – even if they need to.)

- Important parts of the on-screen navigation design should be logically positioned (in terms of the likely movement of the viewers' eyes across the page). For example, many applications use on-screen arrows to help viewers understand that they need to press an arrow key on the remote to get more information on-screen. If the arrows are not positioned near the part of the screen the viewer will be looking at, just before they need to press the arrow key, they are less likely to make the cognitive link between the on-screen arrow and the fact that it will help them get more information.

5.6 A purple on-screen selector. *Courtesy of Carlton Active.*

5.7 A yellow box selector. © *NTL.*

- Abstract icons should be avoided. For example, viewers may not be able to interpret that a hand with a pointing finger means they should press an arrow on the remote for more information. It will help viewers make the connection between the screen and the remote control if on-screen icons mimic the designs and buttons used on the remote.

- Navigation using number keys can work well. Viewers press a number to go to a particular option. The model is familiar to people from television channel changing and analogue teletext. Ideally, the numbers on-screen should look very similar to the number buttons on the remote control, so that viewers can immediately make the connection between the two.

- Minimise the number of key presses required. Using a remote control for selection can be a reasonably strenuous activity (relative to using a mouse for pointing and clicking). 'Instead of being a single action, pointing turns into a sequence of actions that have to be planned and monitored with a much larger degree of cognitive load than when using a mouse,' said Jakob Nielsen in one of the first studies of WebTV usability (in 1997).

- Anticipate the viewer's next selection when they are navigating between pages and pre-set the selector box or highlighter in that position for them.

- The range of finger movement required between different keys on the remote control should be limited, as should the number of keys in use. The more remote control keys that viewers are required to use, the more they will have to look away from the screen to check the remote and the more effort it will take. 'We try to minimise the number of different keys used in navigation and stick to arrows and the select button,' says Matthew Stratfold, manager of enhanced television at digital cable operator NTL. 'In an ideal world, I'd even like to stop using the coloured keys as well, as the viewers have to keep looking back at the remote to use these, which can be time-consuming and annoying.'

- Remote controls can make it difficult for viewers to operate scrolling pages. Some viewers may also find this computer-based concept confusing. Pages that appear in series, one after the other, are likely to be more familiar to viewers, as this is the style of graphic presentation used in television programmes.

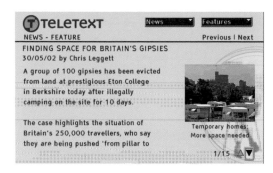

5.8 The first paragraph of the news story on one screen. © *Teletext Ltd.*

5.9 The second paragraph of the news story on the second screen The whole page is updated for each section and there is no scrolling. © *Teletext Ltd.*

- Avoid personal computer or internet navigation devices, like drop-down menus, which viewers may not have encountered before and therefore will take more time to understand.

- Avoid having too many planes of navigation (for example, just up/down navigation options are likely to be easier to understand than on-screen options that require movement of the selector up/down, left/right and the pressing of various coloured fast-text keys on the remote).

Text input

Inputting text is tedious with a remote control. Although some platforms provide keyboards, these usually get to just a small percentage of customers – and, even if every viewer has one, there's no reason to assume they will want to use them. Would you enjoy juggling with a full size keyboard and your TV dinner?

Text input using a remote control, rather than a keyboard, is possible using letters etched onto the remote next to the number keys, in the style of a mobile phone, or using mini-keyboards that appear on-screen, in the style of arcade machines. Both are time-consuming and annoying. An interactive television application that requires lots of text input (a full name and address, for example) may find that the only people to use it are teenagers, who, from constant phone texting, seem to have the muscular thumbs suitable for marathon text sessions. If you absolutely have to get someone's address, it's best to ask only for the postcode, then look up the full address on a database. Then, even better, get the system to remember the full address for the next time the viewer uses the service.

Feedback

Remote controls are used at some distance from the television. Therefore, it's helpful if there is some confirmation that instructions from the viewer are being received and understood. Ideally, there should be some kind of on-screen or other feedback (such as a click sound) within 0.1 seconds of buttons being pressed on the remote control, even if the main response to the key press is going to take a little longer. For example, if the viewer presses OK to select something on-screen and the next screen is going to take a second or two to appear, it's worth considering making the selector box flash once in response to the OK press. This should help the viewer understand that the selection has been registered – rather than risk them pressing the button again during the delay.

If there is likely to be a significant delay in the response following a viewer action (anything much more than one second), this should certainly be signalled back to the viewer, for example, by putting a message on-screen that says, 'Retrieving information now . . . please wait.' If there is absolutely no way of getting the delay below ten seconds, then it's worth considering putting something on-screen that will both distract and give an indication of the time left – perhaps an animated clock, a percentage figure counting up or designing the service so a television channel's video and audio are constantly available to provide some level of entertainment during waiting periods.

5.10 Viewers can press the red button if they get lost on the service. © *NTL.*

It is sometimes tempting to implement a repeat function on remote control keys. With this, an action will be performed many times if a key is held down. This can help viewers perform some tasks faster. However, repeat keys can be risky with interactive television, since some viewers will not be familiar with the idea that holding keys down means the function will be repeated. If it is used, the repeat should take a little while to kick in and should repeat slowly. A fast repeat function combined with lack of on-screen signals for delayed responses can be a deadly combination – since viewers will hold keys down if it doesn't look as if they are working. If key presses are still being registered while screens are updating, this could cause all sorts of mayhem.

Finally, when creating a navigation design, it's worth considering providing an escape route if viewers get lost, bored or press the wrong button. This should be a button or option that will quickly take them back to somewhere they know – such as the main menu. A back button on the remote control can work well for this – but it needs to be implemented consistently across the platform, so that viewers learn that they can always press it repeatedly to back-track through what they've been doing.

Navigational consistency across applications

In an ideal world, all interactive applications would use the same navigation model. Viewers would then not have to go through a learning process every time they use a new interactive television service. Part of the success of analogue teletext is due to the fact that services all work in the same way – using a page number look-up system and hierarchical menus.

Unfortunately, in the United Kingdom, although several industry bodies have tried, there's very little agreement on what a consistent navigation model for interactive television should be. Each producer seems to think that his or her model is best. And interactive television applications are so varied, it's difficult to come up with workable generic rules.

One practical tip: design your interactive television applications to mimic the navigation system used by the platform operator on the electronic programme guide. Viewers are likely to be familiar with this.

Viewer expectations

Television viewers have certain expectations about what a television is used for and how things should work on it. The Henley Centre, Planning for Consumer Change study (2000), looked at how consumers view different devices. The research showed that television is viewed primarily as a source of entertainment and information, while the internet is viewed more as a tool for communication. This is perhaps partly due to television's history of being used in the living room, for relaxation and family activities, and the internet's history of being used at the office and for email. It's probably easier then for interactive television services to be designed to build on these existing expectations than fight against them. And there's some evidence of this being the case: games are one of the most popular applications on United Kingdom interactive television platforms, while email hasn't taken off. Similarly, some standalone interactive shopping services are struggling – perhaps because the weekly shopping task is not associated with television at all.

Furthermore, as discussed in Chapter 3, new interactive services may be easier for viewers to understand and use, and therefore be more popular, if there is a frame of reference from the viewers' previous experience with television. Digital text services in the United Kingdom and Europe have the advantage of building upon existing viewer expectations of analogue teletext. Video-on-demand and personal video recorders have the advantage of building on video cassette expectations. Interactive shopping services linked to television channels, like QVC (as opposed to

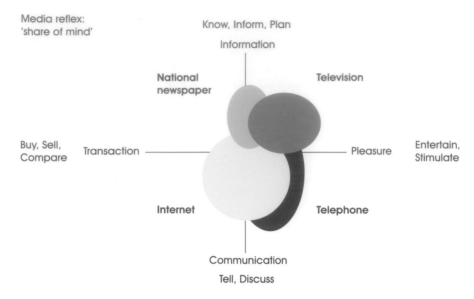

5.11 Share of mind for different media. *Source: Planning for Consumer Change, The Henley Centre (2000).*

standalone shopping services that are not linked to television channels), have the advantage of tying in with an existing activity – that of watching a channel for information then buying products that look interesting.

This is not to say that out and out revolution isn't possible with television, but when thinking about the usability and graphic design of an application, it is worth considering whether evolution is the easier route to take – by thinking about what viewers already know, then building on that.

5.12 This application builds on the existing television experience. © *NTL.*

Viewer demographics

Television is used by a huge percentage of the population – many more people than use computers or mobile phones. This means the potential market for interactive television includes a wide variety of different people. To avoid excluding potential viewers, the design of most interactive television applications should take into account the variety of needs and abilities of an audience that could include senior citizens, children, the visually impaired, and so on.

One way of doing this is to offer viewers a choice at the beginning – for example, 'If you want the easy-access service, press 1, if you want advanced functions, press 2.' It also helps to choose interface styles that most people can relate to and use writing styles that everyone can understand. There's not much point putting a message on-screen that says 'Error #4309303 HTTP', if you want to appeal to a broad market.

Even so, it is always worth bearing in mind that however useful interactive television becomes, some viewer groups may never be persuaded to use it at all. Also, applications aimed at particular niche audiences may not need to care too much about using language, designs or navigation models that exclude those outside their target group. They can be designed with that audience in mind. A pop music service, for example, is likely to want to use design styles that appeal to teenagers and will not worry too much about alienating those over the age of 40.

There's one view on the different ways interactive television viewers can be categorised in the case study from Netpoll at the end of this chapter.

The social context

According to Statistical Research Inc (2000), 60 per cent of living room television viewing happens in a group. And it's the living room where most televisions with digital interactive services are located (the older analogue sets, without interactivity, tend to get relegated to bedrooms and studies). Therefore, interactive television applications intended for use during group-viewing times should take this into account.

One way of building interactive applications that work in a social context is to make sure viewers can get what they need quickly and easily – during advertising breaks, between programmes and during boring bits. The Henley Centre (in 2001) found that 25 per cent of the users of Sky's interactive service went there during television advertising. Enabling quick access means that the interactivity is less likely to annoy the rest of the people watching.

5.13 Semi-transparent graphics overlaid onto video pictures are less likely to get in the way of the programme itself. *Courtesy Two Way TV.*

Another route is to make the interactivity work in such a way that it doesn't interfere with the video programming. This is the main thrust of enhanced television. The less the interactivity gets in the way of the enjoyment of others in the room the better. This can be done by:

- Overlaying information on the video channel using semi-transparent graphics, rather than solid graphics.

- Using inserts, rather than taking up the whole screen. For example, if an enhanced television application has a function to allow viewers to select a camera that follows a particular sportsperson, this may be better done as a video insert into the main picture rather than taking up the whole screen, so other viewers don't risk missing the main action.

- Always keeping a television channel on-screen, even when the viewer is using unrelated interactive content (this is usually achieved by running the TV channel in a picture-in-picture window).

- Providing multiple remote controls and designing the application so lots of people can use it at once. Two Way TV and Sky Digital sell multiple remote controls, so the whole family can play along with enhanced television games.

5.14 This service can be used while watching television in a picture-in-picture window. © *BSkyB.*

In this same vein, there are some interesting possibilities around providing inter-active functionality to accompany the radio stations and audio streams that are available on digital television platforms (these are designed to be played via the television or using a stereo connected to the set-top box). Viewers tend to use these as background noise while they do something else, and the television inter-activity can be designed to complement this fact. Music Choice in the UK already provides an interactive application that allows easy switching between its audio streams. Several UK radio stations are also looking at how interactive content can be used to support their output on digital television.

Time of day

Television tends to be watched by more people in the evening. Therefore, unless specifically pitched at the kind of people that use television during the day, inter-active applications will tend to get more usage in the evenings too. This means that it's worth thinking about providing the best standard of interactive television service (for example, more updates and the biggest customer service team) during the evenings, at peak television viewing times – not during office hours.

Furthermore, in the morning and afternoon, television is more likely to be on while viewers are doing other things. To get round this, television programme makers will often try to structure programmes in such a way that dipping in and out is easy and enjoyable. Niche television channels use the same tricks – they are happy if they get a few minutes of people's viewing time per week. Next time you see a specialist news channel, watch how often graphics come up explaining who is speaking – even if the person had been identified two minutes before. This is done because it's difficult to know when viewers have switched on or started paying attention. You may also notice that morning magazine-style programmes often have much snappier items than the evening magazine-style programmes, and morning and daytime soaps have stories that are easy to pick up without viewers having to have watched the rest of the programme or series.

Interactive television applications can benefit from the same approach. To get viewers to use the service in the mornings and daytime, it can be worth thinking about the kind of interactive content that will provide satisfaction quickly. For example, an interactive television games service could consider running shorter games or ones that can be dipped in and out of during the day. An interactive television news service could promote quick updates and weather in the mornings – and promote more in-depth material at night. It may even be worth changing designs to reflect the different states of mind of people in the morning and the evening – in the same way that late morning television chat shows are often very different in design to evening ones.

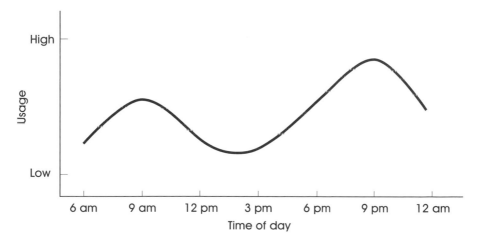

5.15 ITN News Channel iTV service usage figures across the day.

Design checklist

As well as considering the television experience, the graphics themselves for interactive television services need to be adjusted to work on the television set – otherwise they can look really bad.

Set-top boxes and middleware systems make some adjustments to graphics and text. Unfortunately, these automatic processes can't deal with every kind of problem, so it's better to get screens looking right before they are sent to the set-top box for processing (doing this will help the application run faster too). Also, some viewers connect their televisions to the set-top box using poor-quality RF connections, rather than the better-quality connections like SCART and S-Video. This can exacerbate problems with interactive television graphics.

The following is a checklist for producing graphics that will work well on television screens.

Design for the television screen, not the computer monitor

Canvas

So, you're sitting down in front of Photoshop ready to design your interactive television application. What size should your design be? It depends. A regular television screen has a 4:3 aspect ratio. The picture is built up with horizontal lines scanning across the screen – 625 lines with the United Kingdom and European PAL television system and 525 lines with the American NTSC-M system. Some lines are used for carrying signal synchronisation and other information, rather than picture information – see Chapter 2. Interactive television services are left with an available screen size of around 720 × 576 pixels for PAL and 640 × 480 pixels for NTSC-M televisions. This is approximate, because different set-top boxes sometimes use different screen sizes.

Safe area

Unfortunately, every television model is built slightly differently and some show more of the available picture area than others. Therefore, any important information needs to be shown away from the edges of the screen, to avoid disappearing com-

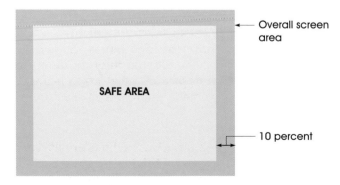

5.16 The television safe area, 20 per cent smaller than the active picture area.

pletely on some televisions – in part of the picture known as the safe area. A background image can take up the whole screen, but any text or important graphics should be within the safe area. There's some debate about what this safe area is, but most broadcasters advise keeping important information within an area around 20 per cent smaller than the full screen – that's 10 per cent off each edge – although it might be possible to get away with a bit less if you don't mind cutting off the edges of your graphics and text on some televisions.

Some middleware systems and platforms will set a specific screen size and force information into this area. Designs that are too big will be squeezed into this. They do this to make sure information is inside their view of what the safe area should be. Some platform operators also include their own navigation or other elements within the screen area, which will restrict the available space still further. Check with the platform operator for the exact available screen dimensions and the recommended safe area.

Pixel shape

If the interactive television design is being carried out on a personal computer monitor, bear in mind that personal computer monitors have square pixels, while televisions have pixels that are slightly rectangular. This means that shapes designed on a personal computer monitor will look a little wider when finally displayed on television – a circle will become an oval. To get round this, graphic work in progress should be viewed on a television screen not a personal computer monitor. Or, failing that, the graphics should be squeezed a little on the horizontal axis before being sent to a set-top box (UK cable operator NTL recommends, for their platform, re-sizing to 94 per cent of the original width, after designs are finished on a personal computer monitor).

Additionally, it's worth taking into account the fact that interactive television applications designed for 4:3 may be stretched further if they are viewed on widescreen (16:9) televisions – making the fonts and graphics appear fatter than they would on a 4:3 television. To get round this, some interactive television producers design their graphics and fonts in such a way that they look okay both on 4:3 and 16:9 – a compromise position.

Avoid detail

The available television screen size in pixels doesn't give a wholly accurate portrayal of the screen resolution. This is because television pictures are built using two interlaced fields (see Chapter 2). The effect this has is that images on television appear softer than they would on a personal computer monitor, because only half of the image is being updated with each pass of the electron beam. There's no point using images with fine details then, as these will blur and television viewers won't be able to see them properly.

Interlacing also means that any very thin horizontal lines are likely to flicker, as they will only be updated with every other pass. Middleware systems and televisions will often have some kind of filter to minimise this effect, although it's still worth avoiding anyway.

Finally, some detailed designs can cause unwanted movement and shifts on-screen known as moiré patterns (one version of this is the effect seen on-screen when someone is wearing a checked shirt). To avoid this, don't use patterns made up of lots of thin lines of light and dark next to each other.

Avoid highly saturated and very bright colours

Saturation

Colours that are highly saturated (very rich and intense) don't work well next to each other on television. The television set can't always keep up with the transition between the two, and blurring or crawling occurs at the edges. There isn't usually a problem in the middle of areas of colour, just at the edges.

5.17 Very highly saturated colours can bleed into each other.

The saturation level of graphics and text should ideally be dropped to less than 80 per cent. Red and yellow tend to be the worst offenders. Pastel colours work well on television, as do blues.

Brightness

Very bright (high in luminance) colours don't look great on television – particularly if used as backgrounds. Pure white is the worst offender. This is because pure white is made by turning up the red, green and blue cathode rays to full blast. The intensity

Television colour terminology

Colour on television is a complicated area, touching on biology, psychology, technology and aesthetics. Here's a ten-second summary of the terminology:

Hue: the colour itself, expressed as the proportion of red, green and blue.

Saturation: the intensity and richness of the colour. The more a colour is diluted with white, the less saturated it becomes (pink is a de-saturated red).

Luminance: the brightness of the image; the brighter the image, the more intense the electron beams will be.

Chrominance: a combination of hue and saturation.

Computer monitor   Television screen

5.18 Very bright colours can cause bloom.

of electrons upsets the electrical balance of the screen and makes the beams go wide of the intended targets – creating wavy effects or curving, known as bloom, around the sides of the screen or around the edges of bright text or graphics. To deal with this cut down brightness levels below 90 per cent.

There can also be problems when there are different colours next to each other with very similar brightness levels. As with the bleeding caused by transitions between highly saturated colours, televisions have trouble keeping up with rapid changes between different colours with similar brightness levels. The end result is blurring between the two. The best way around this is to make sure colours next to each other have different brightness levels.

Note that the NTSC-M system displays colours brighter than PAL, as well as having a different screen size. Interactive graphics will need to be designed especially for each system.

Colour-check tools

Most middleware companies supply PC-based tools for checking combinations of colours for problems with saturation or brightness. These can be really useful, although they should ideally be used in combination with checking the work on a television set (preferably a mid-range television that is reasonably representative of what the viewing public have at home). Checking work on lots of different television sets is an even better idea.

Choose fonts for television

Most broadcasters use font sizes on graphics that are no less than one fifteenth of the screen size. The relative sizes of fonts depend on the middleware and font processing in the set-top box, but as a rule of thumb it's rarely worth using font sizes less than 22 points – and bigger is better. Get a small portable television and see if you can comfortably read the text from three metres away. If you can't – make the font bigger. Moreover:

- Sanserif fonts tend to look better on television than serif fonts. Serif and delicate fonts can break up around the edges.
- Anti-alias fonts as much as possible. Anti-aliasing adds transitional colours between high-contrast colours (like text and its background). This has the

effect of smoothing out the edges of fonts, reducing boundary blur and making the font easier to read. Regular television caption generators traditionally have an incredible number of levels of anti-aliasing.

- Drop shadow (a slightly offset shadow of each character just underneath it) helps pull the text away from the background, reducing blur at the edges and making text easier to read.

- Upper and lower case words are better than all upper case, as the shapes of the letters and words are easier to identify.

- One of the easiest to read colour combinations for text on television is white on blue – as opposed to the black on white or grey that works well on personal computer monitors.

Unfortunately, there may not always be much flexibility with font choices. Some set-top boxes support just one or two different fonts and these are available in a limited range of sizes. Furthermore, most set-top boxes don't have the processing power to do much anti-aliasing on fonts, so they can look a little ragged compared to graphics used in television programmes.

A common font used by United Kingdom middleware systems and set-top boxes is Tiresias. The Royal National Institute for the Blind designed the font to be as easy as possible to read by partially sighted people – and perhaps because of that, it works very well for people with normal vision too.

Next: the future.

Case study: The usability of electronic programme guides

Owen Daly-Jones, manager, Serco Usability Services. Serco Usability Services is the largest independent usability consultancy in the UK.

This case study is based on extensive research that Serco Usability Services has conducted into interactive television services. As advocates of user-centred design, we have learnt many fascinating lessons about how people use interactive television applications such as electronic programme guides (EPGs). In fact, EPGs are particularly worthy of scrutiny from the usability point of view, as their quality may contribute to the overall success of interactive television platforms. Yet little is known about the best way to design these services and there are no established guidelines.

During our research, we have explored user reactions to a range of EPGs to identify the main usability issues and offer relevant insights. We have looked at EPGs available on satellite, cable and terrestrial platforms. Some of our studies have been comparative in nature – users have been asked to carry out the same tasks using rival services. Participants in our research have also been drawn from a wide range of backgrounds. Ages have ranged from 18 to 66, and we take care to talk to users with a spread of technical experience.

The research itself has been conducted in both labs and actual homes. The usability labs recreate a living room environment to support our research. In all cases we have been interested in understanding the users' natural strategies, as well as seeing how they get on when asked to carry out simple tasks using an EPG. Our approach to conducting this kind of research draws on ethnographic techniques and we also encourage participants to think aloud while using services.

5.19 One of the Serco Usability Services user-testing labs. © *Serco Usability Services.*

Keeping things simple

The EPGs available in the United Kingdom market make use of quite different design approaches. Here's what we found worked well with users:

- Navigation by numbers and coloured fast-text buttons works particularly well, probably because existing experience with television remote controls revolves around this kind of control and input.
- Tabbed pages. The key advantage is that the user is not overloaded with too much information on-screen.
- Transparent windows. These support social viewing and allow programmes to be monitored in the background.
- Fairly minimal 'now and next' information. By addressing the needs of most users, most of the time, this represents a classic case of less providing more.

Offering clear signposts

During our research, with new and experienced users, we have often seen people navigate to where they didn't want to go. In part, this is attributable to poor remote control design – people press the wrong buttons. However, another cause is the click-through feature, which allows a user to be taken to a television programme from an EPG listing. One of the biggest problems was that users clicked directly through when they expected to see programme details first. Clear instructions to help users get back into a service will also be essential. In the absence of such cues, some users were unable to return to their original EPG.

In fact, they often navigated to the EPG of a rival. This is frustrating and bad news if a commercial service provider wants to keep people to view promotions.

Another issue is that users do not tend to associate EPG services with specific channels because of their experience with analogue television. In the analogue context, they switch between text and television modes. Where possible, service providers should offer a prominent means of accessing and leaving an EPG via a dedicated *Text* or *Guide* button.

Helping people find what they want

EPGs present programme listings in different ways. The Sky approach, for example, is comprehensive and organises programmes into genres, such as movies, news and comedy, which users react positively to. But care needs to be taken not to overwhelm by displaying too much on-screen. For example, participants in our studies have found Sky's 'all channels' listing confusing. This is mainly due to poor alignment and layout of the information, truncated titles, and confusing channel ordering. Determining what is on should not be a complex visual search task. Present a subset of channels clearly, rather than have all channels displayed in a complicated way.

Users' information requirements depend on the programme type. For example, users want more information on movies, or the guests for a chat show. Programmes with changing content need explanation, whereas a news broadcast or a regularly scheduled series does not. Some users also want added value content, such as reviews, alongside the facts.

In some cases, users were unable to find programme details, due to inconsistent selection metaphors. If *Select* is used across most of a service, then users may not expect to press a separate *Info* button on the remote. If they must do this, then on-screen cues should draw their attention to the fact. Also note that some users did not like seeing the term 'loading' when accessing information, and suggested alternatives like 'please wait'. Interactive television users cannot be assumed to have an internet vocabulary.

Allowing users to consult television listings while watching a programme in the background is a good idea. Pop-up transparent windows support this and are particularly useful for listings that show current and subsequent programmes.

Linking the remote to the on-screen design

One of the key things about interactive television is that it is a three-way interaction, between the user, the remote and the on-screen interface. Far from being a peripheral, the remote mediates the interaction and plays a crucial part in the quality of the whole experience. Yet many remotes exhibit poor ergonomic qualities, and as a result of the poor design users make frequent selection mistakes. In the worst cases we see people operating the remote with two hands, when a television remote control should be a one-handed input device. After all, if both hands are occupied you can't hold on to a drink while sitting in front of the television!

Users are also fixated on the screen; they often only look at the remote when there are no on-screen prompts and they are having difficulties. Despite this, some functions might not be visible on-screen, they are accessed from the remote. Yet users in our studies, some of them experienced with the platform, have problems moving back up through the information, as they are unaware of or keep forgetting about the backup button on the remote. The logical implication of this is that all important options and functions should have some representation on-screen. Remember it is television, a powerful medium that draws in the user's attention. It is not surprising that users look to the television rather than the remote for cues on how to interact with an EPG.

When users do consider the remote, they often expect a direct correspondence with on-screen elements. They look for buttons that have the same symbols, colours and terms as those on-screen. So in the absence of any clear on-screen cues, they may press the yellow fast-text button (with sometimes unpredictable results) to 'get at' an item in yellow. Symbols, colours and labels should therefore be used carefully on the screen, and match elements of the remote only where a direct correspondence is intended.

Conclusion

For EPGs to be positioned as a primary interactive service, they need to be easy to get into, use and return to. Our own research shows that users have difficulties navigating early United Kingdom services. In some cases the interaction model is significantly more complex than listings magazines or other paper-based alternatives.

The presentation of programme information, in terms of the design and layout, may also handicap users' ability to find programmes. Further research into people's natural planning strategies is needed to inform successful designs. How do people currently plan their viewing? How far in advance do they plan? How much information do they need? How do they compare options? What would people really like to do most of the time?

We would suggest that one of the best places to start would be to take a long hard look at how people use paper-based television listings. This would help increase the chances of getting it right based on what most people currently do. Ultimately, creating EPGs that add real value and are easy to navigate requires direct end-user involvement during their design and evaluation.

Case study: User research for interactive television

Dr Guy Winter, senior behavioural scientist, BBC Research and Development. BBC R&D is the BBC's centre for media production and broadcasting technology innovation.

User-centred design (UCD) is important to work at BBC Research and Development (R&D). Fundamentally, BBC R&D is trying to identify and anticipate future audience needs, goals or outcomes, and develop the technology to achieve this. This case study outlines some of our approach.

Our work covers a wide range of projects. For example, European Community Collaborative projects such as STORit, myTV and Share It! were focused on developing standards and services for hard-disk video recorders and have contributed to the TV Anytime Forum. New interactive television programme formats have also been explored, particularly the means of finding and accessing these through electronic programme guides, intelligent agents and other technologies (like mobile phones and personal organisers).

The UCD, or human factors, input aids the defining of the requirements, the description of the users and their goals, the iterative development and testing, and the design of the user-interface itself.

Gathering user requirements

The first effort of the user-centred designer is to gather and shape the user requirements. Within R&D (and engineering more generally), this defines the scope of the development and thus the system requirements. Adopting a UCD perspective leads to quite a radical shift in focus. The emphasis is upon what the user wants and how they wish to behave, and using this to define what a system must achieve. For example, if the users want immediate access to high-quality news clips on their personal computer, then the engineers will strive to develop the technology to enable high-bandwidth, real-time video over a suitable network.

The user requirements usually consist of a number of key components. The first is to define the context of use, that is, the environment into which your technology will be placed and used, and the place within which it will have an effect. In development for domestic technologies such as set-top boxes, personal video recorders, interactive television and so on, a variety of sources of information are used to understand this. Of interest are facts such as the number of people using a technology in a household, to determine whether it is shared or private/individual; what technologies are already in the home; where these technologies are located and so on. It is also important to retain the more usual measures of demographics, such as social and geographical distinctions.

Perhaps most important is an understanding of your potential users' attitudes and behaviours. Models of psychology emphasise the weak relationship between attitude, intention and finally behaviour; thus, it is important to realise that a user may look like an ideal user, they may even sound like an ideal user in interviews, but they still may not use the technology. Research into how media is consumed and how this fits into typical and ordinary lifestyles is vital. From this, it is possible to develop a realistic understanding of how a user in a given context of use might actually use your technology or service. This research relies heavily upon existing knowledge. In addition to this, the results from numerous detailed user tests are extremely important. User testing usually finds faults specific to a particular service, but this broader aim should always be kept in mind.

Early prototyping and testing with users

Once user requirements have been developed, every attempt is made to start early prototyping, and encourage as much user involvement and input as can be achieved. Traditionally, users are involved once the bulk of a system is in place, and experience shows that this is often too late. Users can shape the user requirements more effectively if brought into the process early. This is achieved in a number of ways.

Indirect techniques begin with the development of realistic and important scenarios. A scenario describes a detailed situation and the sequence of events that a user will experience. They can also be used for highlighting alternative ways of achieving the same thing, and this is a useful tool for testing. Two alternative scenarios can be given to users for comment and evaluation to great effect at little cost. Users can also influence the approach to a project through the development of personas. A persona is a stereotypical description of a realistic member of the target user group. The user-centred designer should organise the development of personas and promote their use in all discussions of system design. With time, the persona becomes a means of designing with the intended users in mind at all times, and it is an effective and simple technique.

Early input to refine user requirements can be very enlightening. Techniques such as card sorting are very useful for gathering an understanding of naturally occurring classifications, and the relative importance and sequencing of information. The process is used in many ways, but the principle is simple. Users can either label cards then group them into meaningful clusters, or pre-labelled cards can be grouped. Furthermore, if the cards are labelled with tasks, it can be useful for sequencing user tasks. When done appropriately, this can help design the interaction and information architecture of a system. Web pages, user-interface screens and interactive television menus benefit from determining what items might appear on a screen together (or not), how they are labelled (the terminology), and what tasks should appear where and when.

Scenarios can be tested very quickly and cheaply; and in a similar manner, paper mock-ups of screen designs, structures of information flow, icons, terminology, metaphors and so on can all be exposed to the intended users to generate feedback. The common reliance on full working, interactive prototypes can be mitigated to a large extent by the use of paper prototypes. This is desirable, as working prototypes require considerable coding effort. In practice then, paper prototypes are heavily used to try and ensure that the development of a working prototype will be as successful as possible.

Direct methods of user involvement complement and inform the indirect methods. Primarily, user research that can inform the user requirements should be carried out. Ethnographic, questionnaire, interview and observational techniques are all useful. They are also often expensive, so reuse of research should always be a factor in designing or commissioning this work. A useful means of determining how people might use your system is to user test systems they commonly use, or services that are similar or have close properties to your intended product.

User testing

User testing is important and should be done often in order to create an iterative development process. Methods for testing prototypes vary according to the quality of the testing material, information needs, resources and, of course, deadlines. For initial prototypes, the testing is usually informal and could be described as 'quick and dirty'. At the BBC, potential users are identified from within our organisation (for workflow systems), or may be accessible through a user pool of willing participants, or via an agency. These users are asked to comment informally on what they are shown. Often, a semi-structured interview technique is used to ensure that the resulting feedback is not tainted by variations in approach and questioning, and to minimise the effects of response bias, experimenter and other effects.

In more formal user tests, where the system complexity has increased, user testing is moved to a user-testing laboratory, where greater experimental control can be exercised. The emphasis is upon detailed understanding of what people do with a system, and where errors due to low-level features such as usability can be identified. This is usually exploratory or task-led in outline, the former concentrating on finding out what users do with a system, the latter focusing on tasks we know to be crucial or problematic. Most commonly, a concurrent 'think aloud' protocol is used, where users are encouraged to verbalise their decisions, actions, impressions, attitudes and so on, as they use the system. Task-led tests are often combined with a form of semi-structured interview in order to focus the user on specific aspects of usability, terminology, design and system structure. Finally, a variety of questionnaires and follow-up interviews are used to gather more data and allow the user the opportunity to comment on things we may have missed or failed to attend to. Ultimately, the goal of user testing is to refine the design, and not add a stamp of approval onto a nearly finished project. It is all too easy for user testing to be used for the latter, and the user-centred designer must reinforce this message.

The role of UCD at the BBC

Within an engineering-dominated environment such as BBC R&D, the user-centred designer, or human factors expert, has an important and wide role to play. They must offer expert advice, yet maintain an open mind on what the user would really want. They must be skilled in drawing information from users, with whatever prototypes they can, and they must be able to rationalise and communicate the findings to the rest of the team. Fundamentally, they must adopt the role of evangelist, acting to discover, involve and act as the proxy for users to allow them to have a say in what is developed.

Within the BBC, this role has grown beyond R&D, and the key skills are now being applied more widely. The knowledge and skills gained at R&D have contributed to the early development of more high-profile services, such as Ceefax, BBCi, What's On, i-Bar and other specific projects and interactive television applications. UCD has grown from its modest origins to become an important design driver, helping to develop standards as well as services through the establishment of specific skilled teams. UCD is fast becoming an established *modus operandi* for the BBC.

© British Broadcasting Corporation 2002

Case study: *Hands on TV* – interactive television consumer research

Andy Mayer, former senior strategist, Netpoll. Netpoll is a leading specialist in user attitudes to digital communication platforms. Near the end of 2002 Andy Mayer became business analyst at the NOP Research Group.

Interactive television consumers are television consumers first and interactive second. It is important to get the interactive portion of any interactive television project right; we know, for example, that interactivity increases consumer engagement with the broadcast stream and in consequence has implications for retention and positioning strategy. But it is not yet an end goal in itself. Examples of standalone interactive services that are both compelling and profitable are rare and rely heavily on good television-based marketing support – Domino's Pizza, for example.

But what's the right mix of interactivity and television? Netpoll is one of Europe's leading specialists in user attitudes to interactive media. Our survey work, which resulted in a report called *Hands on TV*, has enabled us to identify a few of the different types of people who use interactive television and how to create an offering for each. This case study outlines some of our findings.

Who are the interactive television consumers?

The life cycle of new technology goes through several phases:

- Early Adopters.
- Early Majority.
- Late Majority.
- Mass Market.

Within the phases, consumer segments tend to have distinct characteristics that help us understand not simply their demographic positioning, but also their attitudes, behaviours and likely responses to new products and services. The United Kingdom interactive television market moved into what could be described as the end of the early majority by mid-2002. *Hands on TV* concentrated around real responses from the first two phases. For this piece, we've also included some insight into returns from some of our broadband research, as an implication to the characteristics of the late majority adopters who will make up the next phase.

Early Adopters

- Generation 'i' – socially active teenagers.
- Armchair Athletes – tribal sports fans.
- Gadget Guy – earliest of the early adopters.

Generation 'i'

> 'I just use it for watching MTV, E4 and Sky One – things like *Big Brother.*'
>
> *female, family, Sky, Nottingham*

Generation 'i' is teenaged, socially active and very switched on to all things 'cool'. Technically confident, they derive the maximum benefit from all of the social and communication platforms available to them. They know what they want to watch and when. Frequently, they are the most confident user of interactive television in the household. As a result, they frequently become the household interactive champion; their behaviour patterns are likely to influence others.

One of the more interesting interactive functions driven by this group is cross-channel SMS voting, particularly true of the music channels (MTV *Battle of the Bands*) and in conjunction with reality shows (*Big Brother*). SMS is already a successful model for taking invisible micro-payments on premium content or services. As a social communications medium, it fits particularly well with the preferred communications behaviour of the teen market and allows them to engage more deeply with social programming (programming that becomes the social currency of our conversations, media and lifestyles). Interactive television voting and quizzes also work well with this group; however, it is questionably a weaker method of raising revenue than SMS. Like micro-payments on the internet, users are reluctant to pay for impulse services if they can feel it happening. SMS works well as a payment mechanism because you don't experience the pain until the monthly bill arrives or you have to recharge the repayment card. Interactive television companies are consequently experimenting with payment schemes that mimic this important psychological factor.

Armchair Athletes

> 'I got Sky for the football, simple as that. I use the interactive for the sports, the girls use it more as a normal television really.'
>
> *male, family, Sky Digital, Preston*

Sport has been a significant driver in the adoption of interactive television services. Almost exclusively male, the Armchair Athlete is an out-and-out sports fan. Passionate about his favourite sports and teams, the range of channels used is relatively limited and interactive services are used only if he can see a direct benefit or enhancement to the entertainment experience around the broadcast

5.20 Armchair Athlete.

stream. Gadgets like Playercam can be perceived as a marketing ploy to entice Armchair Athletes. Armchair Athletes like to be in control and ready access to choice and statistics provides the impression of greater ownership than the best non-interactive alternative. In isolation, these features run the risk of doing little other than make a good viewing experience average. Football viewers generally expect that trained camera operators will know where the action is and Playercam is generally used just a few times and then forgotten. In tennis, on the other hand, court selection is a genuinely value added feature at the early stages of tournaments.

Gadget Guys

> 'I don't have any trouble when it comes to most electronic things.'

> *male, 45, Telewest, Preston*

The traditional early adopter market can be loosely characterised as 60–80 per cent male, mostly aged 25–34, AB dominant and with a mountaineer's approach to adoption – 'I bought it because it was there'. Very at ease with technology, owning the latest gadgets and being able to use them is an important part of who they are. Partly based on innate curiosity and partly on a need to be among the first to explore the new, they respond to interactive television with relish at first when trailing services, but are easily bored when these fail to live up to the expectations generated by their extensive range of alternate devices. Gadget Guys are often over researched and tend to be poor barometers for how services will be used by others.

Early Majority

- Early Clickers – young children with pester power.
- Daytime Dabblers – usually female, at home during the day.
- i-Potato – recumbent channel-hopper.
- Silver Sofas – 50+ with time on their hands.

Early Clickers

> 'I played trivia with mum the other day.'
>
> *female, family, digital terrestrial, Preston*

Early Clickers are children between the ages of three and ten. Some are familiar with interactivity through either school or the home personal computer, and their parents have actively encouraged them to use interactive television and the web, so that they will be more proficient with computers in later life. Young children of technically averse parents tend not to be Early Clickers. In some instances their parents claimed to have subscribed to interactive television at least partly because of the presumed education benefits to their young children.

Games, particularly, for example, those provided by channels such as the Cartoon Network, are a route to interactive access for this group. Their play and on-screen learning with various interactive services provides a path for their parents to improve their own understanding.

With the emergence of successful i-advertising, an emergent danger for parents is that traditional pester power is evolving from 'why can't we buy it?' to 'why can't we buy it now!' – whether that be using shopping cart-enabled toy advertisements or premium content gaming.

Daytime Dabblers

> 'I like to relax and play a few games when my daughter has gone to school.'
>
> *female, family, digital terrestrial, London*

Complementary to the Early Clickers are the Daytime Dabblers. This group is almost entirely female and generally not actively uninvolved in the decision to subscribe. Often the spouse of a Gadget Guy or Armchair Athlete, they were very much a secondary user of interactive television when it was first acquired. Now, however, Dabblers are likely to be establishing their own pattern of use, evolving largely during time alone in the house or with children.

5.21 Daytime Dabbler.

Dabblers account for an early rise in on-screen gaming on interactive television by women who account for between 45 and 55 per cent of all interactive television game plays, not a trend matched in the personal computer and console market. The technical inferiority of many interactive television platforms has, to some extent, removed a barrier for those previously outside the gaming market. Games are simple, usable, and often throwbacks to tried and tested concepts such as Space Invaders and Tetris.

What has been disappointing for the market is that this group has yet to take to the walled garden as a preferred method for shopping. A group traditionally familiar with conventional television shopping (specialised channels and exclusive-to-television products) has not translated that familiarity into browsing and buying behaviour. Most (but not all) television commerce (t-commerce), as offered by retailers and banks in 2002, remains a flawed experience for this target consumer.

i-Potato

> 'There's always something good on one of the channels.'
>
> *male, 46, Telewest, Preston*

The i-Potato we cruelly characterise as generally a male, who can now not only spend his days channel surfing, but also order pizza direct from the sofa, only having to disengage from UK Gold to answer the door. Aged 30–55, the i-Potato is a heavy television viewer, turning into a wide range of programming. Television forms a central part of the i-Potato's life and interactive television represents yet more choice and greater convenience. Viewing is generally passive and the instinct to channel hop rather than switch off when nothing interesting can be found is strong. This group is unlikely to generate revenues for providers before the emergence of one-click video-on-demand. Wider interactivity is just not as interesting to the i-Potato unless it involves no more effort than flicking channels. In that respect, the quality of the EPG and channel choice influence this group (if the household buying decision maker) more than other services.

Silver Sofas

> 'Well I've got eight grandchildren and my sister now lives in Egypt so I tend to send quite a few emails.'
>
> *female, 53, Telewest, Preston*

The final group are the Silver Sofas. Generally 50+ with time on their hands – either due to retirement or the fact that the children have left home. They are drawn to the range of channels relevant to their interest and are open to exploring the potential of the interactive services. In terms of the technical proficiency, they have either gained experience in the workplace or feel sufficiently comfortable with the television to try the different functions that appeal. Although some already use the internet, not all Silver Sofas would be as comfortable with a personal computer.

For Silver Sofas, the principal barrier with any interactive technology is lack of confidence and relevance. Silver Sofas are not hostile to interactive television, there is some pride associated with being able to 'keep up with the grandchildren' and maybe even 'beat the kids to it'. To this extent, the simplicity and usability of interactive television services is very important. Leadership displayed by the BBC and government in delivering enhancements to established programming and local services content is helpful to the Silver Sofas.

A key weakness of interactive television for this group, however, is communication services. Less than 20 per cent of interactive television users have keyboards in 2002 and even those that have access find the traditional layout of a television lounge less than adequate for using the keyboard-based services in a meaningful way. We won't know for certain whether keyboard activity on interactive television has failed entirely until adoption by the Late Majority and those consumers who do not have access to email via other means (15–30 per cent of the market is dependent on the success of 3G and home personal computer penetration). What we do know is that those who do have alternate access, particularly work PC access, don't use email on interactive television unless for very specialised private activities such as managing reactions to recruitment consultants.

What impact will broadband have on the Late Majority?

In mid-2002, there were three Early Adopter groups within the United Kingdom broadband market:

- Gadget Guys (again).
- Hotwired Homeworkers (those using broadband to work from home).
- Fast Families (entertainment and learning orientated adopters).

The first two groups are largely PC-internet fans. However, it is within Fast Families that we believe the greatest overlap will occur with the traditional interactive television groups. Based on analysis of which broadband functions appear to be accelerating in use most rapidly, there are four emergent micro-groups:

- Game Guys (using the personal computer/television for network gaming).
- Movie Enthusiasts (video-on-demand consumers).
- Music Junkies (music-on-demand consumers).
- Push-button Punters (sports betting fans).

Examples of this behaviour are most evident in the nascent broadband interactive television services, HomeChoice and Kingston Interactive. Kingston has led the move away from promoting broadband as an ISP+ fast access service, to using entertainment and choice as a key driver.

Summary of consumer benefits

When we first ran the *Hands On TV* research, we identified seven drivers for the consumer benefit of interactive television services. These in turn were mapped against the seven early user groups.

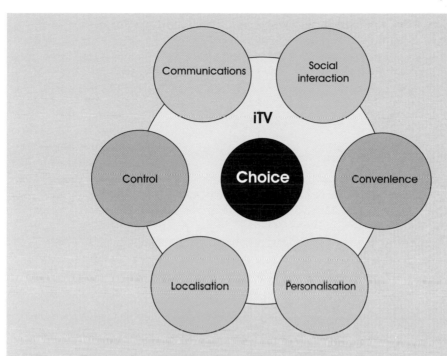

5.22 Consumer benefits of interactivity. *Source: Netpoll.*

User type/ Consumer benefit	Choice	Control	Convenience	Localisation	Personalisation	Communications	Social interaction
Early Clickers	◑	◕	●	○	◔	◕	◑
Generation i	●	◕	○	○	◑	●	◕
Armchair Athletes	●	●	◕	◔	◔	◔	◑
Gadget Guy	◔	●	◑	◔	●	◑	◕
Daytime Dabblers	○	◕	◑	◔	◕	◑	◕
i-Potato	●	○	●	○	○	○	○
Silver Sofas	◕	○	◔	◔	○	◔	◕

5.23 Consumer benefits of interactivity by distinct consumer segment. *Source: Netpoll.*

But all of this must be put into context against the primary motivation for using television – lean-back entertainment. In the same way that the predominant driver of uptake for 2.5 and 3G telecommunications is peer-to-peer voice communication, the predominant driver of adoption and usage of interactive television is good-quality compelling entertainment well suited to the target audience. In the consumer mind, putting a red button on the remote control doesn't alter the fact that the dominant interactive experience is between your eyes and ears and the screen and speakers. In that sense, the enhanced element of enhanced television can't yet compete for consumer attention with the television element.

Conclusion

When attempting to predict the likely success of a new interactive television service, there is no real substitute for audience research, concept testing, usability and usage profiling. However, interactive producers can take heart in some simple guidelines for avoiding inappropriate services:

- Don't assume connectivity means interactivity – if you build it they won't necessarily come.

- Devise content that is right for the medium – social programming and special interest broadcasts will complement interactivity in a way narrative will not.

- Understand the user journey – just like the internet, you won't be thanked for getting it right and you will be punished for designing services that don't take into account consumer touch points at every stage of their engagement with both your service and the context it sits in.

- Keep it simple – creative innovation is fine but no substitute for solid usable design consistent with the standards on the relevant platform.

- Avoid ambiguity – you have even less space than the internet to explain the meaning of prompts and service suggestions. Stick to recognisable icons and intuitive labelling.

- Use consistent brand communications – particularly on 'i'-advertising micro-sites where the television stream sets the standard for what the consumer expects from your brand and is only a button click away.

- Work within the limitations – this means understanding the limitations of your target consumers, not just the technical failings of the platforms. If people don't feel comfortable entering personal information on the screen in the family living room using a remote control from ten feet away, they won't do it, no matter how compelling the content or design.

Above all – ask the customer!

Actions

⊘ Sign up to the www.usableitv.com discussion group. Subscribe to the UsableiTV magazine at www.itv-network.org.

⊘ Check out any design guidelines for interactive television you can find. Design guideline web links are listed on www.InteractiveTelevisionProduction.com.

⊘ Read *Don't Make Me Think* by Steve Krug and *Designing Web Usability* by Jakob Nielsen. These two classic books on web site usability are also relevant to interactive television design, usability research and testing. See also the list of links regarding usability testing tools and techniques at www.InteractiveTelevisionProduction.

⊘ Sign up to the WebTV developers' site and take the course in interactive television design. Although this is focused on WebTV, it has some useful insights across the board.

⊘ Take the usability and design quiz at www.InteractiveTelevisionProduction.com.

Chapter **6**

The future

Chapter 6 in 30 seconds . . .

▷ Interactive television will become must-have television before 2007, but this will only happen if we, as an industry, can get the services right.

▷ Socialising will be an important driver for future interactive services.

▷ Broadcasters need to let go of their traditional models of programme making to let interactivity work for them, or settle for a long slow slide into irrelevance.

" The future is already here, it's just not evenly distributed. "

William Gibson, science fiction author

Hopefully, from Chapters 1–5 you've got some idea of where interactive television production is now. Of course, the industry is so fast moving that parts of this book will be out of date even before the ink is dry. That's the nature of the beast. There are ways to keep up, nevertheless. One is to sign up to iTV news services, like those from BroadbandBananas and Interactive TV Today. The other is to talk to people at the cutting edge about where they think things are going. Here's a sample of thoughts from three people heavily involved in making the future of iTV happen.

Must-have interactive television

Scott Gronmark, head of interactive television, BBC New Media.

One of the pleasures of being involved in interactive television for the past four years has been listening to predictions delivered with all the certainty of Old Testament prophecy. Here are some of my favourites:

- 'Web-on-television is the future – which means you won't have to build any of those horribly complicated broadcast applications any longer' (new media strategist).
- 'If the content's good enough, viewers won't mind waiting 30 seconds for a page to download' (teletext executive).
- 'Television is going to be one part of the experience you get from that screen in the corner of the living room, and probably a relatively minor part of the overall mix' (countless web executives).

Here's my chief prediction: linear television will remain, overwhelmingly, the reason people sit down in front of that screen in the corner of the sitting room. The majority of their time in front of it will consist of watching television without interactivity. But interactivity will become absolutely intertwined with the viewing experience, as viewers increasingly use buddy chat, chat forums and play-along quizzes, register votes, catch up on the latest sport and weather news via text and graphics and video, watch the Olympic event they're really interested in, donate to a charity, get some revision tips, check local cinema listings, do some banking, order their weekly shopping, send an email, whatever.

But if there aren't great programmes available, they won't be sitting in front of the television in the first place. And if the interactive television industry doesn't face this fact, using interactive services will remain a minority activity.

The interactive television we have in 2003 doesn't have to exist in the United Kingdom. We could kill it stone dead and there would be some disappointed games players, gamblers and sport fans, but no great public outcry. As a somewhat ad hoc collection of services, it's in the nice-to-have rather than must-have category. By 2005, ceasing interactivity on television would genuinely disappoint a lot of viewers, who will have begun to rely on it as a means of communication, shopping, entertainment and enlightenment; indeed, some types of programmes will seem strangely bare without an enhanced element. By 2007, getting rid of interactive television will seem as inconceivable as pulling the plug on the web would now. But to reach that state of 'must-have-ness', we, as an industry, need to concentrate on the following:

- Create horses for courses: as a medium, interactive television has barely begun to crawl. But a number of big events, including *Wimbledon*, *Big Brother*, *Walking with Beasts* and *Test the Nation* have all, in their individual ways, thrown light on the big question: 'What do viewers want from interactivity?' Rather than endlessly repeating these early formats, we need to keep experimenting by creating new formats. The richness – and unexpectedness – of these pioneering services certainly grabbed the public's attention; visually, they represented a leap forward for television, something evidently new and exciting. But I'm convinced that the future will be more about finding which facets of interactivity genuinely enhance each genre, and concentrating on those aspects. Just as choosing different camera angles hasn't proved a winner with football fans (highlights and alternative audio seem to be more popular), so interactive viewers will eventually grow tired of 'smorgasbord' menus offering a bewildering variety of choices.

- Create the virtual water cooler experience: when there were only a handful of channels and no web to surf, talking about television was a major feature of our lives. But now, if a programme has engaged or enraged you on television the night before, the chance of finding someone to discuss it with has lessened. We need to provide viewers with the opportunity to enthuse, complain, affect and influence programmes by talking to programme makers, other viewers, or their friends via discussion forums or chat rooms. This process will also help redefine the relationship between the programme maker and the audience – imagine how many viewers might be willing to make their views felt if they could do it without moving from their sofa, via the handset, immediately after the programme.

- Create an effective call to action – or get rid of it: only around 20 per cent of viewers react to the red icon in the top right-hand corner of their screen by pressing the red key on their handset. I predict this figure will drop and lead to some industry panic. By 2007 there might very well be no call to action. Interactivity will be seen as part of the programme and viewers will be expected to act positively to get rid of the enhanced element. If this can't be achieved, then the industry will have come up with an effective call to action that tells you exactly what you'll get when you press the red key. Too often, it's a lucky (or unlucky) dip, with the red key occasionally calling up a menu that seems irrelevant to the programme being watched. By 2007 interacting will no longer be seen as a separate activity from watching television.

- Create programmes for interactivity: currently, almost all interactivity is an afterthought. In other words, we add play-along quizzes to existing formats, take existing audio and video feeds and make them available behind existing sports programming. By 2007 there will be programmes that exist because of interactivity. There will still be linear equivalents that can be enjoyed without interactivity, but full enjoyment of the programme will require access to interactive functionality. The Playstation generation is used to making a difference to what happens on the television screen.

As for 24/7 services – interactive television that isn't attached to a linear programme – these will come into their own by 2007. The majority of on-screen shopping, banking, ticket-booking and charity-donating will be done via the television screen as opposed to the personal computer, and messaging of all kinds will be a major feature of the television. Why? Convenience. Some critics point to early failures in some of these areas – but surely that's the point of experiments; they don't all work. Walled garden areas may not have proved successful, but 24/7 services that contain a heavy local information element and allow for extensive viewer input have a big future.

© *British Broadcasting Corporation 2002*

A social future

Ian Pearson, futurologist, BTexact Technologies. BTexact Technologies helps businesses and organisations get the most from communications technology.

Television was one of the great success stories of the twentieth century. It took decades before it was clear what people wanted from it, as it gradually became less of a formal platform and more an entertainment medium. What will the first decade of the twenty-first century bring?

Current technology limits affordable screen area to typically 1 per cent of the field of view, and to just audiovisual stimulation. We are quite some way from the *Star Trek* holodeck with fully convincing full sensory immersion. Large flat screens will soon hang on our living room walls, though budget constraints will mean most homes will still have screens less than a metre across for some time. Visual immersion is unlikely outside of goggles until after 2020, by which time we will hopefully be able to afford a small room with fully polymer-screen-lined walls and maybe 3D, with the appropriate bandwidth to drive them with acceptable resolution. In this room, we will be able to escape into our fantasy world, just like Captain Picard.

Polymer screens may eventually win out, but the battle will be fought in various niches between a wide range of screen technologies, with plasma and bonded LCD panels being the two strongest current contenders. Screens that are primarily television screens will have many other uses, especially if they hang on walls. They can act as virtual fish tanks, displays for electronic paintings downloaded from galleries around the world, virtual windows showing real-time views out onto a Bahamas beach, or act as life-size video communications panels to allow people to share a cup of coffee across the oceans.

But whatever the display technology, digital television will certainly be the norm soon, and has already captured much of the market. On the back of digitisation, interactivity, indexing, choice of view and commentary, associated information, and video capture and manipulation will make television more interesting. All of these add some flexibility and information depth, but the biggest advantage of making television digital in the long term will be its integration into the computer world. The arguments over whether computers will be integrated into televisions or vice versa are mostly over. Both have happened as costs have fallen. For example, both are used to watch DVDs.

What is less clear is what will happen next. With digital television set-top boxes having high computing capability, providing internet access, games, email, home shopping and information, what is the incentive for a home without a conventional computer to buy one? By contrast, homes with computers and televisions with their sophisticated set-top boxes may still use their computers for the more computery things and televisions for watching television. There may be a strong cultural split in the market.

Interestingly, although most advances in digital technology have been driven by improving computer technology, one of the most significant changes for the internet may come from the television world. Digital video recorders are maturing into home media servers, and these will act as a massive data store for all information appliances in the home, especially television and computer equipment. These machines will happily record television programmes from satellite and terrestrial television networks, but are just as capable of being fed by DVDs or local networks. As DVD capacity increases (holographic or fluorescent disks may hold up to half a terabyte of data!), they will be an attractive alternative distribution medium for television. With smart filters and profiling emerging rapidly, the home media server will be able to provide most of the pages that the user wants to access, so thus will greatly speed up access time. They will have so much storage capacity that they can easily hold most of the really useful and relevant stuff for each of the household members. Real-time internet traffic might be reduced so much by such local caching that its performance increases markedly, so the few sites that change rapidly can easily be accessed quickly too. Such storage-based networking is already being developed. Caches may be filled by using spare network capacity as well as periodic updates on ultra-high-capacity disks, on the front of internet magazines. Half a terabyte is a lot of web pages.

Indeed, it is likely that the internet and television will simply converge, with television being just another internet service, with all the search facilities, indexing, chat forums and, most importantly, worldwide access to any channel (obviously subject to local laws, subscriptions and so on). This will open up the global television market while giving people what they want, rather than just what happens to be shown on a few local channels. Computer agents will be able to organise passive viewing to our taste, acting as assemblers for virtual channels. The agent may appear to the viewer as a friendly face with a friendly personality behind it, which may also have responsibility for non-television tasks too, such as shopping around. With sufficient intelligence, the agent itself may become part of the entertainment, playing live music that it writes in real time, or taking us on a guided teletravel expedition. With adequate indexing and sufficient computer intelligence, it will one day be possible for agents to assemble customised programmes on a particular theme that may not previously have existed.

With an infinite number of potential channels, it will be possible to sit and watch traffic jams in your local town, or remotely sit in at a council meeting, as well as watching any of the many coffee percolators on the internet. Remotely accessing video cameras has many trivial uses, but also allows more useful activities such as allowing parents to check on their children at playgroup. Certainly, community television is likely to grow.

Surprisingly perhaps, computer games are rapidly becoming a spectator activity just like sport and we may see all the same trappings becoming associated with them, such as premier leagues and so on. Watching other everyday activities has already proven successful television viewing in the many real-life docusoaps, and these will evolve well into the internet and digital television.

However, what these mostly point to is that people are content. When we have catered for our basic survival needs, socialising is the next most important human activity and is the primary driver for many platforms. The internet was originally constructed to allow sharing of scientific information. When it matures we will find that the bulk of human use is socialisation. Whether machines talking to machines will dominate even over this remains to be seen.

Power to the people

Andrew Curry, director, The Henley Centre. The Henley Centre is one of Europe's leading strategic marketing consultancies.

In the mid-1990s, I was running an interactive television channel for a cable company in London. One of my tasks was to help broadcasters and television producers understand how interactive programmes were made. They involved more participation, I would explain, but you had to hand over to the viewer some of the control over the programme. After one such session, an experienced producer explained that he expected viewers to watch the programme he'd made in the order that he'd made it. I'd already learnt, as I recruited people into the world of interactive television, that it could take anything from two to six months for them to let go of the idea that they were in charge.

This matters even more now than it did then because we can now see that the 50-year wave in which television was the dominant cultural force is coming to an end. People are still watching, but for the first time, certainly in the United Kingdom, the viewing figures are starting to fall. The energy of invention has moved elsewhere, to the internet and to mobile technologies. As people's media lives are saturated by ever more content, television is being pushed to the edges; the television set is on but people are listening, not watching. There is no shame in this (radio has survived a similar transition) but there is a serious implication, for few of the television industry's business models are designed for ambient consumption, with the exception perhaps of MTV and TNT Cartoon Network.

Michael Grade, the former chief executive of the United Kingdom's Channel 4 Television, once said that 'television is either an event or a habit'. At a moment when the habit is becoming less habitual, interactive television emerges as one of the few propositions that may, at least, make the event more eventful. Against this backdrop, the value of interactive television is that it can make rich experiences richer.

The Henley Centre has identified a trend that is common among much contemporary consumer behaviour: 'elaboration' versus 'streamlining'. The same customer, or viewer, can want each at different times and in different circumstances. So on one day we may drop in to the local convenience store to grab a ready meal on the way home; on another we may linger in the delicatessen trying to decide which of 11 olive oils is right for our special salad dressing. So it will be with interactive television.

At the elaborated end of the spectrum is the football match with the instant replay, the extra camera angles and the modest gambling opportunity, and the music show with the karaoke option. Both are high commitment programmes where the viewer welcomes the opportunity to deepen their commitment. The 'play-along' game show comes into the same category.

At the streamlined end of the spectrum comes the news programme where you can always pick up the headlines and the top three stories, and the sports application which delivers you tailored football results to spare you the effort of going into digital text; the equivalent of the ready meal delivered to the door.

There is a hybrid version. On narrative programmes such as *Big Brother* or *Pop Idol*, the interactivity ('cast your vote') is streamlined but the emotional experience is elaborated; the shared experience of everyone's individual interactive moments *is* the narrative.

All of this, of course, speaks of interactive television that is about enriching the viewers' experience around specific programmes. There is a wealth of possibility here that goes far beyond these examples, which utilises the capacities of the set-top box for personalisation. Nonetheless, these models are still about the broadcaster delivering more, which fits best with broadcasters' traditional delivery model. The next decade will put into the hands of viewers new equipment that will give them more say.

By 2007, the personal video recorder (PVR) should be capable of storing the equivalent of 300 hours or more of video for no more than the cost of the rather limited boxes of 2002. By then we may also have escaped from the trap of thinking of them as video recorders; after all, a hard drive which can store that much video can hold an awful lot more of anything else.

At the simplest level, this gives the broadcaster the opportunity to extend the life of the programme into the home, and extend its range beyond the viewer into their social network. Games played through the television will be far richer experiences than the current digital games, with frameworks downloaded in the background, or overnight. Some will be based on television formats. The future equivalent of *Walking with Dinosaurs* will download, to those who want it, a whole resource to enable viewers to reconstruct (or deconstruct) dinosaurs and programmes alike in their own time.

It is, though, only a small step from there to making the technology your own. Whatever the manufacturers try to do, there are considerable opportunities for playing with broadcasters' content, or rolling it in with your own material and ideas. The day of the video jockey who scratches, samples and remixes other people's content is about to escape from the avant-garde into the sitting room. In such an environment, new applications will quickly emerge.

The second development will be that set-top boxes will increasingly be connected to the network. This offers the same potential for forwarding content as is afforded by the internet. As the American futurist Watts Wacker has described it, 'The future is you're watching *Casablanca* and you remember your best friend who you went to see *Casablanca* with 14 times and instead of calling him up and leaving him a message you send him 30 seconds of your favourite scene of the movie.'

Already we know that one of the most popular applications on the ill-fated ONnet service – an internet to the television proposition – was the ability to send television stills to friends via the internet.

Of course, such usage is likely to be in breach of the United States' Digital Millennium Copyright Act, and the European Union's Copyright Directive. It even challenges our notions of fair use. Lawyers will certainly be involved. But none of this will prevent it from happening.

And broadcasters will hate it. They are among the last of the twentieth century corporations, built on the Fordist model of command and control. Almost everyone else has learnt by now that tapping into the enthusiasms and the connectivity of their customers is the best single way of re-energising their relationship with them. So the battle for interactivity is rather more than a question of whether the technology works or whether people will use it. The technology will get there; we know that people use it. It is a question of whether broadcasters can let go of enough of their traditional models of programme making to let interactivity work for them, or whether they will instead settle for the long slow slide into ambient irrelevance.

This book in 30 seconds . . .

It was the philosopher Eric Hoffer who said that the best way to predict the future is to have the power to shape it. With interactive television, this power is with the viewers and with the people who will produce interactive television services for them. If you are already involved with interactive television production, I hope this book has given you some food for thought. If you are looking at the industry, I hope this book has tempted you to get involved. Either way, start shaping that future.

Actions

- ⊘ Start to shape the future by signing up to interactive television discussion groups like www.broadbandbananas.com.

- ⊘ Visit www.InteractiveTelevisionProduction.com for a list of sites that could help with questions about the future of iTV.

- ⊘ Test your ability as a soothsayer by taking the quiz on the future of interactive television at www.InteractiveTelevisionProduction.com.

Interactive television glossary

There are many useful interactive television glossaries on the internet. Try the following:

www.ETVcookbook.org/glossary/

www.itvdictionary.com/dictionary.html

www.itvt.com/glossary.html

www.OMDtvi.co.uk/f_over.htm

ADSL (asymmetrical digital subscriber line)

A version of DSL. Called asymmetric because it carries a faster connection towards the customer (downstream) than towards the exchange (upstream). See also **DSL.**

Analogue

In television terms, a method of storing or transmitting information, such as video pictures, in the form of variable waves. Typically used in traditional television broadcasts over the air or through cable.

Announcement stream

Part of the broadcast architecture that helps to synchronise interactive content with the video stream to which it relates (necessary for enhanced programmes). It is usually a relatively low-bandwidth flow of data that tells the software in the set-top box when to start the interactivity.

API (application programming interface)

A set of programming instructions that can be used to control software. Interactive television producers tend to deal with APIs that control the middleware layer in the set-top box software system.

Application programming interface

See **API**.

Asymmetrical digital subscriber line

See **ADSL**.

ATSC (Advanced Television Systems Committee)

United States-based alliance of television broadcast companies dealing with standardisation across the industry.

Back channel

See **Return path**.

Bandwidth

In its original sense, the section (band) of the radio spectrum available or required to transmit a signal. However, it is often used to refer to the capacity of the network for transmitting data at speed – the greater the bandwidth, the more data can be transmitted. For digital data, bandwidth is usually measured in bits per second (bps), and for analogue waves, it is measured in cycles per second (hertz).

Bit

The smallest basic unit of digital information. A one or a zero.

Bit rate

The speed at which bits are transmitted. Usually in bits per second (bps); kilobits per second (kbps), which are thousands of bits per second; and megabits per second (Mbps), which are millions of bits per second.

Broadband

A high-bandwidth (usually two-way) connection that is capable of handling a large amount of data.

Broadcast

Distributing a signal from one single source to many destinations.

Broadcast channel

The data channel used to transmit television programmes into the home. Information can be conveyed one way only: that is, from the broadcaster to the viewer. Sometimes referred to as the forward path, in-band channel or one-way channel. Interactivity can be simulated using the broadcast channel by transmitting every possible piece of information that the viewer could request, thus giving the appearance of a two-way dialogue.

CA

See **Conditional access**.

Caching

Storing data temporarily in order to improve access speed. Data that the broadcaster anticipates will be required soon or often can be cached in or near the set-top box. Retrieving content from a cache is usually faster than retrieving it from the original source. Caching can reduce the traffic on the return path and improve access speeds to data from the broadcast channel.

Co-axial cable

A wire carrying a signal surrounded by a layer of insulation plus another wire that serves as a ground.

Compression

Encoding data to take up less storage space or less bandwidth during transmission.

Conditional access (CA)

Method by which broadcasters are able to control access to channels and particular programmes. During broadcast, channels or programmes are encoded or scrambled and may only be viewed by the set-top boxes of viewers who have paid to use them. The technology can also sometimes be used for interactive services.

Digital

A method of storing or transmitting data in binary numbers (ones and zeros).

Digital subscriber line

See **DSL**.

DSL (digital subscriber line)

Telecoms technology that enables digital data to be carried by ordinary copper wire phone lines. See also **ADSL**.

DVB (Digital Video Broadcasting group)

An industry consortium working to develop standards for the delivery of digital television content between the different devices in the broadcast chain.

Electronic programme guide (EPG)

EPGs display information about schedules directly onto the television screen, replacing printed television guides. Viewers can usually select content via categories, access summaries of shows and select programmes directly from the list.

Enhanced television

An interactive application tied in closely with the content of a programme, such as a quiz show or an election broadcast.

EPG

See **Electronic programme guide**.

Fibre-optic cable

Cabling made from flexible glass, and capable of carrying huge amounts of data. See also **Hybrid fibre co-axial**.

Flash memory

Rewritable memory in the set-top box that is used to store data and programmes.

Free to air

Broadcasts available to all without additional payment – as opposed to pay-per-view or subscription television.

Head end

The electronic control centre where television channels and interactive services are prepared for broadcast. Here the signals are processed for transmission to digital and analogue subscribers.

Hertz

Unit of measurement for the transmission of analogue waves expressed in cycles per second.

HFC

See **Hybrid fibre co-axial**.

HTML

See **Hypertext markup language**.

Hybrid fibre co-axial (HFC)

Cable companies in the United Kingdom typically use a combination of fibre-optic cables with co-axial cables (one wire carrying the signal surrounded by a layer of insulation, plus another wire which serves as a ground) in a network referred to as hybrid fibre co-axial.

Hypertext markup language (HTML)

The standard page-description language used on the World Wide Web.

Interactive channel

See **Return path**.

kbps (kilobits per second)

See **Bit rate**.

Mbps (megabits per second)

See **Bit rate**.

Middleware

Software in the set-top box that interfaces with the operating system and provides a standardised system of commands and programming tools. See **API**.

Modem

A device that modulates and demodulates a signal to allow data communication.

The Moving Pictures Experts Group (MPEG)

The group developing standards for digital video and audio compression and transmission. There are several standards for different purposes.

The Multimedia Home Platform (MHP)

A specification developed by the DVB group for defining standard ways for inter-activity to work across different platforms and different set-top boxes.

Multiplexing

The process whereby a range of video and interactive feeds are combined into one stream. Multiplexing is done with a special piece of equipment called a multi-plexer (also known as a mux) and usually takes place at a platform operator's head end.

Mux

See **Multiplexing**.

Near-video-on-demand (NVOD)

This enables viewers to view films at a prearranged start time. Films are broadcast on multiple channels with staggered starting times, say, every 30 minutes. The viewer can then watch the next available showing. See also **Video-on-demand**.

One-screen interactivity

See **Two-screen interactivity**.

Pay-per-view (PPV)

Where viewers pay to watch a particular programme, often a film or a live sporting event. When applied to interactive services it is sometimes called pay-per-use or, for games, pay-per-play.

Personal video recorder (PVR)

The PVR allows the viewer to record programmes onto a set-top box, where they are stored on a computer-style hard drive until required. Like a video cassette recording, the programme can be watched at any time, rewound or fast forwarded.

Platform

A network for distributing video and interactivity. In the United Kingdom, there are three mass market digital interactive platforms (digital satellite, digital cable and digital terrestrial), as well as smaller-scale television platforms that use the telephone network (by means of ADSL technology).

PPV

See **Pay-per-view**.

PVR

See **Personal video recorder**.

Return path

A method of sending data from the user's set-top box back to the broadcaster, thus allowing two-way communication and interactivity. Also referred to as the return channel, interaction channel or two-way channel.

Set-top box (STB)

Device connected to the television that decodes either analogue or digital transmissions and operates interactivity. Sometimes called a decoder.

STB

See **Set-top box**.

Teletext

Analogue teletext consists of text and simple graphic pages, typically composed of television listings, news and weather, and usually transmitted in the vertical blanking interval. Digital teletext offers improved graphics, more colours and enhanced functionality.

Trigger stream

Part of the broadcast architecture that helps to synchronise interactive content with the video stream to which it relates. The trigger stream is often a flow of data that is broadcast with the video signal and contains information about the exact time interactive icons need to be shown on-screen during a programme.

Two-screen interactivity

An interactive television approach, primarily used in the United States, whereby a television programme or programme extras are designed to work in conjunction with an internet-connected personal computer that the viewer is expected to use at the same time (or in close conjunction) with watching the television programme. One-screen interactivity is interactivity designed to work just on the television screen.

VBI

See **Vertical blanking interval**.

Vertical blanking interval (VBI)

The picture on a television screen is created by beams of electrons moving from the top to the bottom of the screen. At the bottom, the beams turn off and jump back up to the top. The VBI is the period in which the beam is turned off. It provides a space in the transmission in which extra information can be broadcast. Initially used just for teletext and subtitles, it now forms the main delivery platform for interactive television in analogue systems.

Video-on-demand (VOD)

This enables the viewer to watch a film or other programme of their choice whenever they want.

VOD

See **Video-on-demand**.

Walled garden

A collection of content providers, retailers and services from various companies offered on interactive television, usually by the platform operator.

Sources

Here is a selection of the sources used to write this book. This list, in hot-link format, is also available on the internet site: www.InteractiveTelevisionProduction.com

Research companies

Barb (UK audience research)

www.barb.co.uk

www.barb.co.uk/TVFACTS.cfm?fullstory=true&newsid=13

www.barb.co.uk/viewingsummary/monthreports.cfm?report=monthtotal

Scarborough Research

www.scarborough.com

www.scarborough.com/scarb2002/press/pr_internetstudy1.htm

Screen Digest

www.screendigest.com

www.screendigest.com/yp_01-03.htm

PricewaterhouseCoopers

www.pwcglobal.com

Strategy Analytics

www.strategyanlytics.com

www.strategyanalytics.com/press/PRDM032.htm

M. Booth & Associates

www.mbooth.com

www.mbooth.com/img/content/mb_trust_survey_2001.pdf

E-Ratings

www.eratings.com

www.eratings.com/news/2001/20011126.htm

EPS Limited

www.epsltd.com

www.epsltd.com/IndustryInfo/Statistics/digtvstats.htm

Forrester Research

www.forrester.com

www.forrester.com/ER/Research/Brief/0,1317,15001,FF.html

Statistical Research Inc

www.statisticalresearch.com

www.statisticalresearch.com/press/pr082801.htm

Ovum

www.ovum.com

Jupiter Media Metrics

www.jmm.com

Reports

PricewaterhouseCoopers, *Global Entertainment and Media Outlook*, 2001 and 2002 (see www.pwcglobal.com).

Forrester Research, *Resuscitating Interactive TV Retail*, 2001 (see www.forrester.-com).

European AudioVisual Observatory, *Statistical Yearbook*, 2001 (see www.obs.coe.int).

IPA, *Digital Interactive Television – Loved or Abandoned?*, 2001 (see www.ipa.co.uk).

Pace, *The Pace Report*, 2001 and 2000 (see www.pace.co.uk).

Interactive Marketing, *What Next for Interactive Television?*, 2001. By Andrew Curry (see www.henrystewart.com).

Accenture, *Pause or Play – The Future of Interactive Services for Television?*, 2002 (see www.accenture.com).

Organisations

NAB

www.nab.org

ww.nab.org/irc/Virtual/faqs.asp#World-Totals

The ITC

www.itc.org.uk

www.itc.org.uk/uk_television_sector/industry_information/index.asp

www.itc.org.uk/uploads/Publics_View_2001.pdf

www.itc.org.uk/latest_news/press_releases/release.asp?releasc_id=535

Television Bureau of Advertising

www.tvb.org

www.tvb.org/tvfacts/tvbasics/basics1.html

www.tvb.org/tvfacts/tvbasics/basics7.html

UCLA Center for Communication Policy

www.ccp.ucla.edu

www.ccp.ucla.edu/pdf/UCLA-Internet-Report-2001.pdf

Companies

Pace

www.pace.co.uk

www.pacemicro.com/pressroom/documentlibrary/2001%20Pace%20Report.pdf

Domino's Pizza

www.dominos.uk.com

Static2358

www.static2358.com

www.static2358.com/playjam.html

Carlton Active

www.carltonactive.com

NDS

www.nds.com

Orbis (part of NDS)

www.orbisuk.com/index.html

Articles

Internet and television viewing

www.fan590.com/MoneyNewsTechnology/nov29_internetsurvey-ap.html#

CRM

www.zdnetindia.com/biztech/resources/crm/stories/45486.html

TV shopping

www.business2.com/articles/mag/0,1640,11604,00.html

Digital television

http://cyberatlas.internet.com/big_picture/hardware/article/
0,,5921_543651,00.html

Canal+ revenues

www.tvmeetstheweb.com/news/shownews.asp?ArticleID=9878

Erik W. Larson and David Gobeli, Organising for product development projects. *Journal of Product Innovation Management*, **5**, 180–90, 1988.

Books

See book recommendations at the end of some of the chapters. In addition to the ones listed at the end of chapters, books used for research included:

Kent Beck, *Extreme Programming Explained*. Addison Wesley, 1999.

Jessica Burdman, *Collaborative Web Development: Strategies and Best Practices for Web Teams*. Addison Wesley, 1999.

Peter Burns, *Top 100 Internet Mistakes You Can't Afford to Make*. McGraw-Hill Education, 2001.

David Feinleib, *The Inside Story of Interactive TV and Microsoft Webtv for Windows*. Morgan Kaufmann Publishers, 1999.

Chris Forrester, *The Business of Digital Television*. Focal Press, 2000.

Ashley Friedlein, *Web Project Management: Delivering Successful Commercial Web Sites*. Morgan Kaufmann, 2000.

Gorham Kindem and Robert B. Musburger, *Introduction to Media Production*. Focal Press, 2001.

Peter Krebs, Charlie Kindschi and Julie Hammerquist, *Building Interactive Entertainment and E-Commerce Content for Microsoft TV*. Microsoft Press, 2000.

Steve McConnell, *Software Project Survival Guide*, Microsoft Press, 1997.

Gerald Millerson, *Television Production*, thirteenth edition. Focal Press, 1999.

Byron Reeves and Clifford Nass, *The Media Equation*. Cambridge University Press, 1998.

Jane Root, *Open the Box*. Routledge, 1988.

Joseph Sinclair, *Web Pages with TV HTML*. Charles River Media, 1998.

Joan Van Tassel, *Digital TV over Broadband*, second edition. Focal Press, 2001.

Magazines and newspapers

UsableiTV

www.usableitv.com

www.itv-network.org

Redherring magazine

www.redherring.com

www.redherring.com/mag/issue81/mag-maybe-81.html

Broadcast magazine

www.broadcastnow.co.uk

Financial Times newspaper

www.ft.com

Quotes used in this book come variously from *Broadcast* magazine, *UsableiTV* magazine, Zenith Media (www.zenithmedia.com), the research sources listed above and from interviews by the author.

Index

Focal Press

www.focalpress.com
Join Focal Press on-line
As a member you will enjoy the following benefits:

- an email bulletin with **information on new books**

- a regular **Focal Press Newsletter**:
    - featuring a selection of new titles
    - keeps you informed of **special offers, discounts and freebies**
    - alerts you to **Focal Press news and events** such as author signings and seminars

- complete access to **free content** and reference material on the focalpress site, such as the focalXtra articles and commentary from our authors

- a **Sneak Preview** of selected titles (sample chapters) *before* they publish

- a chance to have your say on our **discussion boards** and **review books** for other Focal readers

Focal Club Members are invited to give us feedback on our products and services.
Email: worldmarketing@focalpress.com – we want to hear your views!

Membership is **FREE**. To join, visit our website and register. If you require any further information regarding the on-line club please contact:

Lucy Lomas-Walker
Email: l.lomas@elsevier.com
Tel: +44 (0) 1865 314438
Fax: +44 (0)1865 314572
Address: Focal Press, Linacre House,
Jordan Hill, Oxford, UK, OX2 8DP

Catalogue
For information on all Focal Press titles, our full catalogue is available online at www.focalpress.com and all titles can be purchased here via secure online ordering, or contact us for a free printed version:

USA
Email: christine.degon@bhusa.com
Tel: +1 781 904 2607 T

Europe and rest of world
Email: j.blackford@elsevier.com
el: +44 (0)1865 314220

Potential authors
If you have an idea for a book, please get in touch:

USA
editors@focalpress.com

Europe and rest of world
focal.press@elsevier.com

Also available from Focal Press ...

Business of Digital Television

Chris Forrester

- Gain from the research of a key industry consultant, a complete factual understanding of the digital television industry worldwide in one readable source
- See the facts in context, from the key drivers for change through to future applications
- Get up to speed quickly on emerging technologies and complex markets

"Written in an accessible style this book is well documented, its statistics are comprehensive and up to date. The essential facts, data and commentary are all brought together in one single source likely to interest a large and diverse audience."
Bohdan Jung, Warsaw School of Economics, Poland,
The International Journal on Media Management

The Business of Digital Television presents an overview of the digital television industry. Chris Forrester examines the key technologies and developments of the marketplace, with comments on the future from leading industry experts.

Written in an accessible style for the non-engineer, the author covers the issues that are most pertinent to strategic direction, providing, broadcasting professionals with essential facts, data and commentary in one single source.

This book will be essential reading for anyone involved in broadcasting.

You will:
Discover trends in digital TV technology
Gain knowledge about the international marketplace
See an analysis of the financial models
Understand the importance of partnerships
Find out the key drivers for change
Gain an insight into emerging technologies in the future

ISBN 0240516060 • 288pp • 216 x 138mm • Paperback • 2000

To order your copy call +44 (0)1865 888180 (UK) or +1 800 545 2522 (USA)
or visit the Focal Press website: www.focalpress.com

Also available from Focal Press ...

Digital Television
MPEG-1, MPEG-2 and Principles
of the DVB System
Second Edition

Edited By Herve Benoit

Written as an authoritative introduction, this text describes the
technology of digital television broadcasting. It gives a thorough
technical description of the underlying principles of the DVB
standard following the logical progression of signal processing
steps, as well as COFDM modulation, source and channel
coding, MPEG compression and multiplexing methods, conditional access and set-top box technology. If you are looking for
a concise technical 'briefing' that will quickly get you up to
speed with the subject without getting lost in the detail – this is
the book you need.

**After an overview of analogue TV systems and video digitization formats, the author then
examines the various steps of signal processing – taken in order from transmission to reception
– to facilitate an understanding of the architecture and function of the main blocks of the
Integrated Receiver/Decoder (IRD) or "set-top" box. Herve Benoit focuses attention on the very
complex problems that need to be solved in order to define reliable standards for broadcasting
digital pictures to the consumer and gives solutions chosen for the current DVB system.**

- Enhance your knowledge of digital television with this authoritative technical introduction.
- Learn the underlying principles of DVB standard, COFDM modulation, compression,
  multiplexing, conditional access and set-top box technology.

ISBN 0240516958 ● 216pp ● 234 x 156mm ● 94 illustrations ● Paperback ● August 2002

To order your copy call +44 (0)1865 888180 (UK) or +1 800 545 2522 (USA)
or visit the Focal Press website: www.focalpress.com

Also available from Focal Press ...

Digital TV Over Broadband
Harvesting Bandwidth
Second Edition

Joan Van Tassel

"Digital TV over Broadband: Harvesting Bandwidth is a much-needed exploration of this new terrain where mass media and interactive technology converge. Dr. Van Tassel offers both practical analyses and visionary recommendations about the broadband potential. In particular, the business models and organizational strategies offer remarkable and valuable insights into the ways broadband TV will work."
Gary Arlen, President, Arlen Communications Inc.

"Although there isn't much technical theory, Van Tassel has filled her book with plenty of jargon and buzzwords so this is an essential work for anyone determined to get a job in the industry..."
Raymond Marr, What Satellite TV

Digital TV Over Broadband: Harvesting Bandwith offers a clear overview of how technological developments are revolutionizing television. It details the recent shift in focus from HDTV to a more broadly defined DTV and to the increasing importance of webcasting for interactive television. Digital Television examines the recent industry toward a combination of digital services, including the use of the new bandwidth for additional channels of programming, as well as some high definition television. The book discusses the increasingly rapid convergence of telecommunications, television and computers and the important role of the web in the future of interactive programming. This new edition not only covers the new technology, but also demonstrates practical uses of the technology in business models.

- A thorough but easy-to-read explanation of the new digital and HDTV technology
- Discusses the convergence of TV with computers and telecommunications
- Covers the business models and scenarios of DTV adoption, webcasting, and the rollout of interactive services

ISBN 0240803574 • 608pp • 234 x 156mm • 17 illustrations • Paperback • 2001

Also available from Focal Press ...

Guerrilla TV
Low budget programme making

Ian Lewis

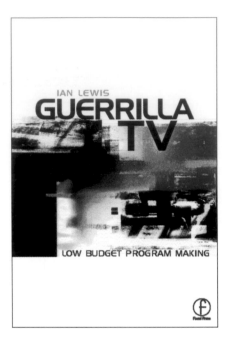

'If you're wanting to make television and finally put your ideas to bed, there is no finer companion for your travels. From its slick design through to thorough content, it should be firmly ensconced in the hand of all DV aficionados. Lewis' copy is witty, intelligent and inspiring.'
DV World April 2001

The world of digital television means hundreds of channels, all trying to be different, all looking for product. But the overall international production spend has scarcely increased. Guerrilla TV shows how to make high quality programs at budget levels, which were previously thought impossible, and how to make a living doing it.

This book is about empowerment; about making things happen. It is packed full of ideas, inspiration and help. The author, an experienced director/producer/writer, provides an insight into the 'real world' of television program making today. He uses many examples of how different low budget programs have been handled successfully with very professional results.

Read this book - take the advice offered and watch your career take off!

- An anarchic look at television program making today
- Offers real life examples
- Covers everything from markets to distributors for your programs and everything in between

ISBN 024051601X • 264pp • 234 x 165 mm • 9 photographs • Paperback • 2000

To order your copy call +44 (0)1865 888180 (UK) or +1 800 545 2522 (USA)
or visit the Focal Press website: www.focalpress.com
